NEW YORK IS HELL

NEW YORK
IS HELL

Thinking and Drinking
in the Beautiful Beast

Benjamin DeCasseres

with introduction by
Peggy Nadramia

UNDERWORLD AMUSEMENTS

isbn: 978-0-9885536-0-6

This edition prepared by Kevin I. Slaughter
for Underworld Amusements.
WWW.UNDERWORLDAMUSEMENTS.COM

Spine and bastard title page illustration by Josh Latta.
WWW.LATTALAND.COM

Introduction by Peggy Nadramia © 2015.
She has also provided three recipes for drinks mentioned herein,
found at the end of the book. This is one instance where it's
recommended the reader "skip to the end first,"
to be properly prepared for the rest.
Her bibulous endeavors can be found at
WWW.COCKTAILVULTURES.COM

Thanks to Pól Cullivan
and Erin Cassavaugh.

*NEW YORK IS HELL is the fifth in a series of books
collecting and reviving the writings of Benjamin DeCasseres.
Other titles:*
Anathema! Litanies of Negation (2013)
IMP: The Poetry of Benjamin DeCasseres (2013)
The Sublime Boy: The Poems of Walter DeCasseres (2014)
Fantasia Impromptu & FINIS (2016)

Further information available at:
ˌWWW.BENJAMINDECASSERES.COM
& WWW.UNIONOFEGOISTS.COM

Contents

BUILDINGS

PEOPLE

BOOZE

BARS

DRINKS

BRIDGE

Introduction

"It's a long lane that doesn't lead back to Manhattan."

IF Hell is other people, then New York is a special kind of Hell. The pressures of its huge and diverse population allow nothing to remain static or unchanged for very long. Like an ant farm, everything about New York is formed and reformed by the lives running through it every day. It's a city of the body politic, and it always has been. Before you assume the book you're holding is a typical rant about why one city is better than another, you should know that the use of the word "Hell" is a huge compliment; to Benjamin DeCasseres, New York was an infernal Paradise.

He came from Philadelphia and his view of it couldn't be more dim; he never passes up an opportunity to take a potshot at the City of Brotherly Love. He makes note of the stingy, staid and priggish ways of the town where it always seems to be Sunday and you can never have any fun.

DeCasseres fell deeply in love with Manhattan. There's simply no other way to present it, for his ardor displays all the qualities of true infatuation—he loves New York from high to low, is charmed and enticed by some of its grittiest aspects, relating his worst experiences in glowing terms and with ridiculous praise. Even as his tongue is jammed in his cheek, you know he's delighted with everything about the place. "I would rather be a lamp post on Forty-second street," he declares in a distinctly Twainlike fashion, "than President of Mexico." He describes the fight for a seat on the subway as free military training, praises the charm and intellect of the stick-up men who fleece an entire restaurant and its patrons, and recalls affectionately

11

the manner in which his neighbors protect and nurture their "pet burglar." An entire class of thrill-seeking jay-walkers comes under his scrutiny, and he seems to dote upon them as mere fun-loving risk-takers, whose antics sharpen the wits and "add piquancy and a certain diablerie to daily life."

The people of New York, from lowly immigrant pushcart salesmen to celebrities and politicians, all display a sort of golden halo for DeCasseres; they do no wrong except when they're enacting or enforcing laws that infringe on Everyone's Good Time. He naturally refers to Prohibition in terms as tragic and mournful as if he were talking about the bubonic plague—but neither is he in favor of curfews or holiday closures or ferries that stop running after midnight; what he loves most passionately about New York is its 24-hour lifestyle and he rails against anything that impinges upon it. He rankles at the idea that people need to be protected from their own foibles, observing that "the definition of human weakness is always the weakness of the other fellow." He vehemently denies any social need for curbing the appetites of his fellow citizens, and his advice is to "legalize human frailties and you eliminate graft."

DeCasseres is not immune to the physical characteristics that define the old island, either, completely apart from the people and their habits. He ferries over to Staten Island just so he can gaze at the twinkling lights of Manhattan. He watches the moon rise over what was at the time the brand-new Fifth Avenue Public Library; the building boasts a "skin" of white Vermont marble and must have been quite a sight back then, when it was still sparkling new and the streetlights weren't casting their orange sodium haze. To walk the grid of New York City's midtown streets could be like traversing the floor of one populated canyon after another, and DeCasseres evokes this beautifully when he says that "the corners of New York are doorknobs that open up to the eye the long vestibule of the streets which always end at a river."

What has truly won my alcohol-preserved heart, however, is DeCasseres' obsession with the entangled triumvirate of drinking, Prohibition and bars. He's the Will Rogers of booze: he never met a drink he didn't like. One can't get through his paeans to German beer, French wine and classic cocktails without wanting to stop for a tipple.

It's easy to see why Prohibition and its proponents would get under his skin so successfully. Not only were they taking away the elixir that sustained him, but they were fundamentally against Everyone's Good Time. He equates the liberal consumption of alcohol with basic Democracy, and describes the post-Volstead Lady Liberty as wearing "gumshoes." When the USA began restricting the import of alcohol and confiscating it as it came off the ships, DeCasseres predicted a new World War over booze, commencing with "dry" Americans being deported from the shores of old friends like England and France. "Keep your fanatics... at home!"

Indeed, DeCasseres' love for New York is in direct proportion to his disdain for the rest of the country. He sees the prissy, Sunday-school nature of the Temperance movement as something uniquely American, but even when drinking was legal, he disparaged the stand-up saloon, where alcohol was quickly swigged in the course of a frantic day: "We sip nothing." He preferred the European style of leisurely drinking, talking, savoring, and was devoted to the famous watering-holes created and sustained by European entrepreneurs like Joel Mouquin and August Lüchow. I'm deeply grateful to have been there for the last New Year's Eve celebrated in the old Lüchow's, immersed in its history, musing on the generations of New Yorkers who had dined there before me, gazing up at the inverted Tannenbaum, and sipping champagne as balloons wafted down at midnight. A few months later it had relocated to a brand-new building in midtown and was an abomination to its own legacy.

DeCasseres was writing about New York a century ago, but his complaints are identical to mine: things have changed - the great watering-holes are gone - you can't have a good time anymore. Don't all we old-timers say the same thing? Surely, the definition of fun changes with each generation, and we have to acknowledge this and let go. My grandparents enjoyed lunches at Schrafft's, and bought beer at a place called "The Hole in the Wall." My parents drank with their friends at Scottie's (before Dad was banned) and went to Katz's at four in the morning for deli. I had my own good times on the Lower East Side, the West Village, and will never forget pushing past pimps and hookers to get upstairs to the China Republic for fantastic Chinese food overlooking pre-Giuliani Times Square. We all have stories. Somehow, it's hard to believe that this generation of New Yorkers will look back fondly on their sixteen-dollar cocktails, on their Fresh Direct deliveries and Citibikes, in precisely the same way. But it could happen.

"I believe in the Spirit of Place; therefore I believe that one place will produce a form entirely different from another place," De-Casseres tells us. In the case of New York, planted firmly on the island of Manhattan, what is most consistent about that form is that it is ever-changing. My childhood was spent in a proletariat New York, full of neighborhoods that were like villages, where there was danger but also tribal protection, recognition, tradition. By the time I left, I felt like a pigeon clinging to a windowsill, forty stories up. DeCasseres saw it similarly: "A chilly city of stone and steel... where 'mum's the word' is printed on every face." When things get that way for you, it's time to move upriver. But oh, the memories.

—PEGGY NADRAMIA
Poughkeepsie, NY
April, 2015

Cubist Candidate for Mayor Talks of His Platform

Benjamin DeCasseres, Choice of the Night Workers, Explains How He Would Eliminate Graft From Politics

IN his candidacy for Mayor, Benjamin DeCasseres, although he does not belong to any party, is neither a Republican nor a Democrat, a Tammanyite nor a mugwump, a reformer nor a socialist, an independent nor a fusionist, a prohibitionist nor an anarchist, he has nevertheless succeeded in attracting the curiosity and, what is more remarkable, the financial support of several prominent persons in the city of New York. A few weeks ago the papers printed an interview in which he announced his candidacy and promised to give out his platform shortly. Now *The Sunday Sun* is able to give an account of that platform. To speak in very conservative language it is a startling document. It is a bold plea for individual liberty: a piece of philosophic literature in the opinion of Mr. DeCasseres' followers greater than any penned by our Epictetian Mayor.

A great many people with a keen sense of humor but no sense of proportions imagined that Mr. DeCasseres was jesting when he announced his candidacy. But it must be said that all such carpers after they have read his platform have exclaimed: "A great platform, the greatest ever, and you shall have our votes!"

The futurist candidate says in his platform: "A vote for me is a vote in the direction of legalized, law abiding, wide open, pleasure loving, sane, human city."

At first the thought is uppermost that a wide open, pleasure loving city would mean the placing of it in the hands of gamblers, racetrack men and thugs. But that is not the case. Mr. DeCasseres says, and he explains, "This platform aims only at eliminating graft as

15

much as it is pin the power of a human to do so, and is a plea for the recognition and legalization of human weaknesses. And the definition of 'human weakness' is always the weakness of the other fellow."

For generations people have tried, but in vain, to abolish corruption in the politics. Now this militant philosopher from the Quaker City, alone, without political influence, without petty ambitions, without moneyed interests to back him, comes along and presents a solution of the problem: "Legalize human frailties and you eliminate graft."

Another plank in the platform says: "Absolute home rule for the city of New York. I am a secessionist and I shall demand the erection of the State of Manhattan."

He begs voters to look at some cold figures. He points out that the population of Greater New York in 1913 is estimated at 5,173,064, of the State of New York at 9,113,279. Deduct the population of New York City from that of the State and you will find that the State is left with barely 3,940,213. And there it is in a nutshell. Four million people of the State trying to boss a city of over five million people. It is as if the tail tried to wag the dog.

The platform further says: "The Mayor's duties to be limited strictly to seeing that order is preserved. A self-chosen moral and spiritual director of five millions of people, the Mayor becomes a Polonius-Pecksniff. The Mayor should be impeached and removed the moment he attempts to regulate the private morals."

True to his principles, Mr. DeCasseres wrote a letter to that effect to Gov. Sulzer and the answer is quoted here with his permission:

State of New York, Executive Chamber.
Albany, April 4, 1913.
    B. DeCasseres, 11 West Thirty-ninth street, New York city.
    My Dear Sir, Your letter of March 27 to Gov. Sulzer has been recieved, the contents of which have been carefully noted by the Governor. Very Truly yours,

Chester C. Platt,
Secretary of the Governor.

On March 27 the Quaker Futurist wrote a letter to the Mayor protesting that he could not get a drink with his food after 1 AM although he was neither a white slaver, a cadet nor a thief. "I am only a night worker. Are we governed by a Mayor or a Czar?" he asked. The Mayor's answer in full was as follows:

City of New York,
Office of the Mayor.
March 27, 1913.

Dear Sir: I am quite prepared to believe that you are none of the detestable things which you enumerate, and at the same time I have no doubt that you will be able to get all you need to eat and drink in the city of New York at any time of the night. In fact I do not for one moment suppose that you are in any doubt on the subject yourself. Very truly yours,

W. J. Gaynor, Mayor.
B. DeCasseres, Esq.,
11 West Thirty-ninth street,
New York city.

Whatever else may be thought no one can accuse the cubist candidate of not being sincere. In fact, his honesty, his logic, his fearlessness are Gargantuan, monumental, pyramidal.

"We shall soon be in the midst of a campaign," says this modern Diogenes. "There will be three or four candidates in the field. I challenge the other candidates to stand on or to answer my platform. Will one of them dare say, 'You are right; it is the only solution to the graft problem?'

"No! They will ignore me and my platform absolutely, though they know that I have offered the only soltion.

"Why will they be afraid to take the stand I have taken?

"Because the other candidates do not want graft elimated.

"The machines that will nominate them thrive on graft. Were is possible, they would Philadelphianize New York."

What manner of man is this Benjamin DeCasseres, who dares challenge the candidates, the parties, nay, the whole nation, like a new David shouting a defiance to mortal combat to the great party Goliath? One might gather from the press interviews and the short, condensed challenge that Mr. DeCasseres was a fireeater, a Bombastes Furioso, a daredevil, or maybe only a borgeois anarchist. But it was a blonde slim gentleman with eyeglasses who recieved *The Sun* reporter at the entrance of his room at 11 West Thirty-ninth street. His calm manner, his gentle and low voice made the reporter ask in surprise:

"Are you really the author of the challenge to the parties and candidates to the Mayorality of the city of New York?"

"Why most assuredly," he answered quite seriously and as if offended by the query.

The reporter also elicited the information that he was born in Philadelphia on April 1, 1878. Mr. DeCasseres boasts of being a collateral descendant of the great Dutch philosopher Spinoza. He was graduated, as he himself says, "from the Philadelphia public schools, the University of the Gutter." And like other precocious geniuses he started after leaving the public schools at the mature age to write editorials for the *Philadelphia Inquirer.* A few years later he was promoted to proofreader. An irrepressible "wanderlust" made him accept and offer of a place as editorial writer on a paper in Mexico city. There under the shadow of the Castle of Chapultepec he wrote stirring editorials and awe inspiring Sunday articles.

One of the most bitterly fought campaigns the city has seen was in behalf of the opening of restaurants and cabarets after midnight. his efforts in the fight were crowned by the defeat of the governor of the Federal district of Mexico City, who had to permit the all night joints to keep open until 1 o'clock. His fearless and incisive campaign brought him many powerful enemies.

One of the most serious charges brought against him was that of carrying a very heavy loaded cane into a bullfight and shaking it at the chief matador while roundly abusing him in perfect Castillian slang for not killing the Spanish bull in a correct and expeditious manner. That memorable incident brought terrific storm upon his shoulders, and the newspapers suggested that he be deported under article 33 of the Constitution, as an undesirable alien, for inciting riot, bloodshed and revolution. Disgusted with the tyranny of the official press and the persecutions of the officials, he left Mexico City and sailed for New York on board a Ward liner from Vera Cruz. As he put foot on Broadway he exclaimed to a companion:

"Thank God I am on the Great Golden Way again! I would rather be a lamp post on Forty-second Street than President of Mexico."

As soon as this pregnant phrase was repeated by his Boswellian admirer he was promoted to his old and beloved job as a proofreader on a metropolitan paper. For over thirteen years Mr. DeCasseres has been living quietly and unostentatiously, occasionally writing articles for the magazines and weekly papers of this country. Some of them died soon after publishing them, but others have survived, and their circulation is not rising in too dangerous a fashion.

The reporter asked permission to glance over the titles of the books in his library. There were observed the names of Schopenhauer, Nietzsche, Epictetus, St. Francis of Assisi, Tolstoy, Thoreau, Walt Whitman, Emerson. To the reporter's surprise, he noted that half the books on the shelves were French. On the table were lying a volume of Remy de Gourmont's *A Night in the Luxembourg* and the plays of Brieux.

"Yes," said Mr. DeCasseres, "I am a great admirer of the French people. They are the intellectual leaders of the world. But to return to our muttons and answering your question, I do not expect to be elected, but I quite expect to be nominated on an independent ticket.

"I can easily get 5,000 waiters, night workers, cabaret dancers and reformers and haters of our philosopher Mayor to put their names on my petition. But as far as the election is concerned, to quote from the Indian bard, that is another pair of sleeves.

"But I am glad to see that my campaign against hypocrisy aroused one of my rivals to make a declaration very much like mine at the Civic Forum at Carnagie Hall last week. I quote from Mr. Whitman's speech: 'When the State provides by legislative enactment that it is right to sell a commodity during nineteen hours a day and wrong to sell it during five hours a day the human mind refuses to accept the proposition as correct, either morally or ethically. It is quite conceivable that a man who would at the same time refuse to agree that there is a reason in a law which makes it right to sell at five minutes before 1 o'clock and wrong to sell at five minutes after.'

"I want the pulque shops, as the saloons are called in Mexico," Mr. DeCasseres continued, "opened and licensed twenty-four hours of the day or closed altogether. If turkey trotting is respectable before 1, why is it lascivious after 1?"

"No, I am not looking for a job, as happened to our silver tongued orator, but like Debs and the immortal Diogenes I shall be a wandering philosopher and perpetual motion candidate in search of an honest man in politics. I don't want to be Mayor or Governor, or even President of this United States. As long as I shall keep jobless I shall be strong, fearless, powerful. The day that I accept a job or succeed in being elected then you will know that I have sold my soul to the devil for a pittance and that I have become a mere mortal, self-seeking, corrupt politician. The votes cast in my favor will represent a mighty voice of protest against puritan pretence and official hypocrisy."

"Have you received any encouragement in your efforts to free the city from graft?" Mr. DeCasseres was asked.

"Yes," he said. "Here is a letter from which you can quote without naming the writer, as he is a very prominent Fifth Avenue man." The letter said:

"I just received your announcement as candidate for Mayor. You will certainly get my vote, and I'd even be willing to go to jail for ten days if I could get two votes through for you on my own name. Hypocrisy in the guise of progress is a wonderful commodity in America to-day. It is on the free list; it needs no protection. It is the one real American product which seems to thrive everywhere in spite of tornadoes and floods, Roosevelts and Gaynors, not to forget all the ministers of the Gospel and all the teachers and publishers and practically everybody else.

"Here's to the Mayorship! I offer my services as the head of the Street Cleaning Department."

-UNCREDITED
The Sun, New York
April 27, 1913

BEAST

New York: Matter Triumphalis!

THE heart of New York is a heart of passion and of song.

Her brain is incandescent. All motion in New York, whether physical or mental, flashes.

The total activity of New York resolved into abstract motion would become lightning.

All energy here is corybantic. All life is nymphaleptic.

Expectancy is on New York's lips and the healthy frenzy for the goods of this world is in her eye.

He who shall write the immortal poem of New York must write it in dithyrambs.

For New York is the Futurist city, the Baden-Baden of that dying stench called Europe, the ironic Gargantuan offspring of the senility, the debilitating spirituality and black breath of the European Succubus.

We in New York celebrate the black mass of materialism.

We are concrete. We have a body. We have sex. We are male to the core.

We have founded our kingdom on the senses, and we glory in it.

We divinize matter, energy, motion, change. We are the sublime reaction against the bigots and hypocrites who libel life.

We stand a menace and a threat to Europe.

What we want we go and take of you, old Jezebel across the seas! You have sucked the blood out of the whole Caucasian race with your kings and wars.

We of New York shall destroy you utterly, for we are yea-sayers, pagans, world-absorbers.

We take from you what we need and we hurl back in your face what we do not need. Stone by stone we shall remove the Alhambra, the Kremlin and the Louvre and build them anew on the banks of the Hudson.

We are the future. You, old trollop that squats from the Caspian Sea to Land's End, are the past.

Come Europe! Into our melting pot you must go. For we are pre-destinate, being of this world.

When we visit you it is because we have a fine instinct for slumming.

"New York is hell," some say.

New York *is* hell. All things exist by contrast. And it is because we live in hell that we shall bring forth poets that shall gash the empyrean with their mighty threnodies.

It is because we live in hell that we shall be transfigured.

It is because we live in hell that we shall carry through the coming time fire and flame in our Promethean fennel rods.

The imagination of New York is unkempt, unshorn.

We wear our opinions pompadour.

We are Homeresque, Dantesque, Hugoesque, Whitmanesque.

On the lofty minarets of Manhattan there stands day and night an invisible muezzin who calls the faithful to the worship of Mammon and Speed. For our religion is a practical pantheism, with energy as the Eternal Substance.

We are the super-city. We are the Nibelungen of the West. We possess the Magic Rhine gold, which is the Holy Grail of Man's desire.

We are Gargantua and Siegfried. The old gods across the sea are graying. Already their Goetterdaemmerung has begun.

Come we, the newer Titans: and we are not yet pubescent.

In the fire and fury of our materialism we are dreaming of diviner Brunnhildes, Helenas and Aphrodites.

Out of matter comes mind; out of New York, Athens shall rise again!

The National
New York Complex

IT was O. Henry who said that ninety-eight out of every hundred Americans dreamed of some day living in New York.

As ninety-eight out of every one hundred Americans cannot live in New York, they have resolved that New Yorkers themselves shall live as they do—"they" being the pronoun that covers the multitude of small towns, villages and hamlets in the Middle West and South that dominate the rest of the country.

The two out of O. Henry's hundred that do visit New York return home with tales of the "iniquity" of the "Modern Babylon." These tales are based on what they see in the White Light district. They snout out the superficial night life of the city with the unerring instinct of all small-towners for the perverse and the vicious.

They air their suppressed complexes here and return to the town pump full of "moral indignation." New York has a thousand eyes— the Middle West and South have but one. And that one is always turned on the great metropolis. They see here just what they will to see—what they want to see.

They have developed the national New York complex. Their suppressed lives turn with venomous yearnings to the essentially pleasure-loving spirit of the big city.

What they cannot do they are resolved that no one else shall do.

The personal-liberty spirit is almost totally unknown in America, outside of New York, Chicago and San Francisco. The herd-spirit, the group-spirit, is the dominating spirit in all the small towns of the country. Persons do not exist in those communities. There are only people. These human groups are almost wholly undifferentiated in so far as individual existence is concerned. Each one of them is a composite photograph of all of them.

The perpetual spying of each upon the other (typified in Philadelphia—which is probably the smallest of all American towns—by the busybody glass) prevents any one from indulging in habits that are not O. K.'d by the group soul.

In New York no one pries into another's business—in fact, no one cares what his neighbor does or thinks. This freedom gets "the goat" of the small villager. Their logic is simple—I am in bondage to a moral code; the New Yorker is not; therefore, the New Yorker is a sinner. Which is something like the famous syllogism of Sydney Smith; Adam way the first man; all men are born of Adam; therefore elephants like peanuts.

The psychological root of the national New York complex is thus founded on envy, which masks itself under a moral camouflage. It is the unity of herd-morals opposing itself to variety and spontaneity—which is the soul of New York. Its slogan is, "I can't—and I'll be damned if you will!"

New York has always been the playground of the nation. The submerged Rabelais of the small town has always come to New York to get the air. Rural deacons and school teachers have visited the city for what William James called a "moral holiday."

Every day is a Philadelphia Sunday in the Middle West and South. In New York every day used to be Saturday night.

Sub rosa, rural America always wanted New York "wide open," no matter what happened "back ter home." It was always to be looked on as a place where one could recover one's sanity from the ubiquitous "Thou shalt not!" of up-State America.

The result of this was that those who were fortunate enough "to take a flyer" in the life of Gay New York went back home with radiant faces and tales of delectable pleasures. Those who listened to them grew sea-green with envy and malice. New York ought to be closed—it was a crying iniquity! It was a place where people really "lived"—therefore it was a scarlet sin and a magenta shame.

If one went deeply enough into the matter, one could excavate from the roots of the Eighteenth Amendment the New York complex. The New York complex is at the root of nearly all the blue laws projected by the Unco Guid Uplifters at Topeka and Washington.

The capital of the United States is now Hayrick. Neb., or Big Pump, Iowa. They froth at the mouth out there because New York has a "jolly time" on New Year's Eve, while they sit indoors and pray the old year out with only a mite of corn whisky in their gullets.

This froth of envy ran over into giant headlines in the provincial Western and Southern press, to the effect that New York was the scene of a "wild orgy" on last New Year's Eve. The Western papers especially went the limit in their charges. If one were to believe the lurid articles which were printed in those papers for two weeks after New Year's Day, and which they seemed loath to discontinue, New York's six million inhabitants—including the babies—were all out on the streets New Year's Eve draining flasks of whisky.

That New York was sea-wet on New Year's Eve is a beautiful and joyous truth; but it wasn't that that disturbed the booze-complex in the souls of the Kansans. What enraged them was that New York was wet and Kansas is nearly bone-dry.

The perversity of human nature that has begotten this national New York complex is exhibited in the way the motion-picture audiences in the small towns throughout the country delight in scenes on the screen that show cabaret life at its worst on Broadway. The wilder the scene the greater the delight. To see the skirtless dance in the Hoochy-Coochy Cabaret!—that's a regular Louvre for the Hayrickians.

Anything that concerns Greenwich Village also tickles their complex. Passing from the call of New York in the dark auditorium of the motion-picture house to the drab, lifeless aspect of their own streets and the deadly routine of their lives, these provincials make a resolve either to (secretly or openly) steal away to New York and give the Old Adam and Mother Eve complexes an airing—or, not being able to do this, to put the lid on New York—by Gum! by appealing to their Congressman to start something.

In the large cities of the country—Philadelphia, which has always seethed with venom against New York, excepted—there is very little hatred against New York. The national New York complex is hardly noticeable in a Bostonian, a Chicagoan or a San Franciscan. It is because these cities have a conception of individual liberty and a desire for healthy self-indulgence in sensuous pleasures which become less and less observant as we move inward toward the smaller towns.

In big cities people grow outward, evolve, effloresce. In the small towns everything is ingrown, secret, unhealthy.

The New Yorker exhales life. The small towner inhales life.

If you compare a Philadelphia Sunday with a New York Sunday you will get an almost visible view of this psychological phenomenon of inhaling and exhaling pleasure.

This ubiquitous New York complex has made of New York city a conquered province of the small towns throughout the country. London and Paris preserve their autonomy. New York has been leashed to the ground by the Liliputians. If left to a vote of the citizens of this city, prohibition and all the blue laws, censorship programs and Sunday laws would be overwhelmingly beaten at the polls.

We are the victims of the inferiority complexes of the small towns.

But there is hope, as a celebrated man once said. It lies in this—that those millions who surge into New York from the small towns of the country during the course of a year are beginning to feel the irk of a closed New York. They *must* have one place to escape from their hideous lives in Mummyville.

As a matter of fact, the Colonel from Kentucky would rather be locked up for the night in the West Forty-seventh Street Police Station when he pays a visit to New York than go to bed sober and cabaret-less at midnight.

Caricature and New York

ART being the record of the self-consciousness of man, New York is naturally incapacitated from appreciating the works of the men who in the midst of the city's mad money-frenzy are doing something for the aesthetic advancement of the American people. New York is not yet self-conscious; the American people is not yet self-conscious. Until the senseless material orgy is at an end and the brain ceases to be the handmaiden of the belly, art must wait.

Especially is this so of the great and revealing art of caricature. The New-Yorker is as temperamentally unfitted for appreciating caricature as he is from experiencing emotion before an engraving of Felicien Rops or a great play like Ibsen's Rosmersholm. Always the finer, the supersensible, the subtle, the ironic escapes his fat mind. He, being still a child, must have the pretty and the pleasant. In matters artistic he is the Candy Kid. To him the truth about anything is a kind of infamy. In caricature, he scents ugliness, missing entirely the intellectual principle, the ironic twinkle.

The exhibitions of caricature which have been given from time to time in New York have been poorly attended. Very little or almost nothing has been sold at these exhibitions. The exhibition which was held here in 1904—an exhibition which gave us the best work of Sem, Cappiello, Fornaro and Max Beerbohm—resulted in the sale of a few of the Beerbohms, probably because Beerbohm's "art" comes nearer the comic Valentine stage than any one else's. And the comic Valentine is still confounded with caricature in this country.

An exhibition of caricature lately held in the Little Gallery of the

Photo-Secession on Fifth Avenue was treated jocularly by a few reviewers and comparatively neglected by the public. These caricatures were among the most remarkable ever seen in New York. They were the work of Mr. Marius de Zayas; and, of course, were caviare to the general. Mr. de Zayas, like Sem, Cappiello and Fornaro, insists that his art must be taken seriously. And why not ? A caricaturist, like a great novelist, a great painter, a great sculptor, sees the human race in his own way, his unique way, his own terribly sincere way. He, like them, is a divinizing psychologist.

The caricaturist has his message. But here in New York it so happens that this message carries at its core the one great sin, which is a violation of the Anglo-Saxon injunction: Thou shalt not commit irony! To the caricaturist the world exists to be sneered at. And this sneer is a serious matter. Swift, Voltaire and Flaubert—their works are a deadly sneer, a cosmic sneer, a ghastly sneer; a sneer rooted in perception. It is so, too, with the great caricaturist. His sneer is the sneer of all wisdom, the unarithmetical sneer of Aristophanes, the kindly-malicious wink of Cervantes.

For the poet the world exists to be wondered at; for the scientist the world exists to be analyzed; for the religious devotee the world exists to be overcome; for the caricaturist the world exists to be sneered at. And to sneer in New York—well, artistically it means to take up your pack and walk.

Then, the original mind in New York has the moral canker to contend with. A thing must be good or evil, it must be tainted with the New England strain; it must be moral. Caricature is the art that is "beyond good and evil"—to use the pregnant phrase coined by Nietzsche. Sem, the great French caricaturist, says it is impossible to caricature a "good" face because goodness tends to stupidity. Where there is character there is always some-thing of evil; that is, pain, rebellion, struggle, life-and-death. "How can caricature elevate the masses?"—we hear our socialistic East-Side workers asking us. A question that is at once stupid and superfluous. The carica-turist comes to slit your mask of smugness and conformity and create mirth in your brain. To him morals are myths.

Nor is the art of the caricaturist an amiable art—and in New

York amiability is a cardinal principle of success. In art amiability is a vice; in caricature it is worse than a vice; it is ridiculous. Sem and de Zayas and Simpson sting and bite. These men are big in so far as they are pitiless. The caricaturist flings your face on paper, and if you shudder at the epiphany of your curtained secrets—as in that wonderful picture of Réjane by Sem—it is because you fear this peering trespasser in your soul. And when he sees the bourgeois shudder—that is the sign by which he knows he has done greatly.

This art is a stringent, peremptory art. It has a logic based on acute insight, a remorseless logic that runs down to its extremest esoteric secret, that hardly perceptible line around the mouth or the wavering look in the eye. And the logic of a face or gesture is seldom flattering. It stings like truth.

It is by this deft distortion—or rather accentuation—of mere fact that the caricaturist shocks. In a single line he will bring each hair to judgment—because each hair, to him, has character. He loves the human race for the mistakes it has made. He is a sneering seer, a prankish Mephisto, with just a touch of Hamlet's malady. If he is sometimes fantastic and grotesque in his work it is because life seems to him fantastic and grotesque; it will seem so to any one who stands high enough up the mental rungs and looks down. And when the New York mind gets out of the gutter long enough and mounts these rungs of perception it will come to understand and appreciate the caricature.

The Physiognomy
of the New Yorker

THE New York face! There is no face like it in the world. It is a mixture of Frenzy and Barter, Power and Servility. It is at once a threat and a promise. In a word, a composite creation, embodying the spirit of the Great Republic.

If poetry is the expression of the hunger for Elsewhere, the New York face is the epiphany of the eternal Here and Now, believed in and conquered, a Here and Now worth so much cash-down on the counter, a Here and Now that is to be haggled for and swapped.

It is a concrete face, a face that believes in "doing things," a face that never procrastinates except on a "sure tip," a face without irony, a face without tears, a face that has just enough imagination to wreck a railroad or out-general a political adversary on the Field of the Cloth of Yellow.

It has something of the sublime in it—this New Face in the world. There is something inexorable in the way the New Yorker walks, the way he talks, the way he looks at a real estate possibility out in boggy Queens. His walk has been called a swagger in the American provinces, but the swagger is the swagger of Juggernaut, not the swagger of the professional "bluffer. '

I would call the New Yorker sublime because he never counts his losses—or other people's. He is an unconscious fatalist. And this fatalism always carries in it the germ of the sublime, and it has passed into the face and manner of its beneficiary—or victim. Points of view differ.

The typical New Yorker is as unscrupulous as a plumber. This trait, Philistia to the contrary notwithstanding, adds to the dignity of his countenance. "Get the goods, but don't be caught with them on you" is his text. It is in his face. It is not a smug, hypocritical face, but one that looks up at you boldly and pronounces those immortal words of Richard Croker—or were they Tweed's words—" Well, what are you going to do about it ?"

Brazenness is in itself not to be condemned. In New York it is a necessary ingredient of success. You see it in the face of the Tammany politician, the Wall-street broker, the hotel manager, the subway director. Brazenness has been evolved in the struggle for existence in this chaos called Manhattan and it sits there in our faces by divine right. It is an asset. It will cow the world in time.

Ah! This is all a terrific indictment of our public men, or, rather of our public Face, the public may say. Not at all. It is a description of what the eye sees. It is a notorious face—this New York face—but it is a great face, for in it there are the traits that mould great empires and found oversea commercial and political kingdoms. Such empires and kingdoms are never fashioned by the soft hand or the weakly honest face.

The New York face! By its very brutality shall it conquer, its moral defects shall contribute its aureole.

It is a rough-cast of America-that-shall-be.

The Resignation
of New York

THE supper was fine and the wine was finer, and still more filling than either was the night, cold, serene, moonlit.

I had heard *The Tales of Hoffman* that evening. Its witchery, its bouquet of dreams, its haunting melodies still had full possession of me. It seemed I had become a ghost wandering through that nowhere land of Hoffman, that Venice woven of strange psychic stuffs, with those grotesque magicians and those unheard-of people, whose unreality numbed the sense of the familiar and made me tread carpets woven by gnomes in strange, nostalgic hemispheres of the soul.

I turned up Riverside Drive. It was 1 A.M. If the Barcarole and the Burgundy and the miasmatic twilight of the Grand Canal had not woven their spells over my brain, the Drive, the river and the Palisades in the distance, all covered with snow and shimmering in the moonlight like the stupendous tombstones in a forgotten necropolis of Titans, would have done so.

It was the magic moment of rare, unforgettable happenings, of vast, infernal doings, of strange and grotesque fantasies.

I sat upon the stone seat surrounding the Soldiers' and Sailors' Monument to gulp in that scene of snow-magic and lunar necromancy and mix it with the Burgundy and the myths of that madman who wrote the Tales and the wizard who translated them into sound.

I had not been sitting there more than a minute when I became aware that something tremendously unusual was going on, or rather coming up, the Drive.

A titanic footfall, like the march of Thor, first came to my ear.

Then another and another. It was heaven-filling and measured. It was the very sound of Doom, the herald of a Finality.

I looked down the Drive and I saw the Woolworth Tower, struck clean from the rest of the building from pillar to dome, coming up the Drive. There was not a light in a single window, but at the top burned a small candle that flickered and sneezed as though it would go out at any minute.

The Tower led the most astonishing procession that ever mortal eye shall look upon. Behind the Tower tramped thunderously the Statue of Liberty. She held her torch, extinguished, in her hand. Then came Diana, from the top of Madison Square Garden; the two Library Lions, the statue of Shakespeare from the Mall in Central Park, the old City Hall Clocks, the Golden Lady from atop the Municipal Building, and last of all the Brooklyn Bridge, crawling along like a tired snake, its cables making a most unearthly racket, which nearly drowned the earth-quivering thuds of the Woolworth Tower and the Statue of Liberty.

As the Tower passed in its tremendous tramp, shimmering in the moonlight and the snow like an alabaster shaft supporting the heavens, it said to me:

"My soul is a series of pigeon-holes called rooms. I am Business. I am Profit and Loss. I am Beauty come into the hell of the Practical. Farewell! I am marching back to the deep-earth quarries whence I came."

Diana, with her arrow, pointed at the stars, said: "I am Paganism, the ancient glory that is no more. What do I here? I have watched the modems of Madison Square with their stupid clothes and ugly faces and unchaste forms till my heart is turned to brass and my breasts to iron. I go back to the Moon to hunt wild boars in the basin of the seas that are no more."

The two Library Lions, with melancholy manes and lack-lustre eyes, said:

"Taken from the jungle, carved into stone, set to watch traffic cops and people who believe wisdom is in books! We are the apotheosis of pacifism. We are returning to Africa, where there is still some freedom and wisdom!"

Shakespeare, his head poised like a planet in the ether, said :

"Farewell farewell to all that humbug called *vers libre*. I return to Titania and Ariel. I cannot dream there in the Mall. It is only the children who have made life livable for me there. Besides, I'm afraid the Rubber Building will fall on me."

The old City Hall Clocks, martyrs to the weather and fire, their gilded letters half faded and their hands chafed and cracked, said:

"We have told our last lie. There is no such thing as time; there are only timepieces. We are going to the tomb of Immanuel Kant at Koenigsberg, he who destroyed the objectivity of Time and Space, and hence abolished clocks. We shall crawl into his coffin and sleep. Sleep! Sleep! That's what all clocks need!"

The Golden Lady from the summit of the Municipal Building said:

"Justice is a dice-box. The rich always win, while the poor get the box. I'm going in yon icy river at a warm spot near Hastings."

The Brooklyn Bridge was making such an uproar that I could not hear what it said.

I leaped upon the bridge, intending to follow that strange procession to the end. But a powerful grip on my shoulder restrained me.

"D'ye want ter freeze to det, hey?"

It was a policeman. I gave him a bundle of cigars I had in my pocket and walked toward Broadway.

But as I left him the policeman, strangely enough, was humming the Barcarole.

CORNERS

The Psychology of "The Avenue"

AMBROSE and Antoine, the two Library Lions, are always worth listening to. They are the historians of Fifth Avenue, the secretaries of Fashion and Culture.

Look at them! Observe their environment! Behind them, in that magnificent library—the Intelligence Office of the Spirit—lies the wisdom of the ages, and all the wit of man and the tergiversations and craftiness of woman.

Books have souls. Books *are* souls. They have auras. They radiate their beauty, their venom and their modesty. Everything is in that marbled magnificence at Forty-second Street—from the obscure magic of the Hindu syllable *Om*, analyzed by ten thousand dead Yogis, to the human-all-too-human stories of O. Henry, the first historian of New York City.

Ambrose and Antoine have breakfasted, dined and supped on this Gargantuan fare for years. Look at the smiles of all wisdom and complacency on their faces. They are glutted with supra-subtle ideas. Their heavy-lidded eyes are argosies of the stuffs of wit and dreams. They are retired Zeppelins of trans-stellar mental zeniths.

In front of them lies Reality camouflaged as Fifth Avenue. Humanity *en auto*. Humanity top o' the bus. Humanity afoot on its multi-mysterious errands. Humanity in eddies, waves, bunches, feminine bouquets. Humanity that smiles, weeps, pushes, crawls, tramples, pays, begs, buys, borrows and gets credit.

It is Fifth Avenue, the velvet-sheathed piston-rod of bellowing New York, the underworld of the upper world, the new Rue de la

Paix, the Louvre of democracy.

So Ambrose and Antoine, like two watchmen of Life, with the ideals, fancies and cynicisms of the ages in back of them and the panorama of the quick in front of them, are to me—the confidant of their conversation and remarks—the very last utterance on things in general.

"The sights and sounds of the Avenue," said Antoine, who had fed too much of late, in the deeps of the night, on the jewelled cynicism of Heinrich Heine, and who was much the more intellectually blasé of the two, "are beginning to tell on me. I need a change. Oh, for a glimpse of Broadway!

Ambrose, have you heard all they say about that magic road as they pass under our paws? It must be a great avenue of yellow light and gayety, of jewels and music, of rouge and lustres, where *décolletté* bulbuls sing all night to lavender ceilings. More artificial, I think, than this road of taxis and careworn smiles, and I long for the artificial. In which direction is Broadway, anyhow?"

"Oh, somewhere over toward the Palisades, I believe," replied Ambrose, tossing his white mane due west. "But you have no longer any imagination, Antoine. My world is right here. I never tire of it. Here is real tragedy, comedy, burlesque, farce and vaudeville. Where have your eyes gone to? You are bilious. Fifth Avenue has become to you a mere smudge of daylight. To me it is a world of fairies and puppets who put on another spectacle each minute. You'll be yearning for a trip in the subway next."

Ambrose is very old. He knows and applies that great apothegm of Parsifal Hammerschlact, the great Roumanian seer, that he who contemplates moves and he who travels arrives nowhere. His imagination is the high road to a Nirvana of ideas and flowery couches on Parnassus. He is a *lion deluxe*. He takes down the wisdom of the gods in the shorthand of his instant apprehension. He smears the jam of imagination over the raw meat of reality.

Antoine, on the other hand, is very young. One can see that in the way he imitates the sinister smile of Ambrose. He is young enough to be a great cynic. He loves the artificial, the concrete. He prefers the scenery of a department store to the heights of Mont Blanc, or even Brooklyn Bridge.

"The psychology of Fifth Avenue," continued Ambrose, fixing his eyes vacantly on a glittering brass button on the uniform of the traffic cop at Forty-second street, "has yet to be done. So far we have only described its physiognomy. There is more than a face here. There is a soul to this mess."

"Mess is right," growled Antoine. "The Maker of Things is not an artist—at least he was not when he hammered out this furious irrelevancy. Oh, for Grand Street on a Saturday night in the good old days. This is only an imitation of that great colored, noisy flash. Look at this ivory tower coming along lit by the crimson lantern of alcohol, and that bit of moral perfumery in pants, and that inspired plumber who writes free verse. Mess is right. They lie like Time."

"A soul to this mess, I said," continued Ambrose, who always listened politely to the charming vacuities of Antoine. "I can see as far south as the Washington Arch and north to the Sherman statue, and what I see is the Champs Elysees of a mightier Paris. The buses are red chariots laden with demigods. The sites of the shops are vast gardens wherein poets and children eat dreams and drink starlight. All New York aspires to Fifth Avenue, and Fifth Avenue aspires to Beauty."

"It is the horizontal Eiffel Tower of the West—all hardware, elevators and tips," broke in Antoine.

"As I have told you, my dear Antoine, you lack the sense of Mystery. You look on this exotic spectacle——"

"Exotic!" sneered Antoine. "Peroxotic spectacle, you mean, don't you?"

"I have noted, Antoine, in my evolution from flesh to marble that all epigrammatists are impolite. They cut into the thread of your discourse with stale puns and abstract piffle. They might learn much from waiters in the matter of courtesy. I said you lack a Sense of Mystery. This spectacle is to you a mere procession of people hurrying for flapjacks or millinery. Your eyes are domesticated; mine are nomad. These crowds are hatted, booted and coated ghosts of the Future——"

"Ghosts of the Future—that's worthy of Lafcadio Hearn, or some of those other dream-peddlers back there in the library." Antoine laughed so loudly that the attendant at the main door was compelled to lift an admonishing finger in his direction.

"Ghosts of the Future," reiterated Ambrose, with the sublime pomposity of an o'er laden Socrates. "And, by the way, why should ghosts be said only to survive the dead? Why should they not also be forerunners of the living? We are such stuff as dreams are made of, and our little lives are rounded with a——"

"'Sleep' in the third race to-morrow looks good," murmured Antoine over his *Morning Telegraph*.

"Wraiths of the future," continued Ambrose, "the raw material of America's magic to-morrow. The alchemic grandeur of these apparelled but unconscious forces, these raw tribes on their way to found a super-Athens! The psychology of Fifth Avenue. These whirling automobiles. I see——"

"Wheels," said Antoine as he composed himself for a siesta.

Favorite Corners

BY their corners ye shall know them!

In a word, which is your favorite corner in New York? At which of the multitudinous crossroads do you like to "loaf and invite your soul" or the bookmaker in to take a—ginger ale?

Corner loafing is an art. In New York it is an art that has risen to the dignity of a sport. It is an occupation not indigenous to detectives, pickpockets, poets or visiting Philadelphians. It has aesthetic and psychological as well as sportive implications.

No less a person than Walt Whitman was a professional corner loafer. Whitmanites of the double-sight variety profess to be able to see his epical heel-print even unto this day at the corner of Broadway and Fulton, where he stood and mentally bagged the human race when he wasn't beering up in the cellars roundabout.

Sam Johnson, that solid pontoon of wooden phrases over which Boswell crossed to immortality, had his favorite loafing corner in London. On the other hand, Oscar Wilde emitted the observation that "no gentleman ever looked out of a window or stood on a corner." But even this latter negation as to the value of corners shows that the word or the idea had some esoteric meaning.

There is a home-like corner for every human being somewhere in this world, and every human being was born to fit in at some particular street corner. Corners seek their human affinities. Humans secretly hanker all their lives to find their ideal corner. Once found, they return mechanically to it, until the end of their lives. It is the Kismet of the city-bred.

I believe a *Theory of Corners* was once a projected book of Robert Cortes Holliday. It was to be a sequel to his long-heralded epic, *The Rise, Glory, and Disappearance of the Bum.* Purely a New York book series, but for some reason or another the great project was given up for the humbler theme of old Broome Street ashbarrels.

The psychological and aesthetic basis of the fascination that corners exercise over all human beings therefore remains guesswork. The great authority on corners, bums, fish, and fireplugs has not spoken. So anybody is privileged to take a hack at it.

The corners of New York are doorknobs that open up to the eye the long vestibule of the streets which always end at a river. Like human faces, there are no two corners alike in New York. There are grinning corners, tragic corners, sinister corners, radiant corners, bleak corners, crazy corners, genteel corners, rowdy-faced corners, open-faced corners, sewed-up corners, baby-eyed corners.

There are corners that literally walk toward you in their geniality. Others that seem to recede modestly and fearsomely before you as you approach them. There are corners downtown with four sky-scraping sentinels that look down on you threatingly. There are other corners, per contra, so completely nice that you take in their four ginger ale emporiums before you pass on.

Suppose New York consisted of one long street—Broadway—which ran without a single break from the upper bay to the Harlem River. The born New Yorker in that case would have no knowledge of east or west. His mind would be of the monorail, unilateral, prohibition type. He would travel to Philadelphia or Brooklyn to visit corners with the same curiosity and pleasure that now drives him to visit the Pyramids or the ruins of the Constitution in Washington. Corners are the elbows of the mind. We couldn't do without them.

There are corners that browbeat your mind and nerves into an immeasurable sense of your own unimportance. Standing at some of the corners, for instance, down in Nassau Street, one has the same feeling that old man Samson had when he stood between two pillars in the Little-Church-Around-the-Corner of his village and pushed the whole business away in order to get a breath of air. No one ever lingers in Nassau Street or hangs around the corners down there. Have you noticed how every one in that street is always hurrying along at top speed either toward the oasis of light up around Ben Franklin's statue or down near the old Curb Market? Nassau Street and its sunless corners create physical panic. If you remember the predicament of the unfortunate radical-minded gentleman in Poe's story of "The Pit and the Pendulum," you will avoid as much as possible Nassau Street and its gruesome corners, for at any moment those giant buildings on both sides of the street may start to walk toward one another and make of your old corpus a gravy sandwich.

Take the corners up and down Tenth and Eleventh Avenues. These are "favorite" corners—but not yours or mine. These are sentinel posts for the ferret- eyed gentry of the underworld—that vast and fascinating region of New York which has put many a Rolls-Royce into the garages of scenario writers. The young and romantic cutthroat and the sleek slit-pocket are the lingerers and malingerers who ornament these corners. Between 7 and 8 at night the honest workingman crowds out the rising generation of those studying for Blackwell University. They crowd these corners along Tenth and Eleventh Avenues discussing the hardships of the six-hour day, and ever and anon disappear behind a frosted pane and a swinging door for a glass of red ukulele water.

Jump to Broadway and Wall. The favorite corner, I wager, of everybody who profiteers and is profiteered upon. It is the Corner of Magnificent Visions. The Corner of the Golden Calf, and, ironically, the end of every man's desire, a quiet graveyard. In spite of the perpetual admonition of Old Trinity to watch your worldly step, this corner is the high-water mark of imaginative materialism. Money is the romance of the age. And here, looking down that fissure of a street known as Wall Street, one glimpses in his mind's eyes the vaulted gold that means road-houses, cabarets, lobsters, "cellars" and things.

On the faces of those who swirl in and out and around this corner is written "I've got it" or "I'm through." Some are heading down toward Broad Street for more; others are heading up-town for a bench in Central Park or a quiet evening on the recreation piers. No one ever lounges at Broadway and Wall. It is a constant movement of human in-fusoria in a vat of hope. There is a cart anchored on the corner where you may buy three pears for 5 cents, but the huckster doing business here wears as grim a phiz as the broker who has just slid down the tobog. with the latest oil bubble. No one ever told a funny story at this corner. It would be in deuced bad taste.

The Corner Philosopher moves up to something entirely different—Sheridan Square. It is not the same New York—which is a city containing thirty-six cities by actual count. Sheridan Square is the new Five Points of New York. Grove Street, Christopher Street, Seventh Avenue, Fourth Street and Washington Place empty their literary tongs and aesthetic schisms into this big corner.

If the Brevoort is the brains of the Village, Sheridan Square is its stomach. It is the Parnassus, the Olympus of bob-haired morals. Looking due Bellevueward from a dressing room in the Green wich Village Theatre, one sees at nightfall the luminous eye of the clock in the tower of the Jefferson Market Police Court. This eye watches over the Villagers with a kind of serene and fateful brutality as who should say "I'll git 'em all finally." The Village raiding squad is secreted in the tower.

In the Village nothing is true but debts.

Going up! We are at Fifth Avenue and Twenty-third Street, which was once the Amen Corner of New York in the days when old Tom Platt and the rest of 'em cracked jokes and prepared the results of the coming election on red velvet lounges and Jack Dunston—now millionaire de luxe—lugged up the claret from the cellars of the Fifth Avenue Hotel, which you could get at 15 cents a spin over the bar.

It is the Flatiron corner, where skirts never cease from troubling and the Old Adam never is at rest. On a windy day it is the bald-headed row in the vaudeville show of New York life. The loungers around these corners have a healthy tang in their cheeks. The crowds move gracefully around the corners of Madison Square as though they all had much "mun in pock"—to use an old Latin phrase.

There are horizons on these corners, and those who do business there have them in their eyes.

Maybe it's the little fountain in the square or the tower in the Metropolitan Building that does the trick. Or is it the goddess that floats so proudly in the air atop the old Garden inviting men and women to a joy ride toward the stars? Or the Only and One Stupendous and Colossal Aggregation of Cannibals and Carnivora that gets inside the Garden once a year to the music of the face of old P. T. Barnum? Anyhow, it is the deckle-edged corner of New York presided over by the famous ghosts of the Fifth Avenue Hotel, the Hoffman House and the Bartholdi.

O. Henry once sat on a bench in Madison Square, and, looking across at the Café de Buttercakes on Twenty-third Street, remarked: "This is the fly-eye of New York; spin it on a pivot and you would see the whole world."

Rather esoteric for Syd, who then wandered across street, but not to the Jardin de Wheatcakes. There is Forty-second and Broadway, a ganglion of streets that fuses into a traffic cop. Men actually live, bolt upright, night and day at the corner of Forty-second and Broadway. It is the crow's nest of a continent—pagan, pagan, all-too-pagan, as Mr. Huneker would say. Formerly the meeting place of the Great Whiskey Soviet, it is now the mecca of all ginger ale psycho-analysts. Have you ever lounged there for a day? If so, you have seen America—the sombrero from the pampas of Texas, the thirsty prohibitionist from Dishwater, Kan.; the wealthy Yogi from Point Loma, Cal.; the dryads and naiads from the Chicago River and the hangover from Philadelphia.

On this corner everybody is going to or from a theatre or a lobster mad-house. It is a full-blooded corner. Least of all 'twas erst before Piggy the Prude and Wooden Face Eben took charge of our city morals. But it is still the Ultima Thule of North, East, South, West.

Times Square is, in a sense, the Gettys Square of the metropolis. It has the air of a perpetual holiday. After 8 o'clock it is nothing but liver and lights. It is the corner where Broadway and Wall comes up to air its inhibitions. To the buzzards of puritanical culture it is a sin. To the healthy, normal, sensuous human it is a sanitarium where one gets rid of his cumbersome health. It is indeed no place for the Neros of Morality and the Caligulas of prudery.

Here are the mountebank, the play, rich and rare wines (maybe), food that would surfeit Gargantua, laughter and song that put beads and bubbles in the eyes of men and women. This corner is paved with the skulls of the brave and the bones of those who loved life well but not wisely—as the great god Pan intended us to love it. Of course, there are a few "dope" peddlers, stick-up men, tappers and seedy touts lying around in the shadows; but as they never worry the police why should we worry?

Have you a favorite corner? Chorus: "Yes; it's the corner where we can sign a meal and drink check."

Right-O!

Lost Corners

"I READ in the papers that the corner saloon must go," said to me, only a month ago, the proprietor of a sub-rosa barroom on one of the corners of Long Island City.

He closed up his bootleggery and moved it to the middle of the block.

A literal, simple soul that obeyed to the letter the slogan of the Anti-Saloon League.

The passing of the corner saloon in New York has changed the whole face of Father Knickerbocker. The corner saloon was the eye, ear, mouth and nostril of the old man. It was here that he saw double, listened to wisdom, spoke with boasting and Rabelaisian tongue and tickled his olfactories with the perfumes of Milwaukee and Kentucky.

These corners of New York that are now no more had a great educational value as instanced in the following story:

"How do you know when spring is here?" asked a school teacher of her class of eight-year olds in the Olden Days.

A deep basso silence. Then up steps little Johnny Walker, aged seven.

"I know when spring is here," lisped Johnny. "Spring is here when Mike puts up the summer doors on the beer saloon on our corner."

Now that the corner with those wonderful B. V. D. doors are gone forever, how is our youth to tell when spring cometh in the big cities? It is like taking away the compass from the mariner or the oyster from September.

We adults had a way, too, of knowing when spring was here before prohibition turned our kitchens into barrooms. In the course of the day each one of us habitually passed certain corners. When the flying constellations began to mellow we looked for the "bock beer" and "May wine" signs in the windows of our corner saloons. These told us that the earth was thawing out and old man Frost was beginning to melt. But now we have got to consult the calendar, like little Johnny Walker. It will be many and many a year before the old goat looks at us again from the corner saloon.

Instead of the goat, the swinging doors or the May wine sign our corners now tell us that "ten certificates are given with each dollar's purchase to-day," or "nut sundaes are down to 20 cents."

Have you noticed how the street dogs of New York run wildly through the streets, stop at the old corners, sniff for a moment, and rush on, seeking for a smell that is no more? These new corners are hard on our loose and harmless canines.

One of the most familiar sights in summer in New York was to see the old mutts *du pavé* put their heads under the swinging doors of your favorite corner saloons, bark gleefully at the bartender and his customers, inhale the fragrance of the radio-active booze, wag their tails in thanks and rush on to another way station.

It was O. Henry who first noted the affinity of the street poodle for the corner saloon. These pagan poodles know something catastrophic has happened to the corners of New York. They stop at the old corners with a puzzled air, look up pathetically at the passersby, then fly on their way towards some Eldorado of sniffs, some Golconda of shining rails and shuffling boots.

Students of canine psychology may take this study up where I leave it. But the canine Old Soak is in a bad way. If you are an observant citizen you will notice that the peripatetic cur is no longer seen on Broadway, where the Good Old Corners have fallen one after the other before the Hindenburgs of morals and the Ludendorffs of indoor Kultur.

That all dyed-in-the-red Old Soaks and master rumsmiths will throughout their lives return mechanically to the scenes of their guzzling is a psychological phenomenon I have observed in connection with the passing of New York's historic damp corners.

You may break, you may shatter booze corners if you will, but the Boys with a Thirst will cling 'round 'em still.

On dozens of corners that I have examined I have noticed the same men standing—leaning against the wall, against the electric light pole or the fire hydrant—day after day. It matters not to them that the corner is now a puff-and-paste restaurant, a soda fizz fountain, a cigar store or a kosher sausage establishment. There they loll, hoping for the impossible miracle. They stand there dully, soberly, a little better dressed, a little worse facially for sobriety, looking blankly at the passers-by with a terrible *"J'accuse!"* on their parched lips.

Give one of them but the half of an opening, and he will grab your sleeve and spin you his Ancient Mariner tale of that particular corner. He knows "where to get it," but it isn't the same. Many of these born-to-the-corner loungers are trailed on their walks—and thereby hangs a raid.

These corner soldiers are going to have a terrible time of it in the Fourth Dimension when they are translated thither. The Fourth Dimension sharps tell us that there are no corners Over There. Everything is on the level. The corner grog-shop soul will have no corner to lay his thirst.

The corner where one receives a constant shock, no matter how many times one passes it, is the corner of Forty-second and Broadway, where the Knickerbocker Hotel stood. This was so long the headquarters of the Forty-second Street Country Club that what one sees there is something almost inconceivable.

The Knickerbocker bar was the meeting place between 4 and 7 P.M. of the *élete* of Broadway. At the corner outside one heard for years only one phrase, "Let's have another."

Hurt pagan souls now hurry by that corner with a hush. There is a lump in the throat. But one can see many of the Old Guard still lingering on that curb. They have died, but they'll never resign. At least, they are not resigned. The Country Club regales itself on salted almonds and sun-kist orange juice. Some are sitting in the trenches at Bimini, while others who have the wherewithal gurgle out their lives in Havana.

New York is coming more and more to look like an overgrown village. It is becoming a Hades peopled by Tantaluses. All our little corners are rounded by a sundae.

"East side, west side, all around the town," used to be the national air of the Empire City. Now it is "Home, Sweet Home"—with a wink.

Look around you now, and behold to what base uses may our corners return!

Summer Days on New York's East Side

MOUNTING to the top of the Woolworth Tower—that white obe-
lisk commemorative of the living life of New York looked down upon
the East Side. It was like looking at the Earth from the Moon. Silence
and the massed movements of infusoria. Canals which I knew were
streets. Flat, uneven surfaces with their silent faces turned to space
which I knew were the roofs of tenements, the lids that covered more
than a half million hells and heavens, human hearts emigrant from
Europe and Asia. Three fallen Eiffel Towers lay across the East River,
monster vent-holes that rose from the earth on the Manhattan side of
the river and plunged into the earth on the Brooklyn side. The rails of
the elevated structures glistened in the summer sun like Milky Ways
fallen to earth. A cross and the minaret of a synagogue, flinging their
mirages of Rome and Zion against the heavens, silhouetted themselves off to the East.

Under all lay that simmering vat of life, that great Oriental ba-
zaar, that Bagdad of the Western world known as the East Side of
New York. It is a theme that three men should collaborate at—Dante,
Gabriele d'Annunzio and Joris-Karl Huysmans.

From the fantastic dreams that are bred in the open skull of
the Woolworth Tower to the glowing reality of the East Side itself
is not a far cry. Hester, Forsyth, Allen, Clinton Streets, Mulberry
Bend, Avenues A and B and Second Avenue, the Bowery, Canal and
Grand Streets, bring us to the dugs of Reality. The chimeras of the
air have vanished and the pictures of a happy-go-lucky poverty crowd
the brain. Here is the far-flung battle-cry for the Dollar, the hoarse

and husky yelp for lifeat-any-price, the grin of a Hope that came to these shores with a household tied in a bed-sheet, the sinister eye of economic vengeance that looks at you over one of Ewer's push. carts laden with plums, and the mythical look of children born to the massacre of Circumstance.

But human nature on the East Side has more of Dionysiac humor than of tragedy in its makeup. The sentimentalist is the curse of the poor. That of which we are not conscious does not exist, and many of the ills that we believe exist Over There, east of Broadway, are fictive. There is a trade as old as the first social busybody, and that is the trade of pitying the poor. A brilliant American writer once said that Victor Hugo and Jean Richepin got rich by pitying the "unhappy." He might have added Dickens and many of our socialists.

What is happiness? Happiness is the art of continuous hoping. Look at Ewer's brilliant pictures, an exact chromatic reproduction of what may be seen any day on the East Side—at Orchard Street, let us say. Put down in front of this picture, or the original itself, an inhabitant from Mars. He would think he had been suddenly flung amid a race of Hyperboreans. It is a fable of color, a gigantic splash of triumphant life, a brave mockery of death, disease and pain.

Everywhere on the East Side Life is affirmed affirmed almost venemously at times. Though Death, Disease, Squalor and Vulgarity stand stark and rigid on every pavement, the inhabitants Over There rollick along with the insouciance of a Neapolitan when Vesuvius belches ashes all around him. Where is the misery on the East Side that is not found in Fifth Avenue? Is the East Side Medusa ? Well, she wears a great rose in her hair. Is the East Side a Social Menace? Well, that is because she is healthy, has the supreme gift of Discontent, and dreams of marble mansions and swishy silks for her unborn.

The most beautiful, the most virile part of New York is to-day almost an unknown land to the New Yorker himself. Stuss, the Black Hand, and the push-cart do not constitute the East Side. There is more silent heroism, more of the sacrificial, more mute drama, more of the stuff that makes for Grandeur, more real supermen and superwomen—those who triumph over themselves and pass on to other immurmurous psychic hells in that purlieu than anywhere else in

New York. Wring out the unfatigued heart of the East Side and you will find nothing of the gunman or the harlot in that, purple vintage; but there you will find gleams and glimmers and skeins of the sublime, that part of us that never gets into print, the unsung, heroic essence of this race marooned on a star. The East Side pronounces from its gulleys all mighty Yea to Life—tempered by the deep bass of Kol Nidra.

Ewer's picture of street scenes on the East Side explode against the eye like a thousand little bombs. The large picture looks like a battlefield of vege tables and fruit painted by a Detaille newly hither-come. Here are types and turnips, sheets and schatchens, maquereaus and melons, green parrots and amber weavers of sleep quaffed by the thirsty Interests of Forsyth and Allen Streets.

It is Business con furies on a hot summer's day, a piece of raw psychology plagued on canvas. You can hear these people talking. Do you think it is about canal tolls or Mme. Caillaux, or Mellen, or the newly discovered pimple on the face of Space beyond Neptune? Non past To this Swarm nothing exists save God and the Main Question. It is talk right from the entrails. What they say to one another is as concrete as a savings fund book. Their once-upon-a-time ivory towers are the parlor, sitting-room and bookkeeper's wicket of their souls. In the synagogue alone they come face to face with Mystery. In the sunlight, behind the push-cart, the Mystery has become Mazumma. They are the Wise Men of the East Side, and they have not listened to Shylock as closely as they have listened to Iago—"Put money in thy purse."

Marvellous race out of the East! Fall as low as they may, there is about them always the Promethean aural light of the Conqueror. It is peep-o'-day on the East Side. The granite bolts of sleep are slipped by the day-demon Must. There is a long yawn from avenue and side street. It is the yawn of the Eternal Return: Work. The sun launches its arrows into ten thousand enclosed holes in the air. It is already as hot as hell's waiting-room. From the fire-escapes—the inverted Jacob's ladders Over There that lead down from the Heaven of Dreams to the Gehennas of Must there rise wild-eyed men and women, hard-ly clothed, who have panted there all night for the air. A mattress is dragged into a window. A flower-pot falls into the street with a crash. A face and two breasts hang out of a casement; a morning meditation in Z. There is a rumble and a rustle. cellar doors open with a bang, the river front sends forth a stench of stale beer and mouldy pretzels. A belated pickpocket ducks into his doorway and a frowsy Aphrodite can be heard splashing in a tub. The great tide of flesh and clothes moves west and north. A new day. A new dream. A new hope. The terror that begets optimism. It is morning—not by Grieg, but by Tschaikowsky and Jonathan Swift.

Noon. Italians, Croatians, Lithuanians, Bohemians, Hungarians, Irish, Germans, and some stray born Americans—"original New Yorkers"—come up like a giant school of fish for air. Union politics, stuss, I. W. W., the bomb found in the wine house in Paradise Park, Becky Edelson, Bakounin and the raid last night in the flat beneath, love letters from across the seas, some smut, the high price of low living, the trip to the Island next Sunday, and socialism, socialism, socialism which is a dream of how the Mills Hotel suddenly became the Biltmore. This is the verbal patter until one o'clock flings its invitation to come back to the Boss. Among the workers of the East Side noon is the "club hour." It is the time of the mental aperitif and the sidewalk cafes wear trousers and petticoats.

It is night. The great human wave ebbs eastward to its home. The cafes on Second Avenue rub the daylight out of their eyes and blink their howdy-do at you. The push-cart has disappeared and the World Over There eats and drinks. There is a band in the park which always begins with Herold's *Zampa* and winds up with *America.* The East River jetties and recreation wharves—the Riviera of the poor—are packed to suffocation. Some one drowns. There will be Kaddish said in a few days or there will be wax candles and a crucifix. Red quilts disappear from the fire-escapes. Instead men and women build a Babel of sounds from them. They would chatter from the rungs of Oblivion.

An anarchist raves on the corner from a soap box and a thousand gobe-mouches believe they are listening to the Thing-in-Itself. Two girls pass, arm in arm, oblivious of this tumultuous, hairy fellow, for they, too, are talking of the Thing-in-Itself--the eternal Him, who will soon buy them ice cream on Houston Street. Nothing more innocent than an evening on the East Side. Outwardly it is the very essence of Law and Order.

But there is another kind of night on the East Side as everywhere else. Yes, it is night, and the thief, eternal representative of humanity, takes up his watch on the corner. The harlot, seeress and sybil, touches her lips with a bit of rouge before she takes up her stroll that will end at the morgue. In the hospitals a vague uneasiness pricks the bodies of the sick and thoughts like black parasols open in their heads. "East Side, West Side, all around the town"—great is New York, and the East Side is its prophet!

The Four Corners of New York

THE corners of New York are door-knobs that open up to the eye the long vestibule of the streets, which end, in whatever direction you follow them, at a river.

There are corners that are as quiet as thought, which point down streets that we are sure must be inhabited by students and recluses and astronomers or cabalistic brotherhoods who entertain behind closed shutters strange men from the East.

There are corners that swirl and toss with human spray—blatant corners, where the sunlight itself seems to honk-honk in unison with the automobiles; a giant maze of humans, who seem literally to pass through one another in their scurry like fourth dimensional beings; corners where the human will bites and gnaws its way from gutter to gutter.

There are corners, west side, east side, that are, day and night, sentinel posts for criminals and the ferret-eyed gentry of the under-world—that vast and fascinating region of New York, which has left us the only land of romance now that war has lost its glamour; that Prester John Land still breedy with tales to make the eyes pop in the telling and fill the ear with resonances of that glorious Italy of cut-throats and slit-purses; these corners have forever the finger on the lips; above the frosted glass of its four barrooms eyes, eyes, eyes, gray eyes and black eyes—come to mere points and slits through years of peering—sweep the horizons for "drunks" and "bulls." At the corner of Broadway and Wall, there is a giant Golden Calf. Of course you can't see it by looking; you must see it by seeing. It is built of the dreams and thoughts and instincts of the great tide of shades that beat around the reefs of brick and granite that raise their ironical heads to the sun.

Broadway and Wall is a great gout of life, a vast but compact spectacle of the Primal Instinct—the lust for the goods of the world. It is the Klondike of the East, the Golconda of the West, the trysting place of Prince Fortunatus with his bravos. This democratic mob, that the headstones in Old Trinity look out upon in such graven irony, inspires one with the pathos of life. For in the faces of these people is the sickly fear of "being done" the foreordained despair of those who dig for gold.

There is about the corner of Broadway and Wall something of the fascination of funerals.

Fifth avenue and Twenty-third street! The Flatiron corner, where skirts never cease from troubling and the Old Adam never is at rest! Here is something of the healthy tang of life. The flow of people is healthier than down below; there is a merrier spark in the eye, more vision and less of visions; the faces here have horizons, and the Will-to-Live, if it marches with slower pace, seems surer of its tread, as though a god—or is it the goddess that floats so proudly in the air atop the old Garden? —had whispered, at this corner "Keep your eye fixed on me."

Here is a sense of the enormous, the indefatigable, the artistic, the vistas of a Parisian place. The Metropolitan Tower, the prow of the Flatiron, Diana, the sages frozen in marble that adorn a great court of justice, a church whose architecture is a memorial to pagan grandeur, a fountain that sings its buried song to the birds in the trees over its head, the fantastic beings who are trying to redeem a beautiful wayward humanity from the summit of a soapbox, the shops of Broadway that show the poor the stupidity of their poverty—why should we not call this corner, where Diana salutes the subway, the Corner of Mysterious Distances?

Humanity at this corner bears about it something of the fugacity of Eternity.

Pleasure—fundamental and primitive, life-giving and eternal pleasure—is essentially Greek. India taught us the sublimities of thought; Greece gave us the religion of Pleasure, the superb gesture of disdain in front of the grave, the worship of Laughter and the Senses. Forty-second street and Broadway is Greek, pagan, full-blooded. It is a heart that pumps with the clangor of a hundred golden tocsins. It is the Ultima Thule of West, East, North and South. It is the corner—mad, rant, clangorous corner—of Perpetual Holidays. To "Billy Sunday" and the sacred buzzards of puritanical culture, it is Sin. To the healthy mortal, not over-moral, not too good, hot too unhuman, it is the way of forgetfulness and the crossroads to pleasant memories.

Avaunt! Neros of morality and Caligulas of prudery! Here is the mountebank, the play, rich and rare wine, food that would surfeit Gargantua, laughter and song that drowns the night in its mountainous billows, puts beads and bubbles in the eye of man and woman. This corner is paved with the skulls of the brave and the bones of those who loved life well but not wisely—as the great god Pan intended us to love it.

Here, on this corner, which bays and calls in a thousand directions, humanity cuts loose and sheds its idealism like a hair shirt. Freshness, expectancy and joy light up the faces after nightfall of those who tread these stones. The Great White Way is the golden shield of the people as they flee Numbskull "Thou Shalt Not" and the old hag Care. Puck and Falstaff are here on this terrace of the House of Pleasure; and Rabelais and young d'Artagnan and Petronius and Robin Hood, if you like, and Scaramouch and Thais, and Ajax Smith, billionnaire lumber king from the far Northland who has come to Forty-second and Broadway in a limousine to be human and terpsichorean and so forth.

It is the corner where all roads lead to the elemental virtue—pleasure.

But still another corner. Bowery and Houston at six o'clock in the evening. This is the corner of Care. A great bat spreads its wings here—wings which shut out the stars. It is, Drudgery. Humanity is going home—eastward—*en masse*. It is a surge of strangled sighs and laughter that rings against the iron girders of the "L" like the fall of counterfeit quarters on wooden tables. It is the corner of the revolution, for these brains have harbored strange chimeras before they were encased in skulls.

Bowery and Houston at six in the evening is a dangerous corner. These thousands of men and women who go east bring not peace, but a sword. Those bat wings shall become wings of fire some day, and these untongued masses of flesh and blood shall begin their march toward the far Meccas of their dreams. The Bowery and Houston is the Corner of To-morrow.

The Corner Where Traffic Cop and Fairies Meet

Just a Few Steps from Fifth Avenue and Forty-second Street:
Wonderland, With All Its Miracles

IF you remember Alice (Lewis Carroll's wonderful Alice, I mean) you will recall that in her second marvelous adventure she walked right through a mirror over the mantel piece into fairyland and the country of Humpty-Dumpty.

That is just what one can do at Forty-second Street and Fifth Avenue, which is, as we all know, right in the very heart of practical, jazzing, money-scrambling little old New York. Only, and still more wonderful to relate, one suddenly disappears through a wall of solid marble into this little kingdom of what Peter Pan called the Never-Never Land, and those who can accomplish this miracle are not only your little believing Alices and Peters but any work-a-day person regardless of age, opinion or previous condition of incertitude about such miracles.

Walking into the Public Library at the Forty-second Street entrance one day and looking immediately down the first marble corridor to the left, I saw many people disappear into the solid white wall as if suddenly dragged in by unseen hands. Investigating, I found a small door set in the wall, and taking the pedal plunge, I was in the children's room, which is situated right at the angle of Forty-second Street and Fifth Avenue.

The contrast between the rip-roaring movement outside, with the jumble of autos, trolley cars, traffic cops, show windows, and moving care-laden and fashionable throngs and this room is astonishing, and, if one is sentimental and imaginative, almost eerie. Here, in one step from the street, was a transposed world of silent adventure, flower decorated alcoves, fantastically colored panels and plates, and a great many kiddies of all ages, ranging from the tiny tot to boys and girls of 12 and 13 years, bent over books of strange and bloody deeds and fairy stories.

I stuck my head through one of the little windows, and, looking at the big traffic cop mechanically mauling his "Stop" and "Go" sign, wondered what he would have thought if I had gone up to him and asked:

"Can you tell me where Mother Goose, Robin Hood, Cinderella, and Humpty-Dumpty live around here?"

Such a question would have, without doubt, immediately tied up traffic. He probably would have given me a smiling, disdainful "once over," and for answer jerked his thumb in a general southeasterly direction toward Center Islip, L.I., where they cage the "bugs."

Everything in the decorative scheme of the children's room is done to remove the minds of the children as far as possible from the realities of life: On the walls are a series of beautifully painted pictures by Nathaniel C. Wyeth which depict the life of that grand old scamp, Robin Hood, and his doings in Nottingham Forest. We see Robin at work and Robin at play—his work consisting of holding up the solid landed gentry of England and his play running to beer and skittles, and all in company with his partners, merry of face and thick in the girth.

There is also a series of paintings, depicting incidents from Robert Louis Stevenson's "The Black Arrow." In glass cases around the walls are de luxe editions of famous fairy stories in French and English, the pages displaying marvelously beautiful illustrations.

On the afternoon in which I made my incursion into this child's world many little noses were pressed against the cases and much whispering was going on as to the strange doings in this silent world beyond the glass, but which was a tremendously live world to these little children.

The library has its fairy godmother, too (what is fairyland without a godmother?). A lady with silver hair and all the other accoutrements of the honest-to-fairy godmother comes into this room each week and, gathering the little ones around her in the cushioned alcoves, spins out fairy stories by the hour to these wide-eyed and open-mouthed youngsters. Her name and position in life—sh-h-h!—remain a dead secret.

By no amount of begging and cajoling could the reporter discover who she was. To give her name, said one of the female attendants in the kiddies' room, would destroy the glamour of her coming and going. She is known to the children simply as "The Fairy Godmother," and it is a great hour for them when she appears suddenly through the marble wall, her eye beaming with wild myths and the latest news from Fairyville.

The Fairy Godmother's store of fairy knowledge is evidently inexhaustible. She often invents as she goes along, and to her and the children gathered around her in this momentous hour the outer world does not exist.

"The Fairy Godmother was here yesterday," said a golden-haired, blue-eyed girl of about seven years to me, "and she knows where Cinderella is."

"And where is the godmother to-day?" I asked little bine eyes.

"She said she was going to visit the Golden-Haired Prince and see whether he wouldn't rescue the sister of little Red Riding Hood, who, you know, is locked in the castle of that awful Bluebeard man."

And she nodded her head significantly at me, as much as to say:

"You just wait and see! The Fairy Godmother will get her out all right."

That the Fairy Godmother had mixed up her stories sadly did not mean anything at all to my little informant. What's a mixed fairy story among children?

I went back into the dazzling light of Fifth Avenue, but the flash from the wheels and the sparkle on the cop's badge and the long array of buildings stretching either way on the avenue seemed to me unreal and of no importance, and that room in the library that I had just left behind was the real thing, and the Fairy Godmother and the little heads concentrated on another world seemed to contain the thing we are all seeking.

"Watch yer step, boob!" bawled a chauffeur at my head as I crossed the street.

It doesn't do to pipe-dream when you leave that room!

Incandescents Declare the Glory of Manhattan

FROM the Pike's Peak of Dongan Hills in Staten Island two Norvals looked, at 8 o'clock (Perth Amboy time). upon the most glorious and mysterious light in the world on this special July evening—the Bagdad-Venice-Babylon of the West (throwing in Northern New Jersey to get over the Babylon end of the metaphor) disappearing under the black counterpane of Erebus and pulling the golden cords on its thousand thousand electric lights.

One of these Norvals was myself, brown and fit from a protracted vacation at the Polo Grounds. and the other was Damon Daguerro, fore man of the camera squad of the Flim-Flam Night-Light Section. whose ten clicks beat as one.

Moving our two cameras—prosaically known in anatomical classes as our heads—on the poles of our bodies, we beheld a jeweled universe.

We didn't look up. The stars were bourgeois compared to the grandeur that is Newark and the glory that is Manhattan and the halo that is Flatbush by night.

Andromeda, the Milky Way, Sirius, Taurus, the Bear and Br'er Rabbit were all bunched over our heads like a lot of twinkling wine-bubbles in an overturned wash-boiler. Mars was making frantic signals to the searchlight at Sandy Hook about the result of the yacht races.

A falling star fell out of its flat in Cassiopoeia—probably old man Lucifer in another dispossess argument with Brahma. Vega, in Lyra, with a blue nose and cold feet, was doing its marathon toward its final pool pocket in the zenith. The usual week-end lawn tennis games were going on on Saturn's rings. Jupiter was singing basso-bluffo in the mu sic of the spheres. Orion was *sinn-feining* around for votes.

"Old stuff compared to this," remarked Damon as his finger pointed to the garter of jewels that encircled our knees. "Night may have a thousand eyes, but the metropolitan district has its Edison and his son, Kilo Watt. If that kid Aladdin could see this sight and he had any imag. left in his Oriental coco, he'd sell his lamp for a ticket to the St. George ferry. He'd climb this hill and rub his lamps instead of his lamp."

The skies above Manhattan burned with a cold fire. It looked like the atmosphere of a great mirage, framed in black. One expects, after long peering, to see Puck, Oberon, Titania and Papa Mephisto grow into form in that lake of molten gold and begin their charivaris.

The bridges are like Milky Ways fallen to earth. Across them crawl lighted cars like interstellar trains.

Brooklyn is a fortress of stars—an invitation to sleep.

Newark is a glittering tiara set upon the wet head of New Jersey.

Coney Island throws is saffron glimmer against the roof of the world. It looks like the outpost of space. It is the enchanted spark on the great Anvil of Light.

Leaving this fantastic scenario, we boarded the boat for New-York.

As we passed the anchored fireflies in the upper bay -and got into the rays from lights of that grotesque and round-shouldered ghost, with her sabots stuck deep into Bedlow's Island, Damon remarked pithily:

"Now I know why it took only six days to make the world—New York wasn't part of the scheme at that time."

Damon wastes them just like that, when he might sell them to Tom Masson.

The sorcery departs when the boat bumps in at the Battery. It is the descent from Horeb. But an other magic begins. The spine of the old giant, Manhattan, Broadway, stretches before you—that spine of which every four corners is a head. The night is hot and the evening vacationists in Battery Park are all licking ice cream cones or drowsing on the grass, some dreaming of Naples and others of "Babe" Ruth's coming ninety-eighth "homer."

From the fairyland of Dongan Hills to the weird at Broad and Wall Streets on a midsummer's night. Silence among the giants.

After Damon and I stood there for ten minutes—carefully eyed from behind gratings by watchmen, the static arsenals of the night—Damon grew whimsical:

"Don't you have a feeling that some midsummer night like this these giants will move silently out to sea and we'll get up some morning to find New York below Houston Street a cow pasture?"

Damon is always thinking up new scenarios like that. His brain is a regular Ritz potpie of Ideas.

After demonstrating to three bartenders in three different places that we knew they had stuff for cooking purposes we reached the East Side.

There is probably-more solid happiness and, comfort in this Vegetable Bagdad than in any other part of New York. No mystery, gloom, quiet or Horebic is stuff here!

Case notes.

The streets pullulate; the fire-escapes look like aerial moving vans; marvelous lady acrobats hang head downward out of the windows throwing in a "goods evening" in the room below; firemen are washing down the streets; while half-naked boys play Swimming the Hellespont in the torrent; an organ grinder is still playing *Annie Rooney*; the girls walk arm-in-arm intoning "he said" ; five Chinamen sit outside of their laundry waiting for the gong of their tong; an offshoot of a man stands on a soapbox prophesying Abracadabra in unsyntaxed Rigmarole, while pickpockets in the crowd wonder whether there is a gold dip or a Waterbury at the end of his leather, chain; down three steps two men are playing dominoes for sticks of Wigley's chewing gum; a painted Aphrodite lolls on a corner wondering when St. Swithin is going to quit.

"A midsummer's nightmare," said Damon, flicking the ashes from his Campbell. "This is neither aesthetic nor olfactory. Let us move uptown. There is no variety among the proletariat—the East Side is all studio stuff, anyhow."

What is a fantasia of New York without Greenwich Village? (I'll bet you on it—this is supposed to be a Fantasia, which in music is a pot-pie of sounds and in writing minced words baked in a crust of a Bright Little Idea).

"A Fantasia of New York without the Village would be like the House' of Commons without a Lady Astor," *bon-moed* Damon, taking in with both lungs the scented ozone from beyond a swinging door attached to an anonymous looking place. Many boots were lined up under a brass rail. We were in the heart of the Village, all right.

The fantasia has all gone out of the Village in the Summer of Anno Volstead 1. The fantasias, I was told by the bartender—who once was assistant to John Masefield—are Summering—some in Rockaway, others on the Island, and a few at Centre Islip Barney Gallant is the only original fantasia left, and he has shaved. Everything is as quiet down there as a stuss parlor before the usual tipped-off raid.

Even a beautiful midsummer's night, with its atmospheric necromancy, cannot stir in a poetic or fanciful thrift in that part of New York, it is as unromantic as the Iliad of a mollusc.

"Suppose," said Damon while we were sitting on a bench on Madison Square cogitating on what a great piece of prose we could do about that bit of dreamland stuck like a glowing amethyst heart between the two ribs of Madison Avenue and Broadway, if we had, combined the brain of O. Henry, "we do the roofs of upper Broadway, the whirls, the frolics, the rounders, the jazz shops; and I know a place—"

"You've got enough 'flashes' in you, Damon, now," I replied. "We'll take a bus up the Drive and have a peep at the most romantic bit of city and nature in the world. There's a full moon about due over the Palisades, and there's the Hudson with its Half-Moons, the dark perspectives, the Tomb, and the sparrows that perch in the basin of your: bangkok, and the red eye on the backs of the auto—"

"Red eye" must have got Damon, for he was off like a shot toward Fifth Avenue, hailing a bus.

The Riviera of Manhattan threw us back into the mood which we had lost when we slid down the Donogan Hills into a ferryboat. It ought to be named, at night, the Avenue of the Will o' the Wisp. Everything flies before you, and yet nothing seems to move. It is noiseless New York.

Quiet, shadows under the trees, shadows that whisper to one another; shadows that lean over the stone wall as motionless as a prohibitionist's brain; boats at anchor, around each one of which Joseph Conrad could build a book by merely looking at them; the funereal hills of the Jersey shore painted on the starlight—Apollo just died beyond and Diana is dressing for her hunt, which will end at au ice cream table in the amusement park opposite 135th Street.

It is all a real fairy spectacle built for people who no longer believe in fairies—bad cess to them!

Hot Tom and Jerry and the Ghost Cop

HAVE you ever seen the Public Library Building in the light of a full winter moon at three o'clock in the morning? If not, you have never seen the Vision Magnificent of New York.

In that wan, mysterious light that Temple of the Brain is like a vision of a palace drowned in an unsubstantial sea. It is a fairy spectacle built for night nomads and poetical policemen. The moonlight washes away all mere facts, and there is nothing more illusory in the world than snow-pallid marble swimming in the ghostly saffron beams of Luna.

As I stood outside the show-window of the cigar store opposite the Library one morning, as the darkness waned, admiring this admirable ruse of Nature, a policeman approached me and said:

"Fine sight, sir."

"Yes," said I, amazed that a Sense of Beauty had crawled into the Department.

"Nothing like it anywhere for sheer mystery." he continued.

I looked at him closer. He was tall, about forty, athletic, a fine, sensitive chin and big brown eyes, with dancing pupils.

"And maybe you'll see it this morning if you watch here a few minutes longer," he said in a low tone. "You evidently know that such things can happen—al least, you do not disbelieve in their possibility." He had evidently been "mugging" me with his mind.

"What things?" I asked, wondering whether I had to do with "one of our finest" or whether the last Tom and Jerry had turned my mind.

"Why, those lions. You may see them rise from their pedestals in a minute or two—if it is their morning to do it. I have been on this beat since they were put there, and I have seen them do it dozens of times, though they are erratic and uncertain. But look!" he exclaimed pointing across to the building, as still as a thought in the brain of the dead.

Both lions had risen to their full height on their marble pedestals, leaped to the long flight of steps, where they ambled to the fountain. They drank long and deep, their manes floating in the moonlight like the golden zephyrs of some ancient, dying sun.

They returned to their pedestals slowly, and exchanging looks full of meaning with their great yellow eyes—eyes that were the mirrors of a city's traffic and vanity—they resumed their marmoreal immobility, while the moon yawed to her bed-chamber in the Dawn.

The policeman had suddenly disappeared. I returned many a moonlight morning to that spot opposite the Library, but never found that policeman again, nor did I ever see the lions take to the "water-hole" in the moonlight.

But maybe that is because I cut out hot Tom and Jerry's.

Ave, Mouquineers!

WHATEVER is has a center. This is a mathematical axiom as famous and as unshatterable as that other mathematical dogma—two parallel lines can never meet; two parallel jags always do.

New York is a queer paradox. It is the only city in the country that has broken over and over the dogma of "whatever is has a center."

New York has centers. It has perpetually moving centers. Its centers jazz and scamper all over the five boroughs, playing hide-and-seek with census enumerators between decade "figgering."

The only center that seems to be kept put and that resists all attempts to dislodge it is the financial center. Broad and Wall and thereabout remain decade after decade the Empire City's Hub of the Cush.

Several attempts have been made to swing it from its moorings. Five-hundred-and-twenty-per-cent Miller some years ago tried to carry the center to Brooklyn. The result is well known.

Another attempt was lately made by a Boston Archimedes—Ponzi by name—to carry the center of financial gravity from this city. Failure marked him for her own.

All other centers in New York, however, keep moving.

The gambling centers move so quickly that they look like a straight line. These centers are pursued by plain-clothes flying wedges.

The Great Whisky Center in these days is having the time of its gay old life. This center used to be around Forty-second Street. The rapid fall of the booze forts around these corners and the rise of the chocolate and soda centers on their ruins is a matter of near history.

No whisky center now lasts more than a month. It moves with

satchel and suitcase so fast to other points on the chessboard of the Big Town that half the time the thirsty have nowhere to plant their gullets. These centers are racing so rapidly in various directions that there are often collisions. Then comes the tug of graft.

The theatrical center, being a slow body, moves with precision and somewhat ponderously. Its objective is due north. I remember when it was at Fourteenth Street and Broadway, with "Mike" Lyons', at Bowery and Houston, for the midnight souse. The geographical center is now at about Forty-third Street. In forty years it will reach Washington Heights with a revival of "The Old Homestead."

The center of population in the greater city has always been a matter of guesswork. It moves with the turning of the earth on its center-pole. Five hundred thousand humans, more or less, clear out of the downtown districts before 6 P.M. to various parts of the urban compass. This causes a violent bobbination of the center of population.

The center of population might be at about Fourteenth Street at noon. Presto! at 8 P.M. it bobs up at Forty-second and Broadway.

In the ancient days we have often thought the center of population of the city was looking at the Futurity. At night the center of population could be placed at Shanley's, Rector's or "Jack's." During the war it moved to the Library steps.

Inquiring into the movements, whereabouts and psychological movements of the center of New York life, I came to ask the question, Where is the Center of Intelligence of New York?

Does the brain of New York move erratically like the rest of the organs of this Titan?

To speak of the center of intellectual gravity in New York City would be a misnomer. One should speak of the centers of intellectual levity. And it is as inevitable as human thirst that these centers are always found in a café or a tavern.

In those days, so far away, when Washington Irving and Fitz-Greene Halleck lived, the center of brain sparkle was far downtown. Literature was literally a floating population then. Poets seldom slept in their own beds—conceding they had one. Their wit often came out of a bottle. Intelligence often moved to the music of the beers.

Most books landed at the Battery from England. There were

"saloons" modeled on the Paris and London institutions, and many times the cream of the center of intelligence held its soirées (if cream can hold a soirée) in debtors' jail.

Old Greenwich Village had always been a center of light unto itself. The light here was rather exclusive. It muzzled its rays, the skulls containing the Sacred Gleam meeting indoors around the big wood fires. Whitman, Edgar Allan Poe and the rest of the literary rowdies of those days were rigidly excluded. Clean linen and a spotless cravat—astounding to relate—were necessary in that circle.

At the time the Light centered in these Ninth Ward drawing rooms a reading out of Sam Johnson was preceded by something on the zither, followed by Gray's *Elegy*. Byron crept in in later years, when the Village began to crack under the poundings of the younger generation from Fourteenth Street who came knocking at the door.

To-day the Village is still a center of intelligence. Its big beam is the clock tower of the Jefferson Market Police Court. It is a shabby-genteel, run-down center, with light-shafts that need scrubbing. The Promethean spark down there is now imbedded in pea coal. The friction of a cop's club on a small sample of pea coal sometimes brings out the sacred spark in the shape of an epigram or a *poème rouge*.

The Center of Intelligence dragged its anchors of gravity about forty years ago and dropped into Gramercy Park. Some of the Light inundated Eighteenth Street and Irving Place and broke violently against the bulkheads of Lüchow's bar, spraying Tammany Hall with some bubbles of intelligence.

The Light took to food in that quarter. It was the glorious era of the Pension, the free lunch and basement red ink. Much brains has been spilled around that section. They still point out the place where O. Henry and "Bob" Holliday first met and where James Huneker and Victor Herbert had the row over Bach's inharmonious sixteenths in the dining room of Mme. Gros-Ventre's boarding house.

New York's intelligentsia at that time carried the banner along Fourteenth Street. The centers of New York's brains? It was the very solar plexus!! Irving Place, stretching from Gramercy Park to Fourteenth Street, was both a Mississippi and a Styx. How many travelers—poets, dreamers and mere writers—have started at the iron gates of Gramercy Park and headed toward the rathskellers on Fourteenth Street never to return! Some were washed over onto Third Avenue all the way down to the Bowery, where the alcoholic gravity was so strong that to this day they have never returned to their parent center.

However, the National Arts Club and the Players still disperse some beams, and these two clubs may still be called a Center of Intelligence, for they as yet have no record of a McGraw Evening.

The Centers of Intelligence got pretty well shot up all over town after O. Henry died, Jo Davidson moved into the Hotel Crillon in Paris, and the disappearance of Huneker (peace be thine, Immortal Jim!) into darkest Flatbush.

At one time all brain-beams gravitated to Mouquin's, on Sixth Avenue. For some years it was a regular Midnight Sun of shimmering intelligence. Every problem on earth was settled there in the evening, and stayed settled until the next evening. Problems, political and aesthetic, have return tickets.

The uptown cafés were pullulating and ululating Centers of Intelligence for many years also. Most of the choice rays in the center at Mouquin's used to trail their garments of glory up Sixth Avenue to "Jack's," where brains wagged till the dawn. Once "Hype" Igoe introduced a ukelele among the bearded Senators and once Trotsky appeared on the arm of "Bob" Chanler in the Councils of Intelligence; but both music and Bolshevism were quickly ruled out by Sir Jack on the ground that they disturbed the intellectual lighting system of New York.

Then came the check, the change, the pall. The war and the Eighteenth Amendment doused our intellectual glims for a while. Can brains meet around the soda water fountain? Is there a Pierian Spring hidden in the tealeaf? Is there an Old Prometheus in Yung Hyson?

The Centers of Intelligence of New York no longer emigrated. They were smashed to embers. Where can we go now to hear Good Talk, to meet Brains, to see our fire-carriers incinerating a score of Ephesian domes of an evening?

Hail, Mouquineers! where do we go from here?

The Broadway Mind

WALL STREET once meant a gut of a street that ran from Trinity Church to the East river. It is now a generic term for the moneyed interests of America: it connotes the Beast of the Apocalypse to the vestal souls of the Farm Bloc, and Paradise Regained to the far-clambering spirit of the ninny-wit bank messenger. What was once a street has become a state of mind.

So with Broadway. From towpath to street; from street to a state of mind. The Bowery is now a legend and Fifth avenue is rapidly transforming itself into a Suit and Cloaka Maxima. But Broadway persists, grows, ferments. A definite chunk of matter has now become a definite state of mind—the Broadway Mind, the antithesis of Main Street, a world-scoop, an outpost of the cis-Atlantic wisecracker.

The Broadway Mind is not indigenous to Times Square. It is far-flung over the five boroughs and its nuances lap over into bucolic Nassau and Westchester. Its psychological sparkle is up-to-dateness. You are ultra-Broadway if you have heard a smutty joke that has not yet penetrated into the speak-easies, if you have been present at a private dress rehearsal of a smart play, if you heard Raquel Meller in Paris or Madrid before she came here, if you know where the Scotch is to be had that only millionaires drink, if you have the low-down on Washington, if you could discuss *Elmer Gantry* before its release, if you can whisper the next move in General Motors, if you know-"Got it straight, kid!"—why the second curtain of *Tristan* at the Metropolitan was delayed a half of an hour in rising, if you are *always* a ringside man at the big fights, if you have never yet been touched in a

Broadway night-club—"Hell those boys know me too well, Charlie!" —and, finally, if you can slap Roxy and Karl Kitchen on the back.

But these things are mere bubbles on the surface of the mind that Scotch cannot wither nor erratic libido stale—or stall. Let me tap deeper. The Broadway Mind is intensely serious. Behind its mask of flippancy there crouches the cunning of the pioneers. You may play between its great paws, but don't fool with its money-maw, or you will get a sudden vicious down-stroke or be slain by a Sam Hoffenstein epigram. In this respect the Broadway Mind is as human and as moral as any other type of mind. To the Broadway Mind money is a spiritual thing, as Don Marquis says. Here, then, is the deep tapping and substratum of the Broadwayite's soul—money. The rise and fall of the box-office (a term which I use generically) is the barometer of the man. What the Broadwayite talks about and what he is thinking about are two different things. He can be glib and epigrammatic (delightfully so) on Mussolini, Ruth Synder, Geneva (not the gin, but the disarmament fraud), Coolidge, Al Smith, McNary-Haugen, Ford, Einstein, Kluxery, three o'clock closing, Bobby Jones, Lady Astor, sea-floundering aviation nuts, or Mexico; but what is really nibbling at his cerebrum all the time like the undying worm is the box-office. It is his preestablished Platonic Idea. Before Abraham was, Box-Office am. The Broadway Mind is thus profoundly American. It is as patriotic as the Sub-Treasury.

The Broadway Mind exudes a form of cynical optimism and ironic enthusiasm which are a combination of Old World disillusion and New World Pike's-Peak-or-Bust hardihood. The Broadwayite's Dionysiac Evöhé is "It's a wow!" "It's a sell-out!" "It's a clean-up!" But his salutation to Success is always tempered by the meditative biting off of a long cigar or a significantly derogatory flipping of the ashes from the end of his cigarette. It is the murmurings of the backwash of the eternal vicissitudes of the Great White Way. It looks like the Great Yellow Way to the outsider, but the Broadway Mind has called it white because those lights also reflect the bleaching bones of those who didn't reach Pike's Peak. He may be next. This ironic enthusiasm and cynical optimism flood the Broadway Mind at all points on the cow-path from the Battery to Kingsbridge. It is an old European mind that is not quite sure of the miracle-money of the Western World. It senses a diabolistic and smiling Houdini behind all the phenomena of wealth and luxury.

II

The Broadway New Yorker is, therefore, intensely concrete in his philosophy. He is unimaginative, literal. Pigs is pigs. He wants the low-down on everything. "Come to cases," "Where do I come in?" and "Show me" are his stepping-stones. The granite and the asphalt have passed into his hide and hair and bone. No star-shooting, no Cockayne rhetoric for him! He is gay, Rabelaisian, generous; but he plants his bottle of Scotch right above the dotted line. Drink—but sign! Here's a Corona-Corona, old man—but don't waste my time; if you're broke, take it out with you and smoke it after dinner. How's the wife?—but his twinkling eyes say, How's your bank account?

Broadway Man believes everybody should be Somebody. Democracy's aspiration to aristocracy is embodied in being Somebody. This Somebody should appear somewhere, somehow, some time in the daily prints. If Somebody's photograph has appeared once or twice, this person passes into the Pantheon of the Broadway Mind. Publicity is the key to a seat in the Astor grill-room at lunch. Publicity admits you to hypostatic union with the supra-Broadway Mind that flows and bubbles and squirts around the tables in the main Algonquin lunch-room, where every face is a mirror of Fame, fame in its Broadway *Gloria in Excelsis* incarnations—amazing publicity stuntists (any obscure being sitting in this room, calmly nibbling his olive, may be called and anointed for the rotogravure section at any minute), the Sainte-Beuves of the weekly book-review sections, the dowagers and the dilettantes of dramatic criticism, the Victor Hugos and Flauberts of the scenario, famous hog-the-close-ups, pontifical Brahmins of the pen who syndicate the doings of the Broadway Mind to the *gobe-mouches* of the sticks, the creme de la skim of sophisticated column writers, the Westchester branch of the *Saturday Evening Post*, pale hangovers from the old Forty-second Street Country Club, playwrights who have made vast fortunes dumbing up Ibsen and Sardou, actors and actresses who played in *Sam'l of Posen* and with Clara Morris, and the younger generation who are preparing to burst the cocoon of obscurity and flit away into the empyrean of a four-column picture on the Sunday theatrical pages. The very Valhalla of Broadway Somebody!

The Broadwayite *de rigueur* must be a member of the Lambs, the Friars, the Greenroom, the Newspaper, the Players, the Jewellers' or the New York Yacht Club. Naturally, he is eligible to all nightclubs. He may belong to anything but the Union League. There are cenacles for the ladies, too. For the Broadway Mind is gregarious, group-proud, and after freely co-educational. Nothing is farther from it than the aloofness of Saint Francis of Assisi. If it has secrets, they are more Rotarian than Rosicrucian. It has a Big Brother air in its unsophisticated moments and a gay minstrel, well-Mr.-Bones expression in its more expansive and sophisticated hours. For a Broadwayite to pass through *the* District—or even Madison Square—and not to shake twelve hands and get three back-slaps a block causes a lowering of vitality and cardiac palpitation. For a Broadwayite to pass through Longacre Square, march north and be utterly unslapped, unsaluted, un-howd'd or un-whistled-to, might cause cerebral congestion. It has occurred to me so many times since Prohibition that I no longer consider myself a Broadway Mind. It is for this reason that I am now silently cultivating my own garden in Gramercy Park—*outside* of the Players' Club.

When Little Rock or Natchez thinks of the Broadway Mind it naturally connotes Gayety (and then spits a large, contemptuous spit nor' nor'-east). Gayety is right. It is one of the elements of the Broadway Mind. But it is a hectic, febrile gayety. It is a gayety that feeds on memories, of which more anon. It is a gayety that always seems to be covering up something—a fence, a mask, a mockery of spontaneous joy. Life in these ghastly funnels called New York is brain-battering and nerve-shredding. New York would be an eyeful for Argus. It is a neurotic Octopus. Father Knickerbocker is gangliopathic. On this physical basis what aberrant flowers of gayety blow! When I try to connote the gayety of the Broadway Mind I think naturally of the flowers of Gaugin and Odilon Redon or the panels of Bob Chanler. It is an alcoholic, a shrieking, a morphinated, an hysterical gayety. It is shoddy dyed to look like gold, like almost everything else in America.

By extension, the term Broadway Mind might cover all of sophisticated, artistic, literary, Ritzy New York. But here also there is no joy found. Life and personal experience do not stimulate its laughter. Speed, noise, alcohol and smut are rammed into the hides of persons at parties, in the theatre or in the jazz-bedlams with gigantic syringes. They all want to be doped. Conversation and wit are gone. Some one cackles an epigram into somebody else's gin-glass. Songs are hiccoughed. They stamp the floor and roll off of lounges, turn nympholeptic flip-flops, bawl at one another from table to table, and hurl chicken-bones at the simpering host or hostess ("high-tea") to convince themselves they are alive. They pinch their consciousness with the monkey-wrench of alcohol, squawk and speed till it screams. Belly-born and brain-born gayety—not a vestige. The Broadway Mind is a camp-meeting of Furies when it lets loose.

III

Ah! but there was a different kind of Broadway once upon a time! (Yes, this is now a Palmy Days wheeze—make the most of it!) There was, in consequence, a different kind of Broadway Mind. Because, I suppose, there was a different kind of America. The New York I first came to live in, in 1899, and the New York of to-day show the difference between Shanley's restaurant and a Nedick nookery. The former had not become, as yet, a giant cash register with the "no sale" card torn out. Its motive was not money, but a gay *laissez aller,* a five-cent-beer-and-pretzel joviality. Machinery had not yet conquered. Those garbage transporters, the subways, were unknown. There were beer picnics in Central Park. The sea-going night cab was as mysteriously enchanting as a trick cabinet. Fifth avenue was Bohemian up to Madison Square (the Brevoort, Fleurot's, Wallace's—conversation and wine that are no more!). Tom Platt kinged it in the Amen Corner in the Fifth Avenue Hotel, while old Dave Grey bounced us out of the Hoffman House bar with a nosegay in his coat and 'McCarthy's Daughter" on his lips. Instead of skyscrapers, a *table d' bite* with free red ink. The confidence man was delightfully conversational. Family beer gardens on the Bowery. Seidel-drinking contests in Lüchow's between Jim Huneker and Anton Seidl. Open barouches up to the Metropole, where you might see Edgar Saltus leaping from the second-story window. God was on his throne. All was well with the Constitution.

The hard-boiled face was not known in New York in those days. The New Yorker loved his city with the same fervor that a boulevardier loves his Paris. To-day the New York air is gone. It is not distinguishable from the Chicago air or the Philadelphia air. No one now ever hears a New Yorker say "I love New York." His face has become ashen and sober. He tolerates New York. It is no longer Little Old Bagdad, but a stern mother-strumpet, an eater of men, Moloch. It is now the City of Dreadful Necessity. The evolution of New York has been from a gay, free, easy-going city to a chilly city of stone and steel, where loitering, sauntering and skylarking are taboo, where "mum's the word" is printed on every face. The soft, beery eye has given way to the hard, cold eye of steel stuck in drawn faces poisoned by bootleg. Once civilized, New York is not even barbaric now. It is Yahoo-Land out of the brain of a Poe.

The Broadway Mind, before the war, was rather an unsophisticated mind, an honest mind. There was no bluff about it. It fought, it talked with bare knuckles. It was Life Abounding. It played the races and poured its winnings down its gullet at Manhattan Beach, Rector's, Shanley's and Jack's. It sang in the open. It looked on business as a means To-day business is an end in itself to the Broadwayite. No one meets another casually. If it's lunch or an evening party it is because some one is going into some one's pocket or looking for a job. In old New York *camaraderie* was sufficient unto itself. Shake, and take a drink, and can the shop. It *was* a simple mind, an hospitable mind, a give-and-take mind in those days. It blew the coin, puked and laughed.

The old Broadway Mind came to its apogee in Jack's. In Rector's, Shanley's, Churchill's and other Broadway places there was always a medley of New York, Chicago, Philadelphia, St. Louis and Al toona. But Jack's was New York. Jack's was the Broadway Mind afloat and awash. It never closed. It never permitted music. It had no clock. For credit—I *know*—the sky was the limit. You could sleep there where you drank—I have. It was a nightly sanhedrin of wine agents, gamblers, actors, newspaper men, jockeys, celebrated writers, newspaper proprietors, painters, sculptors, opera singers, millionaires out of the Social Register, football heroes, prize-fighters. I have seen in one night in Jack's Edgar Saltus, William. Randolph Hearst, Diamond Jim Brady, Booth Tarkington, Harry Thaw and John Barrymore. In those olden, golden days I have heard every subject under the sun discussed—New Yorkers argued in those days and had convictions. The Broadway Mind spilled all it knew. The rising generation of New Yorkers simply cannot visualize Jack's (I was a constant attendant at those all-night services for over twenty years). My one hope is constantly to whet the appetites of their malleable minds to the point where the Boy Scouts will rise *en masse,* toss their radios into the Hudson, and cry to the Fathers in Washington, "Give us back the Broadway Mind that flowered in Jack's!" Catch 'em young! says Mother Church.

IV

A reflex of this Broadway Mind of to-day is the tabloid mind. The tabloids are the preparatory schools for the vulgar sophistication of the Broadway Mind of tomorrow. The girls and boys who devour these sewer-rags in the subway by the million will be the Broadway wisecrackers of another year. Their literature, their drama, their epigrams, their knowledge, their cynicism, their ideals (if any), their very mode of dressing will come out of these neo-penny-dreadfuls. Forth from this tabloid gutter will come the publicity lunatics, the shoddy intellectuals, the smart Alecks, the have-you-seen-mes? the "good showmen," the first-night exhibitionists of tomorrow—a further decadence of the Broadway Mind. Live and verify what I say.

BUILDINGS

The Grandeur and Decay of Home, Sweet Home

WHEN I was a boy home was a place that one retreated to to escape the world and its uproar. It was a sanctum. It was a place of infinite quiet, broken occasionally by the squalls of the new-born sister or brother which I looked upon as natural a noise as the hurdy-gurdy under the window.

The old American home life during the evening was delightful. The classic—and true—picture is the family gathered around the lamp. Mother knits father's socks. Father reads the evening paper and smokes. The children play dominoes or read books. The door-bell, some evenings, rings at never later than eight o'clock. Mr. and Mrs. So-andSo call. At nine o'clock the eldest daughter plays the piano and at nine-thirty the Rising Hope recites "Paul Revere's Ride." Lemonade and cheese at ten. Visitors depart at ten-thirty—never later. All in bed at eleven.

Crash!

Enter—without warning—nerves, jazz, radio, phonograph, home-brew, the lip-stick, petting parties, visiting bottle parties, the fox-trot, the rolling bar, the tin Lizzie, the "movie" magazines, the flapper and the hip-flask!

Far away are those good old days when we awaited with joyful expectancy the visit of Uncle Amos from Vermont and grandfather from Kentucky.

In their places we await with lighted eye the arrival of Uncle Johnny Walker from Canada and Old Grandad from Bimini.

Sister Florence no longer sings on Sunday nights to the callers, "The Gypsy's Warning," but instead she bawls, "Step on It, Kid, While the Going's Good!"

Young Bobbie now doesn't care whether Paul Revere or Phil Sheridan rode. His favorite air is "The Camels Are Coming!"

Ah! how I used to clean up the bottom of the jam-pot! Now, my son furtively laps up the bottom of wine-glasses.

Moving used to be a clean, forthright operation in which everything was, literally, above board. Now the chief problem in moving is how to get the home-brew, the synthetic, the Scotch and the claret into the vans without attracting the attention of everybody and worrying about the thirst and honesty of the movers. (Nowadays every bottle of booze is a "pinch" bottle.)

In the New York home to-day the rooms are still lit up by a mellow glow—but it's not from the dear old lamp.

Mother now damns the socks instead of darning them.

Father no longer pores over the paper. He now pours instead of pores.

And even my two-year-old who used to cry for its "Oh, Ma!" now cries for its Omar.

So the passing of the New York home from its ancient atmosphere of simple domesticity to an atmosphere that is both luminous and redolent and where the cult of the literati is followed nightly is one of the most striking and ominous portents of the new era which we may call provisionally Anno Volstead 4.

Is the change in our home life from the family album to the flying kitchen squad a sign of deterioration or merely a passing phase in the transition of the Republic from Crane to Mencken?

I must leave the question in its deeper phases to those students of sociological problems who write for the greatest good of the smallest number.

Meanwhile I can relate some anecdotes that have come under my own observation as family man, father and host of some dusk-to-dawn non-stop drinking flights which may serve as data for those interested in restoring the New York home to something of its pristine purity and pre-bootleg somnolence.

I will approach my own apartment from the exterior and describe the bottle-fishers in the court. Public bottle-fishing is not against the law, as in our court every tenant has something on every other tenant, so there is a gentleman's agreement to keep quiet.

In the wintertime no one takes ice in our block of apartments. So the home-brew after being bottled is put out on the window ledges, generally in blocks of twelve, to get cold. The bottle-fishers on the third and fourth floors do not brew, but lower noosed strings from their windows when they believe the brewing families are out and pick out three or four bottles of beer.

I have observed the technique of the matter from behind my curtains and have seen my own bottles suddenly take wing and disappear skyward. The tenants of the first three floors thus keep the tenants on the top floor supplied with four percent beer during the winter. The latter are immune, as there is no fishing from the roof; it is too cold.

The art of noosing the bottles may be learned by children. It is the only combined indoor-outdoor game that I know of.

It's an ill brew that blows no one good, as to wit:

The family overhead brews two makings of beer at a clip. One night they left ninety-six bottles, newly scummed from the crock, on a rickety shelf in the kitchen while they a-jazzing went. My wife and I were busy in the kitchen at midnight with the kiddies thermosing the cocktails for the three A.M. party which we expected to blow in from the Roaring Forties when our nerves were shattered by a terrific cannonading overhead. It recalled to me the days of 1918 when the shells were booming in Flanders field. The shelf had fallen and the ninety-six bottles were exploding on the kitchen floor overhead. A river of beer came through our ceiling and walls.

The landlord did our kitchen over in hardwood. As I said, it's an ill brew, etc.

When I used to go to sleep in the old days it was for the night. Now I only nap between visitors. Everybody now keeps a book in his pocket with a long list of house numbers into which he can blow with a gang of mixed sexes at any hour before 6 A.M.

My receptions usually begin at about 1 A.M. They breeze in with their bottles, take possession of the house, turn on the music box, roll up the carpet for a dance, ransack the kitchen for ice and glasses, order taxis over my phone, and stagger out again with the hiccough:

"You've got a cozy little place here, I'll tell the world!"

I probably know the entire name of one person in the whole party. After they leave the house looks like a barroom in the Canal Zone.

They always bring an aged man along who sings "Pinafore" through and a "baby star" just in from Hollywood who'll tell you she put Cecil DeMille on the map and picked "The Covered Wagon" for Jimmie Cruze.

Do you remember the fine old dinner parties we used to give in the olden days? Maybe one cocktail served to your guests before dinner, then a quiet, joyous, full course meal in which you served beer or a light wine. Then you adjourned to the library, and over an occasional highball the conversation ran on books, plays, and the new invention of the Wright brothers.

Now your guests assemble at four o'clock for a seven o'clock dinner. They come with parched looks, and for three hours they sosh up on cocktails, to the continuous making of which the whole family work like subway diggers.

Plastered to the dome, your guests sit down. Continuous service of highballs and cocktails. They do not know whether they are eating whiskey or drinking chicken. Their soup grows cold while the 10,000 horse-power conversation runs to this:

"You're being stung—it's fifty dollars a case—I'll give you his name."

"He was so sober I couldn't talk to him—he! he he!"

"It was at Henry's bar—in Paris————"

"Gawd!—they put everything in their cocktails at Frascati's joint!"

And then after the Bacardi your guests revive the quaint Roman habit of drowsing in their plates. At midnight the dinner ends with half the number of your guests asleep on lounges and in chairs. About that time the post-dinner guests arrive saddled and bottled for action.

In the New Home Life pictures are not the only things that hang on walls.

I was lately a guest at a week-end party down in Babylon of a man whose drawing room is walled with originals of Lawson, Glackens, Whistler and Childe Hassam. Behind each frame there reposed a half-pint flask of rye. He kept his stock hidden in this manner to throw certain prowling guests off of the scent who had on several occasions ransacked his buffet and ice box.

Since prohibition I have been pestered by the reappearance of long-lost friends. Once get a reputation of keeping open house on booze and all the human alcoholic radios broadcast the news from coast to coast. Ralph Waldo Emerson didn't know what a profound truth he uttered when he said that though you lived in a forest if you possessed something that mankind was in need of they would dig a path to your door from the ends of the earth. Many are digging.

My home life is being obliterated by men from Philadelphia, Chicago, Boston and San Francisco whom I have not seen or heard of for years. They enter with the faces of pointers and homing pigeons. I do not know their names—many of them; but there is about them the air of men who have received glad tidings. And some are battered and worn and torn, and in their faces is the pathos of a constantly receding tidal wave of alcohol. They are the Bitter-Enders.

You have read about the man who saw the face on the barroom floor. Well, a long-lost acquaintance called on me the other evening who had the whole barroom floor in his face.

There is a brand-new home game played by a very excellent couple of my acquaintance. It is called hunt the bottle. This game is best played between a spigot-bigot and a scofflaw; and, indeed, in this particular household the wife—a staunch upholder of the ancient ideals of home life—is a spigot-bigot and the husband is a tertiary scofflaw. This, by the way, is precisely as it should be, for a home composed of two scofflaws cannot stand; it would founder in suds and Old Sunnybrook.

Wife hides the bottle from hubby. Hubby's evening is consumed in finding the bottle. If he finds it he is allowed one drink. If he does not find it by 11 o'clock he must go out and buy the wife a pint of ice cream and a box of chocolates.

The children—two of them—help pop hunt the bottle, and the game is so exciting that the youngsters prefer hunting the bottle with papa to listening to the radio talks. And it amuses the visitors.

The bottle is hidden under the mattress, in his overcoat pocket, in the oven, behind books, in the bread box, in the trunk, in the piano. There is a new hiding place each night. And so the evening passes merrily, merrily, merrily.

Certainly, home *was* never like this!

Among the most astounding phenomena of the times is the overturn in social values. Your social position is now determined by the size of your cellar and your generosity in opening it up to visitors. Character, intelligence and even wealth count for very little nowadays as magnetizers. You are measured by celerity and quantity in booze-serving. If your home is as dry as a Sahara, you will be shunned like an oil candidate in a national convention. Your acquaintances measure you alone by the size of the gullet-gliders.

Can the New York home stand the back-wash of bootleggery?

Odyssey of a Home-Hunting Ulysses

THIS is a tale more thrilling than ever related by Gaboriau, more improbable than the adventures of Baron Munchausen, more daring than those of Arsene Lupin, as sordid as the novels of Emile Zola, as mysterious as the dramas of Wilkie Collins, as romantic as a chapter of Poe, as exciting as a volume of Old Cap Collier and as human as O. Henry.

This tale is the truth, which is stranger than prohibition.

It is, in a word, nothing less, and something more, than the Apartment-Hunting Odyssey of a Manhattan Ulysses and his wife.

If I had not been the mental camera man of this "movie" of Life Behind the Doorknob in New York I never would have believed it, although sworn to by Doc. Straton and William H. Anderson on a stack of *Rubaiyats*.

We were new at the game when we started out on Monday armed with twenty-four addresses culled from the furnished and unfurnished apartments-for-rent columns of the daily newspapers and lists from certain real estate agents whose last names shall be Never-more—twenty-four addresses to places in twenty-four different sections of this little island bounded by the Aquarium, Hell Gate and Spitting Devil Creek, plus Staten Island.

We were new at the game on Monday, as innocent of Life as Little Lord Fauntleroy and Little Eva. On Saturday we were as wise as Diogenes and the Queen of Sheba.

Haroun-al-Raschid used to prowl around Bagdad at night disguised as a panhandler to find out what his subjects did behind his back.

If Al ever comes to New York a-riding on his karma, let him apartment-hunting go in broad daylight.

He'll find enough stuff for eighty volumes of *Arabian Nights*, a syndicated bunch of Bedtime Stories and twelve million yards of "movie" tape.

There was, first of all, the Man with the Iron Mask.

He looked at us from behind a basement iron grating in the Far West district of Greenwich Village. His face was a touring car to the Five Deadly Dissipations.

The house was one of those old-style brick affair, stone steps, iron railings, opaque shades and windows that were dirt arabesques.

It was either a "fence" or the home of impecunious genius, we crooned to one another.

Informed of our wants, the Man with the Iron Mask turned around, gave a peculiar whistle to some one in the dark abysm of the back room, stepped to the basement door, pulled out bolts and bars, and let us in.

The "housekeeping suite" was on the fourth floor.

In our passage upward we ran into a howling fight on the second floor in which a man was being propelled through a door by a very stout woman with a black eye.

On the third floor the door of the front room was partly open. Nothing but a bed and a chair in the room. In the chair sat an old man smoking a pipe, studying a spider's web in a corner.

From behind the door of one of the back rooms came the strains of "Anitra's Dance" from a music-box with the tertiary "flu."

As the janitor had a menacing air, we looked at the "housekeeping apartment" on the fourth floor. We dared not go back.

No wonder the price of it was only seventy dollars. Part of the chimney was on the floor and part of the floor was hanging down into the rooms on the third floor, and the closets had no doors—and a lot of things like that.

As we circled down into the basement again the Man with the Iron Mask in his rage at our weak-voiced, "Well, we'll let you know," must have forgotten to whistle.

We saw the claret still in full operation. Oh, you Village Olympians!

We had spotted a place advertised on Westchester Avenue. It was this side of the Arctic Circle. But we never saw the place, although we had our first look at Westchester Avenue, which has been called the Champs-Elysées of the Bronx.

As we appeared before the row of apartment houses which somewhere hid our number, a man appeared on the fire-escape outside of a fifth floor apartment holding a child.

Screams came from the windows. Whistles started to blow. A bullet just missed my wife's Easter hat. Men and boys scaled the fire escapes from every window on the block. Twelve men turned in one fire alarm.

The man with the child was a kidnapper. He disappeared over the roof toward Mount Vernon. A rumor spread among the crowds in the street that "It looked like the boy's own father."

We didn't stop to interview the mother, and the firehose burst right in front of our number.

It wasn't just the sort of place for a summer home we wanted, anyhow.

Lovely, lonely, lackadaisical Staten Island! Manhattan's own little Azores!

In three of the houses we visited the agent boasted that they were haunted, and that in view of the enormous interest in psychic phenomena and the domestication of ghosts he had put on an extra thousand on the yearly rent.

This agent had even practised "materialization" so well that in a house near New Dorp he calmly lit his pipe in the parlor, closed in the shutters, blew some smoke in the air and making a few passages, after reciting a passage from Ralph Waldo Trine, materialized a ghost who was the dead image of Captain Kidd.

"If you go to the northern part of the island you won't get anything like this," he said proudly,

throwing open the shutters, exhibiting a landscape of goats and *mutts ordinaire.*

I gave him a taste out of the thermos and we departed.

We took a gondola on the Kill van Kull, got off at a wild spot, according to the written directions, walked a mile or so through oyster shells and sylvan skunk cabbage till we came to another house surrounded entirely by undulating garbage heaps that sloped away to a murder—for a "movie" was being "shot," or "shooted," just as we rounded the last oyster shell, and found that the house had been rented to the Film-Flam Company an hour before we arrived and was to be burned down in ten minutes.

There were three other places to visit on Staten Island, but we concluded to call it a day, the "movie" people consenting to remove in an automobile what was left of us to St. George.

Home hunting in Staten Island is all right if you believe in the twelve-hour a day daylight saving scheme. He is mad who believes he can discover that isle in a lifetime. It's a fine adventure in eternity.

Friday took us to the upper reaches of west side Manhattan, in the neighborhood of some "swell" apartment houses, where the janitor's quarters in the cellar are far beyond the means of the average wage earner.

The cellars of some of these structures are worlds in themselves—beautiful routes for new subways; all that is necessary is to lay the tracks; or vast underground counterfeiting parlors.

The janitor of one of these marvelous edifices, after giving us the one-two-three over, asked us if we would like a little "recreation downstairs."

As we were both thrillproof and sensation-plugged by this time, we consented with that easy nonchalance of the typical borough-trotters of the greater city.

In the cellar an old-time prizefight was in full blast. We paid the janitor $2 for a box seat—a packing box seat, and we saw a ten-round contest without gloves. There were about 300 spectators present.

We left before the cockfight began. The "soak" on that was $5 a head. Anyhow, compared to home-hunting, a cockfight would be a tame affair.

As we stepped out of the elevator I asked the millionaire warden of the premises if there was a bullfight going on over near the Drive.

Sorry, but he didn't know of any. There was a cellar, however, three blocks up the avenue where a gentleman could take a whiz at the wheel. No, we couldn't do anything with the wheel to-day, thank you.

He filled our thermos up for $20 and we sped away—in a cross-town trolley car.

The proletariat have not only inherited the earth but the cellars as well.

These things will give the gentle reader a bare hint of underground New York—no longer a figure of speech, but an actual reality.

Some day a Freud of basements and cellars will arise who will expound and expose the complexes of our great apartment houses, showing how the janitor is not only the cause of suppressed fires but also the bellows and impresario of suppressed desires.

Saturday brought us to our journey's end.

We rented a houseboat on the Harlem River, guaranteed "to float" until August.

But whither can we float? The agent has it anchored in three places.

Chivalry in Office Elevators

"WHAT a creature is a New Yorker! How ignoble in the subway, in action how like an eel, in polite ness how like a clod!"

I hope the quotation marks will not fall off of the above paragraph in its peregrinations from the inkpot to the make-up man, because it was uttered by Professor Horn Rimm, President of the Washington Heights Branch of the Society for Renovating Courtesy in Elevators and Sub ways, as a poetic can opener to his condensed philosophy, expounded before the society at its usual Thursday night meeting last week at Sobersides Lyceum, up on the Heights.

An uproar ensued. The association was to hear on-that evening the report of the Committee on Male Politeness in Elevators, the report of the Committee on Seats for Women in the Subway, report of the Committee on Rushing the Stamp Window in Sub-Post Offices, and the report of Committee on Traffic Rules versus Lady Chauffeurs.

In this prospective yeast of reason and blow of soul it was not very clubby of the President to delay matters by hurling an uncivic monkey wrench in the Machinery of social uplift.

Mrs. Avoir du Pois, of French lemon extraction, arose to a blanket defense of the population of New York; including the Resident Sons of Oklahoma, untaxed Soviet Ambassadors stopping at the Waldorf, chil dren born on the Far Rockaway deadline, vacationists on the Ile de Blackwell and everybody else not hereinbefore mentioned, untaxed keepers of Holes in the Wall and poverty-stricken prohibition agents not excepted.

It was a furious defense of New York as the politest city in the world, although she fought bet verbal way through a barrage of epithets, interruptions and insinua tions which would argue the reverse.

But that is just what makes of woman a superman—she rides the storm of facts with the gayety of a penniless idealist facing rent day. Professor Horn Rimm finally poured some polite oil on the troubled hot air. He, too, was a New Yorker, he said; born at the confluence of Spuyten Duyvil water with the lordly Harlem; father before him first saw the light of day where the Gowanus rills and purls its way to the sea: grandfather was on the committee that received Lafayette at Pier 1, and so on backward to the day when the Battery was swapped to the Indians for a plug of Battle Axe.

All was quiet along the centre aisle trench after this, and Professor Rimm finished his speech to the subdued music of whispered threats.

Then came the business of the evening. The Committee on Male Politeness in Elevators fussed into their seats while the Quartette de la Wheeze rendered "He Was Polite to His Mother."

This committee had been sweated into life through the pores of many straw hats. Every male whose business it is to travel up and down in the passenger elevators of commercial buildings must face this question many times a month: "Should I or should I not remove my hat when a woman enters the car?"

What do Hoyle, Cushing and Delsarte say about it? His reason and his instincts are at war.

Where does politeness begin and where will a cold end?

Has a man more rights to his headgear in a commercial elevator than in a Ritz elevator?

If business is business, then keep the hat on.

If you are going up to join the Midnight Bounders, why, take the hat off.

Is there a business politeness as well as a social politeness?

Suppose the girl is only a stenog rapher that gets into the car with you in the Woolworth Building. Should you be as chivalrous as you would be in a "lift" at the Hotel della Robberie if Mrs. Fuller Rhino. of Chicago got in?

Profound and ultimate questions of conscience which may yet

bring the Supreme Court to loggerheads.

The chairman of the committee, Less N. Less, arose in his oxfords to read the report amid profound gum-chewing.

He deplored, first of all, that there was no standard of politeness In New York, or anywhere else for that matter.

He had read Lord Chesterfield from end to end, but could find nothing about elevators and hats.

He had gone through fifteen lives of Beau Brummell and Beau Nash, and found that those gentlemen had never even walked up or down steps—they were generally carried. They did not recognize elevators in their day; and the only mention of "lift" in their lives is as aforesaid.

He found the growing necessity for a Muse of Politeness. He would consult the foreman of the "lobster shift " in the Hall of Fame about it.

Coining down to polished tacks. Less N. Less found all of downtown and almost all of midtown New York agog and a-burble over the question, superseding in interest in some office buildings the question, Whose turn is it tonight for the cellar party?

Lower New York is, he found, divided into three camps—the men who defiantly refuse to remove their hats in the presence of women in elevators, those who do (subdivided into two classes, those who do it instinctively and those who do it because they fear elevator opinion) and those who nervously play with the rim of their hat from floor to floor; being all "up in the air" about it.

Many men are polite, but bald headed. Many bald heads are compelled to ride, Winter and Summer, twelve to fifteen times a day in commercial elevators. A draft striking a bald head from a certain angle between floors produces a chill which may run like lightning straight down to the hip pocket.

A beautiful girl steps into the elevator on the second floor. Baldhead is going to the thirtieth. It looks as though the beautiful girl would go the distance with him.

Puzzle: Should Baldhead remove hat and run the risk of contracting pneumonia or violent anti-amendment sneezing or keep his hat on and encounter the mental diagnosis of Beautiful Girl as "No gentleman?"

It was the unanimous opinion of Less N. Less—who enforced the unit rule on his committee on all decisions arrived at by his lonesome—that baldheads are justified in keeping their hats on on all occasions. The society voted a unanimous "yea" after ejecting a minority of ten.

Those other than baldheads who kept their bats an in the presence of women In elevators were roundly condemned as enemies of chivalry. Mrs. Avoir du Pols advocated an elevator, cattle-car amendment to the national Constitution for these men.

Horn Rimm ruled her resolution out of order. He wisely said that the Constitution did not need more amendments, but that the amendments would soon need a new Constitution.

Less N. Less had found that only one man in ten took off his hat in a commercial elevator in the presence of a woman, and that nearly all these men were residents of Brooklyn (Hear! Hear!), and that Southerners and Westerners were rarely seen in commercial elevators, as they came here for an entirely different purpose? (Cries of "Oh! Oh!" and "Tell it!" and "Ha! Ha!")

Touching the third class—those men who fumble with their hats and watch what the other fellow is doing with his—Less N. Less said they were pitiful victims of doubt, neither fish nor fowl nor good red roughnecks.

The cattle-car candidates were, he said, up-stage, while the brim-fumblers were up-State.

This last slur roused the ire of Hastings Tuckahoe, born in Goat's Island, Niagara County; and educated in the public schools of the town of Matteawan.

He denied that the chivalry from up-State was milk-fed. The Republican majority last year was—

He was thrown out at this point by the Sergeant at Arms, Rook E. Kidd, for addressing the meeting with his hat on.

A vote was then taken on the whole matter. It was finally the sense of the society that some men who ride in elevators were born chivalrous, others achieve chivalry, while others ought to be kicked out of elevators and to have their hats thrust upon them.

Arose then in a great clamor as to the precedence of the three other committees on politeness in public getting in their reports. The Subway Committee, the Automobile Committee and the Stamp Window Committee partisans fought all over the floor. Professor Horn Rimm lost control of the Society for Promoting Politeness in Public Places.

He finally put his gavel in the hooch drawer of his desk and declared that, as it was past 11 o'clock, and the currents had been popping for a week in the bottles in the coal bin at home, he would declare the meeting adjourned. But the voice was lost in the tumult.

The police made no arrests, but they gathered up fifty ruined straw hats from the floor—souvenirs of the battle for the Advancement of Chivalry in Elevators.

Discovering Home Life in New York

IN ye olden days (which means any time before 1917) "home" to the New Yorker was a way station between the office and the opera.

It was a place where the business suit was changed for a tuxedo.

It was a half-way house between the last cocktail at the Waldorf bar and the soup at Rector's.

"Well, I'm going to stay in tonight, boys," always meant in those days that you were broke or your laundry hadn't come back."

"They only have latchkeys; they have no homes," was the contemptuous remark of the man from Philadelphia or Kansas City in referring to a New Yorker.

That has all passed away as completely as Halley's comet, rathskellers and the little German band.

New York has within the last year or se become a City of Homes—so much so that if anybody is now seen on Broadway after midnight he is immediately spotted as a Philadelphian or Brooklynite with a roving commission from the folks down ter home to "find out the place where they've got it and arrange."

New York has, in fact, gone in for the Philadelphia Plan. Philadelphia, as we have gathered by the statistics lately put forth by both the Democratic and Republican machines of that city, is the greatest home-loving city in the world, especially on Sunday.

Some families used to spend their Sunday giving Herbert Spencer afternoons and Sarah Grand evenings. Chestnut Street was given up to snoring cops and promenaders from the Eastern Penitentiary who had broken jail for the afternoon with their keepers.

Of course, the old Philadelphia Plan has not yet invaded New York in its full moralic grandeur on Sunday or any other day. Knowing the New Yorker so well—his riant rantankerousness and his plangent pa-gantudiosity—am convinced that the ultra-homing instinct of the old-time Philadelphian will not invade our pleasure-loving souls to the extent of doing any final damage.

The renaissance of the home in Manhattan may be only a passing craze. To paraphrase Bryan,. Our heart is in the café, and we must pause at borne till it come back.

Heaven help us if "Home, Sweet Home,. should supersede our own national island air, "Where do we go from here?"

Prohibition, the prohibitive cost of outdoor life, especially at night and on Sunday; the growing craze of burglars for dumbwaiter rides, the spread of canned music and the passion for the materialization of spirits over the ouija board and in the kitchen—these are the main factors in unearthing the lost home-complex of the New Yorker.

The only thing, in fact, that can now drive a New Yorker out of his apartment at night is an invitation from an Atlanta or Terre Haute friend to join him at a theatre party. It is a fact that the Uitlanders from the South and West keep all the shows alive in New York. At most, the New Yorker finds the time to get away from the Watch on the Rhino at home to go around the corner to see Bill Hart, always leaving some one of the family behind him to watch the fire escape, the dumbwaiter and the bonded investments in the bookcase.

If you live in a regular house with a regular cellar, you have given up your out-of-doors and street life entirely. Many New Yorkers of the latter lucky class have, in fact, moved their business offices into their cellars, telephones and all. Call Extension Chaser H20 and you can get them any time of the day or night.

But it is the middle classes and the proletariat that this short sociological survey touches on and appertains to. They are the spine, the muscle and the hip pocket of our island civilization. It is they who have barricaded themselves by the million against the call of the street and the summons of the court.

The village chimes from Old Trinity and the thunder of the landlord's boot on the old oaken door come dully to their ears, as from beyond the walls of a monastery.

Pop holds four aces, and mother and little Willie serve the bonded investments. They should chafe!

Sweet are its uses, as was said aforetime by the melancholy Jaques as he stared into the rill of aqua pura near the village of Arden, which had just voted dry.

Prohibition holds yet a rare jewel in its head. It is the lucky Hope jewel of home brew, -which is the main factor in driving the New Yorker back to the home.

The yearly lease used to be the cornerstone of the home; it is now a recipe. The Little Red School has gone; the Little Red Nose has come.

The usual 10 A.M. conversation over the telephone between our goodly housewives used to begin, "How did you enjoy the show last night?" It now begins, invariably, "Has it got a kick in it yet?"

Papa, who now no longer loiters with tile boys downtown after 4 P.M., used to be greeted at the door by mamma and the children with kiss-puckered lips. Papa now enters his door unwaited, for the whole family is busy bottling In the kitchen.

He used to bring home a jag, flowers and candy. He comes now with a new still under his arm, a brand-new pack of cards and three new shimmy records.

At about 8 o'clock the new Indoors Life of New York begins. The tables are spread and the cards are laid. All signs of unnecessary prosperity disappear. It is best to have the air of Just Making Ends Meet. In this new life of the times one-half the world must not know how the other half doesn't live. Pull down the curtains or you may be "pulled."

Casually remark that you think "you can dig up a drop or two." Keep your one "cracking" guest—there is always one nowadays In the party that is "cracking"—as far from the kitchen as possible. Lock the bookcase; he knows that that set of Thackeray in front is merely a smoke screen. I have noticed that the expansion of the olfactory and visular senses among certain persons since the appearance of the Volstead lesion in our liberties has been phenomenal.

I have noticed also a general air of suspicion in almost all the new vogue Home Parties. it is like an atmos phere. To allay everybody's suspicion that you have vast quantities of "goods" stored, always assert you have just been "cleaned out" by burglars, and By George! they got the rum and beer.

It is a cruelty, these days' to have the air of Vast Gullet Promise. The New Yorker, so open, so free, so forthright heretofore in all matters concerning food and drink, now wears the solid mahogany face and the buttonhole eye when he greets the friend who has " just dropped in to say hullo."

This is not the least of the nuances in the changing manners of our citizens since the home has become the last retreat of liberty and normalcy.

But prohibition is not the only cause of the decadence of healthy out-of-doors life in New York and the recrudescence of life under the lamp, where you can watch the moth singe his wings or your neighbor akin your wad.

It pays to stay indoors—that is, if you wish every night. To go anywhere nowadays you have got to be a moving picture actor or a revenue agent. The man with the average salary is beginning to move in the outer world through his newspaper. Even walking is no longer free after certain hours. You are likely to hit a crime wave at every other corner. To be caught in one of the traveling crime waves means that you will be fined for about all you have on you by the only persons who can now indulge freely and to their heart's delight in the joys of out-of-doors New York—our street hold-up men.

Before prohibition these pagan spirits used to Congregate at bars and in back rooms, where the rites of the glass became so pressing and insistent that most of us could get home at night before they took to the open road.

Now they've got to get out early to earn the price of a drink, reversing their hours. Another nuance is the study of changing manners here about. Prohibition and high prices have upset all the schedules of civilization, especially that elder branch of it which consists in the expropriation, transposition and sequestration of wads.

The police having become only a vestige of a former social usage—the vermiform appendix, as it were, of the body politic—every householder now polices his own flat. The new home life is not complete without a policeman's whistle (which, at the most, may summon another gang of burglars), a crowbar, ten padlocks, an automatic, a rifle, a sharp butch er knife and all your trench tools. Sleep with your souvenir helmet from the Marne on your head, the telephone within arm's reach and Spring 3100* graven on your brain.

All this is a brand-new experience for the New Yorker, and he is not adjusting his canty ego to the Home Idea without a good deal of friction, fret and flurry. His life used to be a Hungarian rhapsody; now he listens to one of them in his pay-as-you-catch-me music box.

From the ebullient and Rabelaisian jazz-room or tavern seat he used to look with satisfaction at the quietness of his home and the sanctity thereof.

Now from his parlor barroom and his dining-and-poker room he looks with longing eye to the sedateness and refined atmosphere of the café.

All values are changing and what used to be counterfeit is now genuine, and what used to be genuine is now counterfeit.

And worse to come. Under the coining Matriarchy, the lady inspectors of homes will do away with the New Yorker's poker parties, home-brew and bonded investment evenings and the delightful shimmy rag records.

Cheero! The spelling-bee, Pussy-in-the-Corner and the candy-pull are to come.

---

*   *ed*: SPring7-3100 was the phone number to call the NYPD at the time.

An Adventure in a Tenants' Community Council

EVERY Thursday night, when our Community Council meets, I get a good look at all those people who make those mysterious noises which seep through the floor, wash through the walls and percolate through the ceiling into our hallroom apartment.

A little touch of rent profiteering has made the whale world skins.

But it was, also, a little touch by the landlord that has made the whole world of tenants kin.

The Community Council is as near as New York has come to communism.

Communism as you know, is a political theory wherein everything is given to him who hasn't and absorbed by a club from him who has.

All landlords in New York until lately were communists. They came around every month and absorbed and dispossessed.

The tenant was merely the soft boiled egg that laid the golden goose—the landlord.

This communism was at last broken by a Bright Little Idea that entered the brain of some tenant who watched his home brew and other household necessities being deposited on the sidewalks of New York.

He conceived in the only part of him that could not be dispossessed—his brain—the idea of the Community Council.

His name is lost with the inventor of the thimble and the discoverer of the Cosmic Soul.

But he was the Sam Gompers of the Bitter-Enders among the tenants of New York.

"In union there are leases!" was his motto.

Before this cry fell the banners of the Amalgamated and Cemented Order of Gougers, on which was inscribed, "E Pluribus Bonus!"

The Community Councils in New York are now business organizations of district tenants which meet once a week in a library, a church, a hall, and even vacant gin mills.

They employ lawyers, listen to their local Assemblyman, call some of the judges names in dialects that are pure Esthonian, and talk.

Every one comes with a grievance or the shadow of one to come on his or her face. Coming rent days cast their adjectives before.

If you don't show up at your Council meeting after the notice has been put in your letter box you are looked on askance. You must be landlording on the side, and your regular job is only a blind. Or you have concluded a secret covenant, whisperingly arrived at, with the Beelzebub Leasing Company.

It would be better for you to drop your pipe and copy of the Hard Set at 8 p.m. and get around to your local Council meeting.

It has its advantages, even though you are selling so many epigrams and scenarios that you really don't care an unfermented grape akin what your rent is.

Since I moved up into the ragtime-graphophone district of the island I have had an itching desire to see what some of my neighbors looked like.

I heard, further, that the man in the apartment below, who has in his possession a poodle that can make more noise than Cerberus at the gates of hell when he sees a "Dry" leader trying to edge his way in to the Haig and Haig cellars, would be present.

Then I wondered whether wouldn't come face to face with the man across the way who breaks into "Sola Mia" at 7:30 Sunday morning and whose voice splits fifty-fifty.

I'd have a quiet word with him.

If you think sociability is the Psychological reason for these packed Community Councils—sociability plus rent troubles—you are mistaken.

Quite other. Each neighbor wants to identify some other neighbor, take his Bertillion, put some mental thumb-prints in his brain, and "mug" him for future reference.

All mankind loves a scrap. I verified this axiom at my first and only appearance at the Thursday night meeting of our Community Council.

The meeting was presided over by Doctor Novocain, expert on ills of the molar plexus, and incidentally the proprietor of a seat in the Assembly at Albany. He is noted for his political fence and bridge work.

He had not got very far in his opening discourse, in which he averred he was prepared to answer any question pertaining to rent, die-Possess or ropeless dumbwaiters, when a lady rose up and said:

"Your Honor—"

Sibilant snickers from all over the ball.

She glared around, readjusted her elbow on the head of the little bald-headed man sitting next to her, and continued:—

"Your Honor, suppose one of my neighbors persists in beating carpets in the courtyard, and the agent will not—"

"We are not here to discuss carpet-beating!" yelled a deep baritone from the back of the hall.

"The question is not on the carpet, madam," smiled back Asssemblyman Novocain.

This pun caused a gust of laughter all over the hall.

"Say, you, that broke up the lady over there—aren't you the guy that throws papers down the fire-escape at 632 West?"

"This is a rent meeting!" shouted a young man, who had leaped to his feet. "I have some questions to ask—"

"That fellow is a regular Pest." whispered someone in my ear. " He comes here every Thursday night with the same questions. He's trying to get the community lawyer to get him a rebate on his income tax."

Doctor Novocain's hand went up for order. He flashed his teeth around the hall His bald head nodded gently.

"We must stick to our work," he said.

He had just begun again on his masterly exposition of the enacting clause of the latest rent law when a terrific commotion broke out on the side of the hall overlooking the five-cent furniture store.

"Sneak!"

"Grafter!"

"Throw him out!"

"Lynch him!"

"Let me get at him!"

It seems that, ensconced in a corner, there was a live landlord present. He was taking notes.

A tenant who was noted for always minding his own business if it wasn't in his own apartment had looked over his shoulder and saw the landlord writing down the names of those present who were among his tenants and putting large black crosses opposite their names.

Policeman Rook E. Kid, the friend of all the peanut stand proprietors in the precinct, fought his way into the corner. Mr. Kid was in civies, but, fortunately, he had his nippers with him.

He handcuffed the Judas in our midst and dragged him out into the hall. He took off the handcuffs and whirled him out into the street, thus saving the landlord's life.

"You did great work there, Rook, old boy," I said. "That man is certainly a low-down sneak to edge in here; but we must have law and order."

Mr Kid looked at me sidewise.

"He's my landlord, you boob," he whispered. "I saved his life. I'll live rent-free for six months."

There was comparative order for a while. Three Judges had been ruled off the bench by popular vote. One man was advised by Assemblyman Novocain that be could not be put out of his house during the week that the cat had kittens. A woman was advised to "keep her shirt on" (hasty and blushing apology by the speaker for the faux pas).

When suddenly a man rose up from the very middle of the hall and announced that he had voted for Abraham Lincoln and every Republican nominee for President since, and that he was not going "to listen to any more of this here boolshevism."

Another uproar in which no damage was done. Old Abe's elector was assured that be was among 110-proof Americans.

So the evening wore on until 11 o'clock, when the Secretary announced that there were ice cream cones for sale on the floor below, after which the meeting stood adjourned until the following Thursday, which, he said, was to be Leaky Roof Evenings

That was my chance—to find out what I had come for.

Although I questioned every male going out of the door whether he could sing "Sola Mia," or had at any time attempted it, near my house, I could get no one to admit it.

What's the good of trying to be a Good Citizen?

I shall bring this question up at the next Community Council I attend.

Subways: The National Gym

IF you are like myself and a few other millions of citizens of the United States, Europe and Asia, a constant subscriber and reader of Mr. Frank Hedley's Subway Sun, you must be pretty familiar- with all the reasons as to why you ought to pay 8 cents instead of 5 for riding on the Sardine Express and the airy mountain-climbing locals, with their roomy observation car in the extreme fore and aft.

The editor of *The Subway Sun* is a bright man. He marshals figures, italics, underscorings, deadly parallels and coal statistics that please the eye typographically and move the mind to combative argument. But they do not convince. Nothing can lie like figures, except it be a motion-picture camera.

Now, there is an overwhelming reason why there should he an 8-cent fare on our subways. Why has the editor of *The Subway Sun* never guessed it? Probably because the reason is right under his nose. When he gets into the subway the elbow of the reason is literally rammed into his back.

It is the vast crowds and the rush-hour jams that have put all the travelers in the "tubes" under great obligation to the owners of the subways. The latter have given us a substitute for universal military training. They have developed a sense of direction second only to the homing pigeon's.

They have opened and kept going at their own expense the greatest outdoor physical training school for both sexes that the world has ever known.

The body is molded to graceful lines by the constant pressure of each on each.

The subway develops stoicism and self-control in the face of most exasperating circumstances.

It lengthens and hardens the muscles of the arms by compelling them to maintain an upright position for miles and often hours.

It straightens out knee sag by planting one firmly on one's legs—there being no room for knee abutment.

It develops politeness and graciousness in the most confirmed grouch. If any forward individual with a home-bruise face tries to "start anything," he is literally smiled into a tranquil state.

It has raised the morale of New Yorkers and outsiders one hundred percent

The football rush, the strangle hold and the tug-of-war are among the useful sporting exercises which this great institution reserves exclusively for its patrons of the morning and evening rush hours.

It inculcates patience—for many expresses are called, but few are chosen. There is a growing sect among subway philosophers called Local Addicts. They are the weaklings. They have chosen comfort to struggle and discipline.

All these advantages and more are open to the public of a great nation for the small sum of 5 cents. It is worth 8 cents—yea, 20 cents! For you may enter the subway at Junius Street. Brooklyn, a moral and physical weakling and emerge at Van Cortlandt Park an iron-muscled and an him-jawed Man—if you take your training during the preferential rush hours.

The above may seem like glittering generalizations. But concrete testimonials can be adduced to prove that our subways are the greatest mind and body trainers in the world. What Chautauqua is to culture the subways are to the body.

(Ex-Fatty) Roscoe Arbuckle—have you noticed him lately? He is edging away from the vulgar *nom de ventre* of Fatty because he is becoming normal in girth.

I was curious to know bow he began to lose his Hippodrome.

Three years ago Mr. Arbuckle was hard to get at. Now he is easy to approach. His ramparts have fallen.

"The subway did it," he said, sitting in his high chair, looking directly at his watch charm, an inconceivable feat three years ago.

"When I came to New York I left my machine behind and rode up and down in the trains at the rush hour every day for months.

"Nothing wears down fat like those crowds. Men go to Marienbad to fight fat; others go out to Tom Taggart's, and some take to golf; but let me tell you that the greatest obesity cure on this old planet lies right on the old shuttle trains between Times Square and the Grand Central Station or a Van Cortlandt express at Times Square at 6 P.M.

"I started the cure on a hot Summer day. With all my pores open I had melted two pounds away be tween Times Square and Seventy-second Street In ten minutes. I rode back and took the shuttle over to Grand Central and had three more pounds literally shoved into me.

"That was the result of the first day at your underground Muldoon's. Thereafter I began to decline regulary.

"I was once caught half in and half out of a car, with the side door closing on me. My back looked north and my stomach south. I rode three stations that way—it was an express—with the door actually pressing the in. It was most delightful. I assure you. I emerged ten pounds lighter on that trip. I understand I set a fashion in this sort of riding.

"Yes, indeed, I was always ashamed when I lay down my nickel each day for my exercise. Why I would gladly have paid a hundred dollars a day for the privilege. I can't conceive why *The Subway Sun* has got to put up such a fight for an eight-cent fare. It is only the selfishly thin who insist on that ridiculous five-cent fare."

Another great booster of our subways as an athletic school is Charlie Chaplin.

"The way I learned to swim," said the celebrated comedian to me, "was In the good old way of being tossed into the water and told to swim or drown. I swam.

"I advise the *sauté* method for weaklings among the younger generation. If you are a father and have a weakling son, get three or four huskies to drag him into the subways at the rush hour and bud him into the crowds, where he will soon learn the manly art of self-defense. If there is a potential Dempsey or Sandow in him it will come out. It will seem to him at first like a wildcat scrimmage, but he will soon learn that there are hard-and-fast rules in the game which he must obey or lose his hat, his eyeglasses, his wrist watch, or whatever else he may wear.

"I learned some of my most intricate and mystifying bodily contortions by daily exercise in the subways. By hanging head downward with nay feet in the straps I got that trick which you may have seen in one of my pictures.

"No, sir, the subway is not a railway; it's a gymnasium."

And now I bring forth royalty itself to testify to the benefits of con stant subway traveling.

The Prince of Siam—one of the keenest observers I ever met—told me that the one thing that impressed him above everything else in New York was the heroism of women in the rush hour trains in the subway.

"Nowhere else in the world," said His Siamness, "have I seen such feminine hardihood. In the crush of millinery and the wreck of veils at Times Square I saw the prophetic dream of a great race of athletic women of your Walt Whitman come true. They can give the Battalion of Death—what do you call it? Cards and spades?—yes, cards and spades.

"On the platform for three blocks your women fight like the fabled Amazons for a chance to enter these electric chariots. And when they get in they stand proud and erect for miles while your weaker sex read the sporting columns, reclining easily on their cushions.

"Such women, daily trained in such a school, must give birth to a glorious generation of athletic youngsters. There in nothing in the world like your subways for inculcating feminine self-reliance.

"Ah! We of the East have coddled our women too much. I must introduce your subway in Siam."

The fume of the Rush Hour in our subways has spread to the West and South. I lately read in a Western paper that a See America First touring agency In Minnesota had organized what they called Weekly Subway Excursions to New York.

This advertisement bills our subways as a rare and novel sport. Going under the Falls In the Maid of the Mist is played out for Grade A thrills. The subways at the Rush Hour are the thing! Parties of ten (so the advertisement says) will be taken from the New York hotels be tween 5 and 6:30 at night in tow of an experienced guide and sent into the maelstrom. Pneumatic coats will be supplied to the timid.

It Is curious that the editor of *The Subway Sun* has not played up these incontrovertible arguments in his campaign for an eight-cent fare, which would be a ridiculously small fee to pay for thin greatest of sub-pavement sport.

At five cents I feel like a deadhead at a world's series.

PEOPLE

The Exquisite Manners of the Newer Gunmen

I WAS sitting in a restaurant late at night not long ago in the Anti-Nordic delicatessen belt of upper Broadway when two young men entered who immediately attracted my eye.

Although they both carried pistols which they leveled in a rather neutral manner at all of us, this in itself would not have evoked any surprise on my part, for there is nothing more common and even boresome nowadays than for two or three young men with pistols drawn to enter your favorite eating place after midnight and go to work.

What particularly interested me and sent me into a profound meditation while I held up my hands and was being relieved of some of the roots and spuds of all evil was the delicate, almost poetic, movements of these two young men. Their entry was dramatic but courteous, something in the manner of Rudolph Valentino or John Barrymore entering a ballroom set.

They were dressed in what the French would call the *dernier cri*. They were perfect blonds. Their trousers were creased and the cuffs from their silk shirts protruded from the sleeves of their coats in the approved two inches as laid down by the master fashion moulders in Heilweber & Bruner's.

My eye remarked to my brain:

"We are being held up according to the inflexible rules of the new aestheticism in the fine art of public filching. These young men are veritably of the Fifth Estate and during the day are either gentlemen bootleggers or white collar workers in an office that codes and decodes oil night-letter wires."

And, indeed, as they approached us—there were about six of us crowded to the rear of the restaurant —everything went to bear out my quiet auto-observation.

On their faces—smooth shaven, delicately chiseled, blondish— there played the smile of inflexible social necessity. Their eyes were lit with a quiet humor as though they had wished to say:

"Pardon the intrusion while you are at table, but necessity, over which, according to the high authority of the great Greek tragic writers, the individual will has no power, compels us to follow the fashion of the time of getting ours either by—forgive the phrase—hook or crook."

From their overcoat pockets I saw two magazines protruding. They were *The Dial* and *The American Mercury*.

So my first impression had been absolutely accurate. I was in the presence of the Bunthornes and Brummels of the Neo-Hold-Up Movement.

The one with a face that might have been the face of Shelley reincarnate began in half-apologetic tones:

"Do not be frightened, ladies and gentlemen" (there were two women present); "we certainly will do you no bodily harm, and will, if you will be strictly advised by us, reduce your mental tension to *nil*. These pistols that we point at you are only for self-defence. Besides we carry pistol licenses procured at great trouble and with some circumlocutory pull, so we are strictly within the law.

"The ladies will remain seated and may go on eating, as we do not intend to molest them. *Au contraire,* if either one of them is in need of monetary assistance, we will be pleased to assist her.

"Now, if you gentlemen will kindly fold your hands over your heads we will as quickly as possible relieve you of your valuables, which for aught we know may have been as questionably come by as this little operation of ours would suggest.

"Dear me, who was it said—Proudhon or Emerson?—that all property is robbery? We, you will note, are Pragmatists in regard to that astounding epigram, which we of the Society for the Restoration of Public Confidence in the Arts of Stick-Up accept *in toto*, with all its implications and ramifications."

While he of the Brummel gesture and Shelleyian face was telling us this, both of them went through our pockets so dexterously and with such an air of by-your-leave-sir that no one of us felt that he was being robbed. *Au contraire,* as the disciple of the Newer Aestheticism in Friskery would have said.

We really felt that we had received the intellectual and aesthetic equivalent of the treasures (which are not laid up in Heaven and which moths and rust might consume anyhow) of which we were being relieved.

One of the women—I fear not of the Vere de Vere breed, but who had rather the air of a character out of Paul de Kock—having finished her coffee at the suggestion of this Admirable Crichton of public expropriation, said slowly but decisively :

"Gawd! Times have changed since the big days on Fourteenth Street! They batted up your phiz in those days for a dollar. Now there're college courses for yeggs and dips! Gawd!"

"Madame," replied the other young fellow (who was so quiet and refined looking that he would not have been permitted at the "Follies" or a Shubert revue), "there is, as my friend here intimated a few minutes ago, a movement among what you are pleased to call the yeggs and dips to regain the confidence of the public and the police in a profession that is as ancient as I must ask your pardon—a certain other profession which Goethe said was as old as the world and with which, unfortunately, some of your sex has allied itself.

"All human activity is about the same under the sun in all times; but technique *does* change," he went on, as he gracefully removed my diamond ring, "and in the change, or evolution, of technique we have what we call progress, which, as Chesterton says, is an illusion of direction.

"Now the society to which we belong are sticklers for improving the technique in our trade. You may have read in the papers of late that though the number of hold-ups and burglaries continues to rise, the casualties are less and less. That is because our association is taking in a better class of members and because we insist on *politesse—politesse at any cost.* It is, in fact, the fundamental doctrine in the

NeoAesthetic Movement of those among us who, like many artists and poets in Greenwich Village, refuse to distinguish between *meum* and *teum*—mine and thine."

Removing the watch and chain from the pockets of the man next to me, he went on in his caressing tones:

"Our technique differs among the various strata of the social organism. All of you here belong to the middle classes, from which both of us here have risen to our present position of supermen. Our rougher confreres, those who still adhere to the vulgar and outmoded knock-'em-down and drag-'em out school, call us the Two Blond Angels—but let that pass.

"We do not handle the proletariat with the same degree of politeness that we display here. They are lower in the scale, and I fear they would not appreciate the lighter touch. As we go up the scale we find we are better understood and meet with less resistance, all other things being equal. *Noblesse oblige.*"

"You have never murdered any one," I ventured.

"Good gracious, no!" they both said at once with shudders of horror, which I was astounded to note were not feigned. "We have fired in self-defence but only when pursued to a wall which must be over twenty feet high, as the old English law demands. We of the newer school of gunmen, to use the vernacular, discountenance murder— even of policemen—under any condition.

"We are steadily improving the house manners of our burglars," he went on, as he put back into the pockets of one of the men some cigar store coupons with a low "I beg your pardon."

"This improvement, I admit, could not have been brought about without the co-operation of householders themselves. Insurance of household goods is almost universal now, which has brought about a greater tolerance in regard to our trade. We have even noted a disposition among certain of the well-to-do to assist us in our work. They leave things around that they once put under lock and key, knowing the insurance companies will pay.

"Booze alone is still padlocked, alas!

"All this has had its effect in softening the manners of our burglars. You know that when we enter a house we have no intention of making a noise or creating a disturbance of any kind if it can be avoided. Householders have only of late recognized this. We desire to expedite matters coolly, silently and without interference. Is not that the *sine qua non* of all big business?

"As an instance of our growing gratitude and the softening of our manners, Reggy [pointing to his Shelley-faced companion, who was putting back some private papers in my wallet] and I were compelled a week ago to make an entry on the Drive. We found a husband and wife asleep in bed. They continued to sleep while we worked quietly in the other room. But when we left I had some doubts as to whether they had really been asleep and whether they had not been watching us from under their eyelids. But if so, they were perfect in their behavior because they did not report our work to the police—at least it never got into the papers.

"Well, we were so grateful at this recognition of the excellence of our work and the gentleman-like qualities we showed in the execution of it (we did not touch the ready household money in the secretary) that we sent back to the man by special messenger his costly watch and to the lady the most expensive basket of flowers we could purchase. You know that *quid pro quo* and *savoir faire* are now recognized *mots* in our trade.

"The trouble in the past," he continued, putting into his pocket the day's receipts of the restaurant which the smiling cashier handed him, "both as regards hold-ups and burglaries (I still use the vernacular), has been not with us but with the attitude of the public toward us. It is they who have made all the fuss and feathers. They have protested. They have resisted. They have made all the noise. When we were relieving them you might have thought they were being murdered. They denied the right of search and seizure—until the government itself pronounced it legal.

"It was this unfortunate attitude of the public that caused so many unfortunate *contretemps*. And it also caused a decline in the manners of those engaged in our business, which in the days of Robin Hood were *comme it faut, as* you know."

"Gawd! I'll tell the world things is changing!" sighed the lady out of Paul de Kock.

"Bergson and Heraclitus, madame, both have averred that other than Change nothing is—and, that being so, do you think that the manners of the greatest profession in the world could stand still, like Joshua's sun in Ajalon?

"We, too, are in the Cosmic Stream, and the Society for the Restoration of Public Confidence in the Arts of Stick-Up is moving toward its goal—an intensive aesthetic of prehensility, which the lady may comprehend better as putting the soft pedal on the frisk."

Silence. Then it dawned on all of us that both the pistols of the Neo-Aesthetic gunmen had been lying on the table right within our reach ever since they began operations.

But we were all too completely hypnotized to take advantage of the situation.

Finally I said:

"Haven't you both been afraid we would grab your guns?"

The young fellow with the face like Shelley said with a smile:

"No, sir—they are both empty, but we have a couple of loaded ones in our pockets.

"You see, we merely suggest death. You were never really in danger of it. Another one of our new rules.

"The science of suggestion in the realms of the Higher Psychology is only in its infancy."

They put the empty guns in their pockets and with a gay *"bon nuit!"* they vanished through the door into a taxicab.

"Gawd!" said the lady out of Paul de Kock, "I'll bet neither of them highbrows had a loaded gun on them!"

Have You Your Pet Burglar?

IT was six o'clock in the morning last week.

The place was Washington Heights, the third-story of Manhattan, the subways being the first-story, the streets the second-story.

I insist on the above paragraph because this is a second-story story laid in the third story of Manhattan, and directly concerns the life, the fortunes and the sacred interiors of every person who lives indoors.

I was finishing a *vers libre* poem called "To a Speedway" when the silence was gashed by a symphony of police whistles in semibreves, demisemiquavers, supertonics, sub-mediants and Dutch Babels.

I threw on my denim duster, took down my Indian pog-a-ma-ha-gen from the wall and hiked out into the street.

At the corner of another corner at the end of the street a big crowd was congregating—made up of cops, night watchmen, a wire-protective association and citizens hurriedly demobilized out of their sleep, many not yet in "civies" and some of the ladies without all of their accoutrement.

In the centre of the melée were two young men of a goodly mien that the officers of the law were tapping on the back and otherwise manhandling.

The citizens were tugging at the cops and watchmen, evidently trying to free the two young men. From windows and fire escapes came threats directed at the police with sporadic cries of "Leave 'em alone!" "Beat it, boys!" and "Up this way; we'll take care of you!"

I jammed my way into the mess and saw our two Neighborhood

Burglars fighting like madmen, making desperate appeals to the citizens to rescue them.

I wedged myself between them and the cops, who, seeing me, desisted—in fact, ceased.

I turned to the cop who looked like the leader of his gang and said:

"What do you fellows mean by arresting these two young men who have been doing a business on this block for six months without harming a hair on anybody's head? You're a bunch of fine rookies all right to try to arrest the regularly constituted Neighborhood Burglars of this district. These men visit us every night. They only take what rightfully belongs to a burglar. We are used to them, like them. They understand our ways and we understand theirs. Put these boys away and the Second-Story Concessionaires of New York city may put in a couple of Brooklyn roughnecks up here, and we will have to show them the game all over again.

"Now, you cops beat it! These are perfectly housebroken yeggs, reserved, discreet and noiseless."

The cops and the watchman slunk away while the crowd in the street and hanging from the windows jeered them for arrant boobs. Which shows what a little civic sternness will get you when your rights are invaded by a badge and a club in the hands of the rookies that do not know the rules of the game.

We washed off the faces and straightened out the clothing of Tony De Vere and Mike Montmorency, our special pride, and gave them a good breakfast, promising them that if they continued to enter our apartments in the same noiseless and gentlemanly fashion as they had been doing nothing would happen to them.

Isn't there enough noise in New York anyhow without destroying the only sect that practices silence?

The Pet, or Neighborhood, Burglar—and every district in New York has one or more—is a growth of the last year or so brought about by the great confusion that existed for years in this necessary and important branch of transportation.

Ten years ago there was a total lack of system. Every time there was a shake-up in the Police Department there was a corresponding shake-up from the headquarters of the Second-Story Concessionaires.

Burglars assigned to certain districts no sooner got the lay of the land and the shape of the roof in their section than they were transferred to some remote street in one of the five boroughs, which worked not only a hardship on them but put the householders to a great deal of inconvenience in readjusting themselves to fresh conceptions.

It wasn't fair to have a man study the fire-escapes on Riverside Drive and when he had them all down pat to jump him to New Dorp. Then, too, in those days there were no regular afternoon or night shift, and some hard workers were compelled to go on at one o'clock in the afternoon and remain on duty till six the next morning.

Now everything has been specialized. Burglars have their rights, and they can pick their districts, and may operate there as long as there are no complaints about rough stuff from the citizens who live in their districts.

If your apartment has not been entered yet, you are certainly a poor fish. Nothing so betrays a man nowadays as the confession, "I have never been robbed." It practically means you have no furniture, dishes or clothes in your home. It is humiliating in the extreme to have all your neighbors out on the sidewalk bragging to one another that they were cleaned out to the tune of five thousand or so the night or week previous, and there you stand silent, abashed a self-confessed poverty-stricken voter.

Cigar-store and restaurant hold-ups have been idealized and systematized in the same way. Two fashion-plates enter your store, tie you up with expensive silk ribbon, wait on the customers while you are temporarily motionless, wrap your day's receipts in their real pigskin wallets, read you a chapter from their pocket Dante, pass the baseball gossip with you or shove a Carolina perfecto in your mouth and light it—and then walk out of the store leisurely, turning on a Vincent Lopez, if you have a music-box, so that you will not feel the pangs of solitude while waiting for the cop, who is studying the box score in a hooch kitchen.

So long as you have got to be robbed, you may as well have some one to do it you'll know when you see him.

There is a place on Thirty-ninth street where there dwells a celebrated writer the back of whose apartment looks out on a certain street of ill-repute. He is so used to being robbed that he lays out articles that he has outworn or outgrown—like an old fur overcoat or an antiquated Jules Jurgensen timepiece—on the fire-escape every Thursday evening, which is the clean-up night of the special Neighborhood Burglar who has the census enumerator's job in that district.

It is just like spreading crumbs on your windowsill for your pet pigeons.

One week the regular visitor got sick or had to attend a meeting of the Welfare Club up in Sing Sing, or something, and he notified the celebrated writer on Tuesday that he had a "sub" on for the regular Thursday visitor. Please let him know whether the latter got fresh or bothered his best customer. And would he protect him from the "rookies," whose business, the regular averred, was to watch all flask pockets and street ball players.

One rainy afternoon my writer friend was sitting in the front room of his apartment pounding out a big syndicate editorial entitled "Honesty : Its Cause and Cure" when he heard the sad and silken rustle of a purple curtain in the back of his apartment and a foot that had unthinkingly stepped on a peanut from the previous night's carouse.

He walked back and saw an old style burglar—one of the disappointed lower classes of the profession—gathering up his umbrellas and canes.

My friend knew this was all wrong. It was not in the regulations. He caught him firmly, but not too firmly, by the wrists.

"Excuse me, boss, but I didn't know you were listening," said the poor fellow sheepishly.

My friend had him transferred to Brownsville. He also received an apology from the headquarters of the Second-Story Concessionaires.

Everything is being done for the comfort of our burglars. In certain sections of the city the midnight or matinee callers are so popular that kind-hearted housewives lay out a meal for them on the dining-room table on the afternoon or evening on which they are expected. Their dressing-gowns are hung for them on a hook in the hall marked "Charlie" or "Aubrey" or "Guglielmo," or whatever their names may happen to be, and felt slippers are laid out for them under the lounge in the "study" so that they can work foot-free and not disturb the baby.

In our neighborhood we are getting up 3 A.M. block parties for them this summer. The fire-escapes will be decorated with paper lanterns and kept lighted all night so that no accident can happen to them. A fall means an ambulance, and we want to avoid any "extras."

So many timid citizens have put away their valuables during burglary epidemics that there is even talk of a Housebreakers' Drive to reimburse those who will go broke because of this weak-minded holdout of many taxpayers.

The Police Band have volunteered their services and John Held, Jr., has offered to get up a poster in color of the famous patron saints of the Guild Burglarious—Bill Sykes, Jeremy Diddler and Jack Sheppard.

In an apartment where I had dinner the other evening I was struck by the signs in the halls and the rooms—it was a very large two-family affair—that met my eye. I thought I was in the subway.

Some of the signs were exact duplicates of those used in the big subway stations."

"Follow the green line to the fire-escape."

"Follow the brown line to the safe."

"Follow the red line to the silverware."

"Follow the blue line to the negotiable stock strong-box."

"Follow the black line to the telephone in case you need assistance."

"Why have them upset everything when they get in?" said my host to me. "As a matter of fact, the block burglar called on me one afternoon and asked me to have them put up. In years gone by there has been so much excess damage done by visitors that I thought him very considerate, and took his advice.

"A charming fellow and he has his own philosophy—our block mover," continued my host, setting aside the burglar's evening bottle of Crow y Haig. "On his regular monthly visit he sometimes gets so interested in my books that he forgets his business. But then I am the gainer. Every month take stock of what I haven't left, and you have no idea how little I lose during cold, hard winters."

Society soda-counter luncheons for pet burglars have become quite a fad in some of the more exclusive sections of the city. They make a great to-do over them on the big stool over the sandwich and the grape-juice. Sometimes, with the burglar's permission, the afternoon cop is invited in to join the circle, and adventures are exchanged.

The New Bleedem has even caught on among the Master Minds. The good old rough stuff is gone forever. The police vie with the citizens of New York in crook courtesy.

Pinch a few million in bonds, hire a touring car, go to another city and there, surrounded by lawyers and private detectives, negotiate with the home District Attorney for your terms of surrender—just like Villa, Jesse James and other lords of the profession.

Capitulate with dignity when you have dictated your terms, gear up the car and ride back in state to home Police Headquarters. Present your card at the door, surrender with grace and pick your cell. Our manners are really becoming as soft as a "movie" hero's.

There is one final anecdote I must relate before I close this tribute to the First Gentlemen of New York—the burglars—and it is one wherein there is contained a warning.

A burglar entered the studio apartment of an artist friend of mine and while rummaging around had the ill manners to startle my friend out of his sleep.

My friend unfortunately lived on a block where there was no pet second-story man. They were all pure *bourgeois* in that block.

The artist when he heard and saw what was happening reached for his revolver, but the intruder covered him first.

"Have you a householder's permit to have that gun?" asked the burglar.

"No, I have not," replied my friend.

"You know the Sullivan pistol law, of course," said the burglar.

He 'phoned the police, made a charge against the artist of having a deadly weapon in the house without a license, and only consented to drop the matter on the condition that my friend would back him for Neighborhood Burglar.

Civilization "may be going to smash," but there is a distinct improvement in the manners of the Lower Ten.

Our Sublime Bums

NEW YORK, like all big cities, breeds three kinds of lizards—the lounge lizard in the hotels, the corner lizard, and the bench lizard in the parks. The lounge lizard is the Brahman of lizards, the corner lizard ranks below him in the caste system of loafers, while the common garden variety of the park bench lizard is the proletarian among the tribe.

The bench lizard is a European product. In Paris and the Italian cities the open-air squatter traces his descent back to the Middle Ages. The right to loaf in the open has always been recognized in Europe.

In Paris the parks and squares have their regular guilds of bench lizards. Paul Verlaine was, by common referendum, elected their President in his lifetime. This great poet was probably the most famous of park idlers in his day. He chose, we believe, the Gardens of the Luxembourg as the Parnassus wherein to air his absinthe-perishing body when he was not sleeping in a wine cellar or getting pressed out in a hospital.

We wonder where Francois Villon, gunman, burglar, parasite, poet and pickpocket, aired his limbs. Probably somewhere around the old Sorbonne, where the theological discussions inside, such as the number of angels that could stand on the head of a tack, would tickle his fancy; for Francois, like a great many crooks who write ballads, was of a religious turn of mind.

We must not skip Socrates, either, while seeking the origin of the park loafer. Socrates gabbled morning, noon, and night in the public squares of Athens to any one who would listen to him. For work he substituted wind. He refused to support his family, and it was not an unusual sight to see him cut short while expounding his doctrine of the inside of words by a flying wedge of scrubwomen, led by his good old hausfrau, the gentle and unreasonable Xantippe, who was always being served with dispossess notices by some stern-brained landlord.

Sometimes the flying wedge let fly a barrage of pots and bricks at the head of the sublime bum of Athens. He was, as we all know, deported to jail as an undesirable citizen and as a man existing without visible means of support.

Villon escaped the gallows several times by the skin of his wit. But his philosophic ancestor was not so fortunate. He warmed the bench for a while in the Tombs of Athens, and finally drank the perfumed wood alcohol handed to him for violating the Eighteenth Amendment of the Grecian Constitution, which prohibited philosophers from loafing around the village pump and talking without a license.

Every park and open space in New York has its peculiar race of bench lizard. The hot-air Soviets are in session day and night. Only a Jean Richepin could do them justice. These strays and wastrels by the hundred have chosen their special park or square by a sort of instinct peculiar to the open-air liver. The Battery Park lounger talks quite another lingo from that of the shabby-genteel woodwarmer in Central Park, and those that have elected Bryant Park never mix with the sedentary dreamers of the Bronx.

The Battery Park Chapter of the Ancient and Illustrious Order of Worknots is the most cosmopolitan of the whole batch. The members of this council constitute a study in international sociology and racial ideals. They are culled from the eight corners of the world. The sea is in their eyes, and they are pickled in liquor from many lands. They have played poker with the Turk at Aleppo, chinned the Sphinx in Egypt, rubbed down the fat of the rich at Marienbad, trekked it through Whitechapel and shot craps in Thibet. You can get enough "stories" out of these young and old soldiers of fortune and misfortune down around the Aquarium to make your fortune in the "movies." It is well, however, to leave your long green at home. They have a way with them.

"Salty Mike," for instance: I interviewed him one hot August evening just as the 6:30 boat for Coney had cut loose from Pier 1. "Salty Mike" he said his name was, and he spoke a perfect semi-American. Italian by birth, he strung me along to the tune of having taken a boat when a boy that put out of Genoa for some Chinese port. It was many years ago, when mutiny was in fashion on the high seas, and when the marlin-spike settled all disputes with the first mate. "Salty" got into one of the altercations, and although he was, I believe, ethically right, he was adjudged legally wrong, and spent a few years thinking it over in one of the hallrooms in the county jail at Yokohama. He worked his way to San Francisco, where, looking over America afoot, he finally settled on Battery Park as his home.

"Salty" washes dishes in the restaurants around the Battery when he is pushed by the hunger germ, and even peels potatoes when the thirst comes on him extra strong. When not occupied he is a Socialist—Left Wing. He said he had chosen the park down by the sea wall for his five-year loaf because it combined the advantages of both seashore and country.

Washington Square is strictly highbrow. The bench lizards here are all Idealists. A Manet might paint any one of the habitués of these benches and label the picture "Thought Sitting." The fascinating dreamers of the hourless workday and chanters of the far-off divine event to which all arid artists move cling to their wooden thrones with a tenacity that makes a mollusc look like a buzzsaw.

On the afternoon I spent among these pallid and dark-haired Olympians I heard the twittering in back of me of a vegetarian poet who was reading his penciled thunders to a lady who—one had only to look at her—was Leading Her Own Life in Her Own Way without any parental restrictions. It was good stuff, but not quite according to the rules of that taxidermist of words, Harry Kemp.

Near the buses an artist was doing an "open air," Union Square, sad to relate, is purely socialistic. The loungers here are all waiting for the Grand Upset that will land each one of them in the foremanship of a State-owned factory or bank. The Right Wing squats down on Fourteenth Street and the Left Wing airs itself toward Sixteenth Street. The Secret Service men are corralled in the center of this historic grassplot. Union Square has always belonged to the proletariat.

I have seen the same bench shiners there year after year.

It was on one of these benches that Hippolyte Havel, patrician of vagabonds and the anarchist with the fatal baby stare, exfoliated his theory of rent-jumping which finally penetrated to the Bronx. I never knew an anarchist who didn't love music, flowers and babies. There are many of this type to be found in Union Square each day. And there are memories of George Francis Train and John Masefield, not to speak of O. Henry.

Madison Square is the refuge of the solid bourgeoisie. In the afternoon the benches are graced by the tired night worker, who reads his paper, smokes his pipe and meditates on Sam Gompers. In the evening the still soldier bourgeoisie sit around the fountain, sometimes *en famille,* sometimes lonesome, bachelor or spinster like.

Everything is proper here. The faces are cut and dried and the epigrams are stately and prim. The Philadelphia Sunday spirit suffuses itself everywhere. One recalls Tioga or Overbrook or the sweet little parks of Camden in post-Whitman days. Unlike Union Square and Washington Square, one seldom sees the same face here twice. It is the spot par excellence in New York for the upright meditation and the legal reverie.

The magnet in Bryant Park is the Library. These benches—many of them—are the open-air sofas of the bookworm. They read everything from Darwin to Fanny Hurst, from Freud to Julian Street. The horn-rimmed council of highbrows meets every day around the smiling countenance of Washington Irving, who bears such a striking resemblance to the lions in front of the big marble pile who gaze benignly and serenely upon the wealth of the avenue—sweet, pacific faces, pretty Bryans in marble. In fact, the loungers in Bryant Park are strictly pacifist.

Quite another story from all this in Central and Riverside Parks. These two parks are show places.

Riverside Park is the Riviera of Manhattan; Central Park is the Bois. The benches in both of them are patronized by the *élite*—often the glass of fashion and the mouldy of form. Beau Brummel (first stage) and Lady Clara Vere de Vere (middle stage) here sit cheek-by-jowl.

I once saw at dawn in Central Park, one summer day, something that, far-away, looked like Lady Godiva in her classic uniform. She sat on a bench, dabbling her toesies in the lake near Fifth Avenue. But it may have been an optical illusion—I had lingered late over the ukelele water.

Have you ever noted the total absence of happiness in the faces of the Central Park sitters? Many of the titled nobility of the Old World are here, but you can observe, if you have the Balzacian eye, the ravages of baccarat Over There.

Thousands go into Riverside Park to watch the sun set over the Palisades—on a clear evening the most magnificent sight in the East. The benches should be set as though for a feast and they should be made of onyx and jasper. The drama of the heavens is given free for the asking, and your aesthetic bench lizard in the park is seeing something for nothing that was never dreamed of in the philosophy of Ford or Hylan.

The Merry Suicides

THE Jay-Walkers' Club of New York, lately organized, has taken for its slogan the famous saying of Nietzsche (whom some critics call the greatest spiritual jay-walker in the history of philosophic literature):

"Be hard—and live dangerously!"

The Jay-Walkers' Club is composed of men and women who, being compelled to stay in New York the year round, find life under the Nedick Dynasty growing less and less dangerous.

They are romantics who are death-gasping under the incubus of sanity. They are the daredevil souls who flounder in the fogs of common sense—the Hot-spurs whose nights used to be filled with boozic, but who now are groggy with yawns.

They declare that there is only one form of danger left in the old town—the danger of being killed by an automobile, a trolley car or suffocated in the subway.

These *blaséists* welcome the titillation of braving death even in front of a Ford.

Their psychic thermometer rises to the blood heat of pure ecstasy when a subway train is stalled under the East River.

They wait with bated breath the oncoming of the non-stop mail wagons.

They skirt the Rolls-Royce juggernaut with the cackling gusto of a boy who has thrown a match in a pile of shavings under a Chautauqua meeting house.

It is said the Mexican wouldn't know he was alive if it wasn't for the fleas on him.

That is the melancholy condition of New Yorkers to-day, the Jay-Walkers claim. They wouldn't know that they were alive if they weren't threatened with physical dismemberment or violent death from the very moment they leave their houses.

The Jay-Walkers are propagandists—following the high usage of the times.

This is the age of propaganda. You've got to ballyhoo for something; you are a dead one if you do not tin-horn a Cause with all the power of Brobdingnagian lungs. Not to care, to be smilingly indifferent at the Way Things Are Going, like George Jean Nathan, is a form of anarchy.

The only crimes are to believe that the Lord knows his business and to mind your own business.

The Jay-Walkers are intensive propagandists in the art of cultivating jay-walking in the streets.

They are Fundamentalists when it comes to taking a chance in Times Square.

As opposed to the Die-Hards they are the Die-Easies.

In a word, they have revived and teach the grand old doctrine of monkeying with the buzz-saw.

To obtain membership in this hedonistic organization one must show battle scars—in place of the bottle scars which used to be a requisite for membership in this organization when it was known in pre-Volstead days as the Cork and Carstairs Club.

You must swear to some hairbreadth escape from automobile, trolley car or subway accident. Better yet, if you can show a deleted finger, a broken ankle, a squashed ear or an armless sleeve.

"Throw away your medals—show your scars!" is another one of their slogans.

One of the stunts cultivated and practiced by the Jay-Walkers is walking in back of a street car without first looking to see whether there is a car coming in the opposite direction.

This rule is founded on the dogma that the greatest joy in life comes from surprise and thrill.

To walk in back of a car at Forty-fourth and Broadway while in a brown study on Pragmatism in its relation to modern landscape painting and suddenly to be yanked out of your intellectual mood by having to dodge death in the twinkling of a rabbit's eye gives an exhilarating bounce to the nerves that may even be a substitute for the evanescing cocktail.

No Jay-Walker will stand still on the curb to wait for the signal from the traffic cop to go ahead when he can comfortably ensconce himself between the north and south tracks, getting the delightful thrill of having automobiles and trolley cars graze him on either side.

This develops the self-preservative instinct to its highest point. It refines and purifies the acuteness of ear and eye. The Jay-Walkers call this "stunt" "getting the tingle."

If you can perform the feat of keeping an umbrella up while standing in this position or manipulating it so that it just misses a motorman's eye—why, you may be elected treasurer of the club for the most daring feat of the year.

How near can you stand to the revolving wheels of a taxicab without losing a toe?

Some of the members of the club brag of having had the soles of their shoes ripped off. Others tell of miraculous flat tires that have passed over their toes, leaving nothing but a bruise.

Persons in nowise allied with the Jay-Walkers' Club indulge in this hilarious and tantalizing sport every day at Thirty-fourth and Broadway. To achieve the best effects stand right in the street in front of a sewer as a machine rounds the corner.

During the theatre hours the Jay-Walkers assemble in groups on the pavement and start across the street coolly and haughtily just as the cabs and cars are told to go ahead by the traffic cop.

To be stalled in the center of hundreds of flying taxis and street cars gives them the sensation, they say, of being in a Mack Sennett comedy.

Playing tag with Death and flirting with the ambulance sharpen the wits, cause the emotions to simmer, kindle the brain, dilate the consciousness and add piquancy and a certain *diablerie* to daily life.

There is one ultra daring member of the Jay-Walkers' Club (who is also a member of the Court-Death-While-Smiling League) who takes his morning "constitutional" every day—rain or shine, Yankees win or Yankees lose, come Michaelmas or Candlemas—down Sixth Avenue from Fifty-third Street to Eighth Street.

But instead of walking on the pavement he walks the whole distance between the north-bound and south-bound car tracks. He has done this for two years, and has escaped with only the loss of two toes, one ear and a bit of his scalp.

He (I withhold his name at his request because of certain errors in his income tax blank) recommends this walk to all sons of all mothers who have backward sons.

He claims, and rightly I believe, that courage is an art and not an instinct. He also says that heroism is merely the fear of being caught running away.

The Court-Death-While-Smiling League was organized to bolster up the morals of those who lose their nerve or, indeed, express any emotional interest in life when suddenly confronted by the sure prospect of losing it.

This phenomenon of self-preservation has been noted in those who are face to face with an oncoming express while stalled in an auto in the center of the track; in the faces and actions of those about to be run down by a red racer; of those whose boats suddenly turn turtle in a cloudburst off Coney Island; in elevated trains that get tired of forty years on the tracks and leap for a long rest to the street below.

The league's motto is: Die Smiling.

The members are taught for an hour each day to visualize every kind of violent death with a smile on their faces. The league members claim it has worked out beautifully. They even think of starting an Italian branch for the people who live in the shadow of Vesuvius.

The growth and propagation of these ideas show us to what sublime heights the innate optimism of the American can soar.

Our patron saint should be Harold Lloyd and our *Iliad* his five-reeler, "Safety Last!"

Mike and Priscilla: Cronies at Last!

FROM childhood wives have been taught to look upon the bartender as a pariah, a disreputable being set apart from his fellow-men, a being who had horns and a cloven tongue, who lured millions of husbands from the fireside to the Hades of intoxication.

The white apron of Mike and the white apron of Priscilla have been hereditary foes for ages.

A husband in pre-dry days might bring any one home for supper or for the evening pinochle game—a baseball player, the corner bootblack or even the man who ran the poolroom around the corner. But a bartender—never! He was never allowed to darken the threshold of home, sweet home. He was the Beast of the Apocalypse.

But the wheel has turned around since 1920. The wives of America have come to understand as never before what a hero Mike must have been in those days. In her pity she has come to understand. She has been compelled to shoulder all his woes and learn his gentle, patient ways. For she is now compelled to play the bartender to her husband and is often nightly the victim of the great gas barrage that swept over the bar and drove weary Mike from the spigot to the bucolic quiet of his own home, where he could tune in on the voices of his children and drink his bottle of beer in peace with his wife.

And now lo and behold! the white apron of Priscilla has come strangely to resemble the white apron of Mike!

After the "party" was over some nights ago at our house, after my wife had wiped dozens of glasses, mopped up the tables just as Mike used to mop up the bar, and after she had taken off her white apron spotted with home-brew, she said to me:

"Why do not the women of America build a memorial to the bartender heroes who went down to defeat in that bloodless battle of 1920? I'll throw in my dollar.

"There they stood behind what you used to call the solid mahogany like smiling cherubs, the silent recipients of all the bunk, bluster and blab that you turn on us now.

"My dear, I used to visualize Mike the bartender as a being with a flat nose, terrible jowls, pin-point eyes, a brow that receded from the top of the nose, with a long piece of lead pipe in his hand. Now I see him as he really was—the dear thing!—a kind-faced, smiling little man, with snow-white vestments. behind his altar of oak, a sort of confessor to all the hokum in the world.

"When those little doors swung open you must have seen a neat, fastidious sort of man, a sort of Dutch housewife to male wayfarers, who mixed and shook and polished and scrubbed and tinkled his way through the evening.

"He listened patiently—as we do now—to stories he had heard a thousand times. All the operas and popular songs were poured into his ear. He must have listened to tenors, bassos, baritones, and falsetto-bluffos sing *Annie Rooney* and *The Sidewalks of New York* so many times that all the dear little Mikes were never bored after he got home.

"Ah, my dear, there was peace in the home in those days when you poured all your complexes and troubles into the ear of Mike. Mike, dear Mike, I salute you as a brother across the social abyss that divides us!"

Thinking my wife exaggerated my own foibles during the era of home-brew and also her own troubles since taking the place of my favorite bartender, I instituted an extended and exhaustive inquiry about the matter and found it only too true that the immaculate white apron of Priscilla and Penelope has become stained with bardrip and that our wives have been going through a complete psychological overturn in relation to their thirsty and home-brewing mates. The dainty French heel follows nightly the patient, plodding brogans of Mike.

In some homes I even found that instead of the centuries-old greeting of "Good evening, Charlie, your slippers are under the bed," husbands are greeted from the kitchen with, "Hello! What'll you have?"

Ever since the war women have been grabbing off the jobs of men. But the bartender's job was wished upon them. It looks like a subtle frame-up of the lost bartenders of America to get even with their most inveterate detractors.

"You thought we had an easy job of it, did you?" they seem to be saying from their exile in Cuba, Mexico and Paris. "Well, the pleasure is now all yours, ladies. You'll see what made us bald before our time. It wasn't rum; it was gas. Get me?"

Our wives, the queens of the kitchens, are surrounded now by more than just pots and pans and carving knives. Their kitchen treasures have had some strange additions in the last four years. They are now surrounded and preside over "jacks," "crocks," "shakers," new and curious cork-pulling devices, "tubes," "feeders" and "rinsers." There are new kinds of stewpans—and the "stew" is often "panned" when he sends the mousetrap and the dustpan down the dumbwaiter instead of the garbage.

While the cook crochets the food for the dinner party our wives are seen in the kitchen not as of yore, tasting and testing the chicken and the soup, but we envisage her behind a trench-work built up of six-gallon crocks, Gargantuan stew-pans, ambushed behind beer bottles, punch-bowls, siphons, cocktail shakers and unlabelled claret bottles.

"What great psychologists those bartenders must have been!" said a charming housewife to me as she put on her apron to wade through the kitchen. "Since prohibition I see all the little emotional cogs and wheels of my husband for the first time. Why, do you know that the bartenders knew our husbands better than we did!

"To-day our men who do all their drinking at home unmask all their grouches, enthusiasms and hidden didoes to their other half. Home-brew and the kindly corner bootlegger have taken the masks off of them. Our once-upon-a-time fireside companions, our chivalric husbands and fathers and sons, spill the beans to us after their third drink.

"I never suspected my George had a poet, an orator, a colossal world-shaking statesman sewed up in his bean! He's a positive genius after 10 o'clock. All his hidden emotional complexes litter the house at midnight like the Sunday papers. He is a wild, star-eyed lover, a great actor. He can weep like a baby and storm like an oil investigator. What a vaudeville show we wives missed in those grand old days— and no wonder no bartender was ever known to go to the theatre!

"Where now are the dignity, the silence and reserve of George? When he felt his periodicals coming in the old days he used to go to the little sanctuary around the corner with other sinners, where he shouted and sang and moaned, wept, indulged in self-accusations of all kinds, beat himself and others with the whipcords of abuse, and then came home and slept like a dove. Now I get it all! I have even put a mirror in his den so that he can talk to himself when I'm exhausted—just as he did down at Mike's."

It is true that the introduction of liquor into the home and the transmutation of our wives from mere hausfraus to champion bottle-holders has destroyed the illusion of our importance. Our mates are wiser than the bartenders, before whom we used to swell up and brag. They do not now believe very much in those "weighty problems of the time" that used to keep us out till 3 A.M. They see that we were not "overworked" as much as we used to be. "At the office till midnight tonight, dearie," no longer goes down. We now arrive home just before cocktail-time—sometimes long before. We seldom bring a "business friend" home for dinner any longer. "Let him find his own" is our inmost thought. Besides our wives have found out they were not "business friends." They were just bar-lizards.

"Not only have we become our husbands' bartenders at home," said a friend's wife to my wife while I pretended not to be listening in, "but we have become his friendly cop when he goes out. I find most husbands are afraid of stag parties under prohibition and I always am invited everywhere with Harry when it is a question of a hooch or high-tide dinner party.

"Well, it used to be the friendly cop on the old booze routes who used to pilot our husbands home or pass them from hand to hand like a load of dead hog. The last cop to handle them—often a good-natured rookie—generally took them to their apartment and sometimes put them to bed when the wives were visiting mother in Wilmington or Springfield.

"Now, since the hooch dinner party has become the main all-night social event of the spring season throughout the country we wives are the cops. We hustle our muzzy halves into taxis, unload them in our arms and guide their wandering footsteps into the elevator or up six flights of a walk-up. It is good athletic exercise, I find, and personally I have developed a regular Dempsey muscle.

"Then," she went on, "where are those quiet evenings at home when you found time to go over some old library favorites, darn the socks and tell the children bedtime stories? Instead, my dear, we have to polish up glasses, rinse them and hunt for lost flasks that the gang blew in with. Why, I actually think of putting sawdust on the parlor floor and laying down a portable brass rail under the mantelpiece! On several occasions I have had to act the part of that odious being known in the old days as a 'bouncer' to the obstreperous ones. I can see why the barroom had to go. But why did they wish it on us?

"Ah, those late crowds that blow in now with merely a rapid-fire, 'We're on our way!' over the 'phone! They roll in with their bag of complexes hidden on them like a kit of burglar's tools. They roar, they rant, they scrap—and wind up by weeping on one another's collars, swearing they are going to buy the Ritz for the missus the next day. My dear, did those dear bartenders have to go through that in pre-Volstead days?"

"They did! They did!" I whispered softly from the next room, my whole being wilting into tears at the vision of the trials we had put upon those very excellent beings, bartenders and wives.

"It's curious," said my wife, now that this had turned into a kind of wives' experience meeting, "the tipsy dimension that men enter. They get the first peep in after a cocktail or two; then they take the shuttle which is run on highballs and find themselves in No Man's Land with green and red arrows running slantwise everywhere. All straight lines are forgotten. Everything is topsy-turvy, a-tilt, cut on the bias, a-slant, askew. They lurch and sway and sidle, dodge automobiles and street cars and hang over subways in what appears to be a miraculous manner. They have found some great secret. There are different laws of gravitation for men who can make this grade and reverse gear. They are as babies and no harm can come to them.

"In one of these moments if you see your Sevres vase swaying on the edge of the table make no outcry, have no second sober thought. Walk bravely away and leave it to these masters of this tipsy dimension, and ten to one nothing will happen.

"Conversation at some of these new evenings at home is difficult for the lookers-on-the wives. Husband No. 1 will continue his talk on the Ruhr he began a week ago. Husband No. 2 is keen on labor and Ramsay MacDonald and a third on the prizefight he saw and the Big League stuff. They talk inordinately to each other, never for a moment hugging their subject, quite unaware that when one shouts, 'Who are the great American poets?' the other will answer in the same tone of voice, 'I tell you it is Labor sitting on the throne of England!' and then there is a fade-in of 'Oh, I'll tell you that was the cleanest, prettiest scrap I ever saw in my life.'

"It is the wife's business now to haggle with the bootlegger. All the experience we ever got from thread and pin sales, the Yankee intelligence we used to such advantage in the past, we are now compelled to turn in this new channel. Women no longer take the interest in the dry-goods sales they formerly did because of the new field opened up to them in wet goods.

"Our dainty hand-tinted address books are now filled with strange new 'phone numbers. When you demur at meeting these friends of your husband all your objections are overruled with:

"'Would you stand in the way of culture? That fellow is bootlegging his way through college. One case of Scotch will mean a milestone in his career.'

"So to lift up the culture of the land you do your bit and ring up the lad to send you a case.

"Perhaps one of the hardest blows wives have had to endure is to see the tea-wagon they waited so many years to possess become a portable bar. It is trundled proudly from room to room with the master's stock. And the new vanity case that was given to you by your husband at Christmas time and that made you cry out with joy—well, you were somewhat surprised and disappointed on opening it to discover it contained a very small compartment for your rouge and powder because of the amount of space given to three bottles that nestled down soundlessly in the lovely silk lining.

"Well, my dear, these last few years have been a terrible blow to women's illusions. They know now that their power is supreme as long as they have a flask in the sideboard; their busbands will cling closer to the wife's apron-strings than they ever did to the bartender's. They know that men are the liars, the boasters, the braggarts of the world, the chanticleers that believe they make the sun rise when it is only the yeast they cause to rise.

"And we wives now also know that the bartenders were the greatest heroes of civilization—that is, those who survived the years and years of gas barrage from our husbands."

Feeling as guilty as a debt, I tiptoed out of the house. As I got on the pavement I met a seedy and haggard-looking person. It was my friend "Curley Bill," old glass polisher in the Mirror Café.

"No—I don't carry it, Curley," I replied; "but if you come inside with me my wife will fix you up—she tends bar in our house."

Psycho-Analyzing "Pop" Manhattan

IT was an off-day in the Film-Flam "movies" studio, so the whole bunch took a trip to the Woolworth Tower with the camera.

From this platform in the air you can take your vacation mentally in any number of States lying loosely around. You are "swept by ocean breezes" and stung by the air from the pine-needle zone. You can, mentally, fish in a pool in the Dongan Hills, line up for a ginger ale with a sarsaparilla chaser over in New England or flounder around in the sea where no lifeguard can bother your suicidal instinct.

It was a perfect day, and by dint of looking one could make out the outlines of the moon, half-full, hanging prophetically over "Jack's."

After taking a "close-up" of the Liberty Bell, over in Philadelphia, we all looked down on "Dearie," Pearl White's nickname for Manhattan.

"Big Bill," the camera man observed that everything had been filmed in that curious little island entirely surrounded by Brooklyns, except the inside of the sub-mud tunnels and the interiors of Trinity graveyard.

The director, whose imagination could not boast of anything over a 2.75 "kick," hurled into the empyrean the definitive aesthetic judgment on Manhattan that it was "certainly cigar-shaped, all right," an observation borrowed, we believe, from the secret memoirs of Pete Stuyvesant.

The famous star of the Film-Flam Company's last big "hit," *The Waiter from Joel's*, said that Manhattan was a grocery store where the chief stock in trade were nuts and chickens. But stars can afford to be

147

cynical—their contracts give them that privilege.

Sue Marie, the heroine of a thousand and one automobile accidents at Fort Lee, the actress who did so much for the Liberty Loans and so little for Art, said that if it had not been for the Manhattan cocktail no one would ever have heard of the name—"New York" was good enough for her. Manhattan and the Bronx, she continued, were both named for cocktails, and Brooklyn should have been called Dry Martini.

Sue finally confessed that she had been born in Prohibition Park, Staten Island. Her little dinky island, she said, was a kind of coming Alsace-Lorraine, and some day it would cause a great war be tween Brooklyn and Newark for its vast beer and rye deposits.

Everybody was getting bored and the portside of one of the thermos bottles was running low when the doctor, alias the surgeon of the company, said, his voice clearing itself with an effort of vast thermos injections :

"None of you see Manhattan, and there it is lying right under your eyes, your brain, your feet, and the camera. Manhattan—New York if you want to call it such—is a being, a living, pulsating being, a vast giant, who grows by lying prone on his back. Lying on his back *apparently,* I should say; it is an error of perspective.

"You know the tricks we do in the studio, where an automobile runs up the side of a house and a man falls down the side of a mountain, and the other stuff? Well, that's the trouble with Pop Manhattan. We are tangled up in a wrong, a tricky, visual perspective. He isn't really lying on his back. He is standing up straight, but to reproduce him that way in the camera would require one that could cover a surface twelve or fifteen miles high instantaneously, and Bill would have to station himself in a stationary plane at about three miles above the level of the fountain in Madison Square Park and at criss-cross rectangle-triangles from the old bar in the Central Park Casino."

"Doc, ain't there a parallelogram or an icosahedron somewhere in your super-camera? I dote on 'em," said Sue, petulantly pulling a cylindrical hair from his hirsute awning.

"Then," continued the doctor, who neither saw nor felt the verbal and tactile incursion into his flight, "you would see the most astounding of all things—a living being twelve miles high without flesh. The network of streets are his arteries—look below you and see if they do not look exactly like veins and arteries—and you and I and the rest of us who live or work in Manhattan the moving, living, warring corpuscles in his blood."

"Looks like that just from here, come to think of it!" shouted the director, who acted like a Columbus who had just discovered his first America.

And everybody leaned far over the marble balustrade to see the human corpuscles racing up and down the great network of arteries of Pop Manhattan.

"Red corpuscles, white corpuscles, yellow corpuscles, true-blue corpuscles, and—" murmured Bill the camera man, whom the doctor had put into a philosophical frame of mind.

"And," broke in the Doctor, "phagocytes—who are the street-cleaners and uplifters of the blood—parasites, bacteria, and all the rest are there."

The Film-Flam bunch looked at one another self-consciously. An uneasy moment. What were they? But they all remembered with that miraculous interlocking consciousness that comes from close quarters in the "movie" game that just then they were not down there in the arteries of Pop Manhattan, but standing on the summit of his world-famous pimple.

"Now," continued the doctor, who had drained the rye side of his thermos and who dropped automatically into his best clinical pose, "this vast being, like all other beings has his complexes—if any of you know—where's our title scribbler?—what a complex is—"

"Oh," said Sue, in ecstasy, "he's going to pull that dear old Frood stuff on us—wishes, dreams, complexes, and all the rest of it. Lovely, lovely!"

"A complex," went on the doctor who had begun his address to the five boroughs and the two Oranges, "is that mixup in the ego of motives, wishes, conscious and unconscious, and their expression. It is curious that 'camouflage' and 'complexes' began to get into print about the same time, for a great many of our complexes have to be camouflaged. Almost every complex breaks some law—it's indecent, runs counter to one of John Roach Straton's gawps, or has not the O. K. of the Society for the Suppression of Things. So we camouflage it in tailor-made subtleties and put a white nightie over its bareness.

"The New York complex, or the complexes of this vast being Manhattan," maundered on the doctor, "is to-day the most interesting psychological study in the world. Interesting because it is now suffering from a series of suppressed wishes and dreams.

"The most restless, nervous, dynamic, the most hopelessly alive city in the world is bound and gagged like a Gulliver tied down by a band of Liliputians whose assembled wisdom might possibly rise to the importance of an epigram in the mouth of Young Gobbo or Tom Noddy. They have gagged the old man and put his healthy, natural complexes into straitjackets. His human corpuscles no longer circulate freely on their own foreordained orbit because his blood is full of traffic cops imported from strange south-by-west zones who arrest them for the slightest speeding on the streets of their wishes."

"The soul of Manhattan," went on the doctor, "is ecstatic, material, jazzy, pleasure-loving. In a word, liberty in the widest sense of that word is its heart-note. The corpuscles take their time from the heart-beat. But somebody has been feeding the old man with vast quantities of bromide of potassium and the whole machine is running down."

"Bromide of what?" shouted Bill. "Watered ale, you mean."

"Right," said the doctor, "watered ale in the complexes, and, as with water in the gas main, the light of old Manhattan is flickering, sputtering and puts fearsome shadows on the walls of our brains. Joyous old Manhattan is pussyfooting around these days, and on the brow of the Statue of Liberty should be written the new motto of New York: At the Sign of the Wink.

"Greenwich Village, which is the art-complex of Manhattan, is raided nightly by the phagocytes of morality. Now, the village is suffering terribly from suppressed wishes and submerged bacchanals. The result is that Bolshevistic erysipelas is spreading all over Pop Manhattan's most picturesque complex, and the great thought-ganglion on West Fourth Street is beating funeral time.

"The dance-complex and the drink-complex, two root-complexes of New York, are on the fritz, Forty-secondly speaking. At the Sign of the Gumshoe, near Times Square, curtains are drawn and every waiter is a breath picket when you leave. The corpuscles in the old man's body up around the old White Way are all turning white. Vanilla ice cream soda is beginning to tell on the complexion of the face of Manhattan.

"Now, suppose we put the X-rays of psycho-analysis on the financial, sex, crime-wave, and sporting complexes of this vital, beautiful beast in which we live and move and have our————"

"Let's all go down and ride up Pop's alimentary canal, Broadway," suggested Sue, as the doctor sat on the floor of the tower, quite aw-rye.

Keep Smiling!

YOU can't go into any public place in this country without meeting with the command to "Keep Smiling."

It seems to be the Eleventh Commandment in the American Decalogue of Thou Shalt Nots.

It is the only one of our national commandments which at the present time is written affirmatively.

You will find it stuck in elevators, over the cash registers of restaurants, on bootblack stands, in business offices and wherever there is danger of the tax-ridden, blue-law ridden public puckering its face into quite a natural scowl.

Is there any other country in the world where the grouch and the peeve have so sculpt the human face that in order to avoid a national epidemic of facial ugliness we are practically ordered to keep grinning?

Even when things were at their rottenest in the State of Denmark Hamlet did not advise his subjects-to-be to "Keep smiling, damn yer!" As a matter of fact, he added that a man may smile and smile, and be a villain.

Can things be worse beneath stairs (figuratively speaking) in America than they were in Denmark, when kings were slipped off before the cocktail with a little wood alcohol poured into the ear by an ambitious brother?

We New Yorkers were once a buoyant, happy-go-lucky, smiling race. When you and I and Edison were young fellows it was not necessary to order us at every minute to keep smiling. We were so chock full of life, liberty and the pursuit of pleasure that the buttoned-up face, the efficiency scowl and the solid mahogany glare were almost unknown.

But to-day we all look like frightened children about to have our pictures taken while a smug, seraphic mug grins at us over the camera, telling us to look at the comical rubber face which is manipulated with the photographer's free hand.

Something has gone out of our lives. We have become glum, solemn, morose, irritable. The change in the nature of the New Yorker seems to have been coeval (and co-evil) with the ukase of the Invisible Empire that "moral holidays" (as William James recommended for every human being) and the deliberate and occasional unbalancing of the moral equilibrium (as Herbert Spencer advocated) were to be abolished.

Saturday nights used to be carnival nights in New York. It was the night on which the city regained its sanity and normalcy by losing it for a little while.

Cheero! was in the cup. And out of the cup it flowed in a buoyant stream for the next six days.

But there are no longer any abnormal releases and explosions for the abnormal and feverish lives we live in New York.

The result of this perpetual depression is a swarm of cheero yogis, hopesmiths, smile brokers and psychic joy doctors. They pound out their doctrines of Cheero in syndicated editorials, advertisements, correspondence schools and Pollyanish books. They get rich beyond the dream of bootleggers. In fact, they are the bootleggers of happiness. The real thing being verboten in this country, these culture rings will slip you something that tastes and smells like the real thing for a small price—and something guaranteed to go down every boob's gullet.

It was, I think, the late Edgar Saltus who said that Victor Hugo and Charles Dickens made a fortune by pitying the poor. The Cheero School of American philosophers (not thinkers) have got enormously rich by yowling Cheero! Keep Smiling! and There is Hope! in capitals, italics and double-leaded brevier. If they uttered their "messages" in solid agate they would have no customers.

A platitude is known by the type company it keeps. Buy no agate wall mottoes. Insist on embossed thirty-six point type with gold lettering.

Nothing is wanted to-day in the magazine, on the stage and by many newspaper syndicates but Messages of Good Cheer. Hope, cheer and twitter are urged on you pathetically (almost venemously) from every direction. Avoid substitutes like personal liberty. The Devil of Reality lurks there.

You can grind out the bunk by the yard. Here is the recipe. I have written thousands of editorials, epigrams and advertisements by following it.

YOU can do the same!

Buy a Roget's Thesaurus. Turn in the index to the words "smile" or "cheer." Pick out these words in the book:

Good humor, sunshine, rejoice, carol, chirrup, blithe, sprightly, palmy, buoyant, forward, clean, lilt, merry and phrases such as Never say die! Hence, loathed melancholy! and Begone dull care! There are thousands more. Incarcerate these words in large-typed paragraphs surrounded with suitable adverbs, adjectives and prepositions, which you can also find in the thesaurus or dictionary. Don't forget exclamation points and dashes when brain-fag hits you.

Make a word drawing of a human's face before and after taking your dose of cheer or your hope pellets. Always say that a pessimist has a bad liver. Insist on exercise in Sweetness and Light. Tell them care is spiritual dandruff.

Hammer this into them and you will receive thousands of testimonials telling you how they beat the other fellow to it. The "other fellow," of course, is always a heavy drinker, a time-clock knocker, a "dope fiend," or a reader of Schopenhauer.

In your masterpieces always put the word "you" in gigantic capitals. It creates the air of a private conversation and inspires confidence.

Many years ago I got $500 for this:

> Behind the clouds the sun still shines!
> It is so in life!
> In YOUR life!

YOU are a sun, not a cloud!
Never admit defeat!
Napoleon never did!
YOU are a Napoleon!
Be a sun!
Be a Napoleon!
ONWARD AND UPWARD!

My father tells me I was born singing this:

For what is the use of repinin'.
       For where there's a will there's a way!
Termorrer the sun may be shinin'.
       Although it is cloudy terday!

Little did I know that it was to become the marching song of the Neo-Cheero School in America.

Then there is the roaring flood of Buck Up books which have sicklied o'er with the pale cast of age Parcel Post Pete. A certain big bookstore on Fifth Avenue has almost a whole floor devoted to the litter. They sell like Scotch at a revenue agents' fair.

I pick up one haphazard. Here are a few planet-jolting epigrams from this tumescent tome:

The Mind is Master until—until the Mind is mastered.

Getting riled never pays.

Be sure!

Work for Prosperity!

When Ann Hathaway's husband died the greatest Genius of our world died.

To live in our vital individuality means much.

Moral Courage comes from Resolve and Reason. Occupation, Employment, Business will keep you out of mischief.

The "movies" in this country have conspired to keep us smiling ad nauseam. Most of them seem to have been made to iron out the wrinkles on the brow of the Tired Business Man and the hollows in the cheeks of Efficiency Ezra. The "movie" with the final cheero! fade out is essentially American. The rest of the world after viewing 20,000 of these films believed us to be the Happy Harrys of evolution. It has only lately come to suspect the truth—that there is something suspicious about our chronic optimism. Are there no unhappy endings to anything in America?

Meanwhile, in the schools for salesmen, Cheero! is still the slogan. The way to sell a pair of socks to a legless man is to firmly fix in your thought the sweetness of your mother's love and smile with poise.

With cheer in your morning heart you can drive any competitor to the poorhouse. Remember, the bass voice and the open Waterbury face turneth away the boot—if you are a book agent.

Always serve a dispossess notice in a low voice and cry "Greetings!" to the baby.

Smile and it shall be given; smirk and ye shall lift.

When the blue law loonies have at last achieved their ends we shall no doubt have a Secretary of Cheer in the Cabinet. His inspectors of faces will swarm over the land like cops around a real-beer spigot. It will be as dangerous to wear a gloomy expression on the face as it is now for a physician to carry a pony of brandy to a dying man in the streets.

Children may wear smiles for the same reason that Victor Hugo's Laughing Man did. Why not! Long faces breed peeve.

The wisdom of the Cheero, Buck Up, Keep Smiling School! It is like radium—it gives off endless force and light without decreasing in density.

When that well-known traveler from Yap sits on the ruins of the Library Lions and meditates on America of to-day—what will he think?

Great heavens! let us not think on't. Keep smilin'!

The Triumph of
Shame Over Darwin

THE Darwinian theory (that in the struggle for existence the fittest survive and the weakest go to the wall) is being violated and undermined every day in the subways of New York.

During the rush hours, when all of New York is battling with brawn and brain to get home, the unfittest—at least physically—survive to a humiliating degree in the battle for seats, straps and standing room.

The lame, the halt and the blind, the aged and the children, with the connivance of the guards and some sentimentalists, are given an unfair advantage over the well, the strong and the hairy of both sexes in the titanic struggle for seats and ingress to the cars.

How to beat the lame, the halt and the blind, the aged and the children to these seats is now a daily problem that confronts the athletic and robust New Yorker.

If every one is entitled to a seat for his nickel, it is clear that these seats first of all belong to the healthy, agile, athletic citizens on whose shoulders rest the might and the fame of New York City. After a good day's work they alone are entitled to consideration. Their strength must be conserved. The prosperity of our city depends on muscle and tussle. It is an outrage to ask the physical flower of our city to engage in a vulgar battle for rest in these cars after a long day in the office or the trenches of Queens.

I have seen an old woman engaged in a regular death-clinch with a six-foot automobile salesman for standing room on the platform. The unfittest survived. He gracefully waived his nickel-bought privilege after she had knocked his hat off.

I have seen a child in arms, egged on by its mother, viciously pluck at the beard of a captain of industry who had valiantly fought and gained his seat at South Ferry. This was at Times Square. The C. of I. rose shamefacedly and the weaker vessels squatted. The triumph of shame over Darwin.

I saw at another time a shuttle train guard threaten to arrest a 200-pound tired business man who had gained his seat by striding over a hunchback. The T. B. M. was impenitent. He held to his seat, while the discourteous little cripple held on to the door knob. My admiration for the solid specimen of the struggle-for-life knew no bounds.

The stupidity of the weak and the aged in daring to try conclusions with the flying squadron of New York's athletic seat squatters is in evidence in all its crass shame at Times Square when an "empty" pulls in northbound during the 5:30-6:30 cockpit hour.

This is a curious moment in the history of mob psychology. The moment the ten "empties" draw up 10,000 years of civilization vanish. Eyes grow big at the rows of empty seats glimpsed through the windows—like eyes clapped on Paradise. Sinews grow as hard as the old Nemean lion. The glory of battle surges through all breasts. Fists are clinched rigidly. The thews tighten like steel. Cheeks pale and become taut. The blood recedes from the lips of 2,000 beings and becomes as cruel and thin as a water drinker's. Coats are buttoned tightly, hats are pulled way down over the eyes, like men going over the top. Each one picks out the weakest looking being nearest to him, resolved to smash him if necessary.

The doors slide open in a sinister manner. The Paleozoic smash is on. We kick, we scratch, we laugh hysterically, we grasp the air—walk on it in fact; we swarm in as though we are taking an enemy dugout. The "preferential standees" gnash their teeth and glower at those who captured the seats.

It is here that the physical underdogs of both sexes show their inherent bad manners. They battle with the "fit" inch by inch. They butt. They rend. They upset the equilibrium of stoical business men. They survive, upsetting Darwin's law as completely as old Doc Bryan.

"Why don't they take taxicabs?" is the natural question on the lips of strong men and women.

Then they meddle with our consciences—we who are strong and get our seats in the subway by a kind of divine right. Who can ever surmise the great mental battles that go on in the brains of the fittest as from behind their papers or from under their eyelids, as they pretend to drowse, they watch some little old woman glancing around pathetically for a seat?

"Why should I get up?" asks Left Lobe. "I am tired, I have a long way to go, I have won my seat by the primal law of fists, shoulders, stout stomach and alertness. Maybe the little old lady has been shopping all day, or maybe she's the mother of a prohibitionist. Would she get up for a drunk?"

"But," says Right Lobe, "she's looking right through you and she is shaming you. That's the reason you are pretending to drowse or read your paper. She knows you are faking. You know perfectly well what she is calling you!"

These battles of conscience in the brain of the man who has slugged his way to a seat are the insidious vengeances that the weak and meek standees wreak on the strong. They generally end by Right Lobe and Left Lobe going to the fifteenth round, when it is time for the sittee to get out. Then he arises and, with a grand flourish, offers his seat to the little old lady, lolling in front of her for a minute or two, as though he had just discovered her and had to ride five miles further. He goes out sore on himself.

It is in this way that the weak torture the strong in the subway.

I have myself studied this question—of how to outwit women and children and cripples—at close range in the Queensboro elevators at the Grand Central terminal of the shuttle. Between 7 and 9 in the morning and 5 and 7 in the evening people are literally catapulted in and out of these elevators like thousands of tons of "movie" dummies. To beat the women, the children and the crippled into these perpetual-motion sardine boxes I find that the elbow is the most powerful and effective weapon. As you are being lifted off of your soles in going into the cage get between (if you can an old woman and a woman with a baby in her arms. Suddenly let them both have it with your elbows. This will keep them out of the cage if you are on the last line of defense and enable you to reach home (or work) the same day.

It is, however, in the Queensboro elevators that the physically weak put up the most terrible battles against avoirdupois and muscle. It is a shameful exhibition of the alleged meek and lowly. Only a few days ago I saw a lame man raise his pine stick to strike a giant long-shoreman who had a knee buried in his back. Fortunately, I deflected the blow, which struck a six-year-old who was struggling through the legs of his father. Some one said, "Children should travel between Manhattan and Queens in airplanes."

There is a rare sort of being whom I observe ever and anon in the subway crushes. This being is sometimes a man and sometimes a woman—more often a man. He is always the last to go into a car and the last to go out. He is buffeted, mauled, crowded out, and often waits for the next train. I do not understand his game. Is he a gentleman or a pickpocket? Does he know how to play the game or does he simply refuse to play it? Is he one of Us? Is he a weakling or the superman? He is evidently not a Darwinian. He simply will not struggle. He is a menace—a growing menace. He is an enemy of the great New York sport which makes the weak stronger and the strong weaker.

I am getting up a circular entitled "A Thousand and One Ways to Lambaste Your Way to a Seat, with Notes on the Art of Choking Women and Upsetting Cripples."

The Seven Lost Arts Of Manhattan

An Examination by the Dodo Club Into Life and Living Now and as They Were in the Good Old Days

THERE are hundreds of curious clubs in New York City of which one never hears. They avoid publicity not only because they are personal but because they are eccentric.

They are shy centres of esoteric discussions that would wilt beneath the word "nutty." Few of them are "red" many are pale blue, and some of them are as white as the soul of a new-born pacifist.

Like all odd indoor and eccentric things, these clubs and their meetings are interesting. Rarely is an outsider admitted to their discussions; rarely, too, does an outsider apply for admission, for these clubs are generally without a bar or a community locker.

There was the old Stowe Club of Brooklyn, which used to meet every Saturday night to discuss the psychology of "Uncle Tom's Cabin." Does it still exist?

The Geranium Club of Fordham used to meet every Wednesday night up on Fordham Road and discuss suicide among the flowers and plants.

Staten Island had its Inner Circle—the Atlantis Club it was called—which collected and dilated on the folklore of the lost archipelago between the Battery and St. George, of which Bedlow's Island and Robbins Reef are now the only vestiges.

I was once the guest of honor at the now defunct Hoax and Humbug Club, which used to meet in a building where the Hotel Astor now rears its arid head. The standing theme of these rare spirits was, What have you done this week to promote the art of lying?

The influence of the stub pen on Mid-Victorian literature was the curious standing theme of the old Rutherford B. Hayes Society, which held its meetings up in Harlem.

There were many others whose whimsicalities I do not recall. The times are low-brow and concrete—even ghosts are as common as ashcans. New York has grown strenuous and commonplace, which is probably the Why of the organization several months ago of the Dodo Club, which now meets to discuss the Seven Lost Arts of Manhattan.

According to the constitution of the Dodo Club, life in New York is in a bad way. Spirits are at low-ebb. The character of the inhabitants has undergone a change for the worse. Something has passed away since 1914 never to return—maybe.

New York is suffering from something—everybody knows that. The Dodo Club has found out. Its Sociological Committee returned last Monday night with a Report—returned from Bath Beach, where it had doped out the whole tatter.

The Seven Lost Arts of Manhattan, according to Gus O'Toole, who is the scholarly Secretary of the club, are:

LIVING.
DINING OUT.
POLITENESS.
EXTRAVAGANCE.
IMAGINATION.
LENDING.
WALKING.

The Sociological Committee of the Dodo Club finds that the psychological strata of Homo Manahatta have fallen into the cellar. The phiz of our souls has changed. The "New York manner" is extinct—even as the Dodo.

We were once a great painting done in oils, under which sang the title, in incandescent bulbs, "The Joy of Life."

We are now, according to Gus O'Toole and his colleagues, a chromo done in water-colors. Was it prohibition, war, landlords, food profiteering or the ouija board that was the cause of our downfall?

The Dodo Club has not gone very far into causes; it sticks to facts.

Living is, of course, one of the Seven Lost Arts of Manhattan. No one "lives" in this city anymore. Whoever is moves; and having moved you exist till you are evicted, dispossessed or otherwise tortured.

The Old Joy of Life is floating around like an empty whisky bottle. The old-time Manhattanite enjoyed life for the sake of itself. Easy-going, careless, sing-songy, he literally sweated life. A bare subsistence, such as satisfies the Philadelphian or the Brooklynite, was never the dream of the man of the Big Borough.

He often lived a way beyond his income, but he "lived." New York was an interlocking loan soviet. Money, like umbrellas, had almost become common property. They were the happy days of the Communism of Touch.

Living was the Art Perfect! To-day livings is only a device—a kind of guess-work from rent day to rent day; hand-on-the-trigger existence; a watchful waiting for old man Doom, who may assume the shape of a deputy sheriff, a home-still rustler or the furniture replevin.

Dining out! This most ancient of Manhattan arts is as dead as a bar-fly on a prohibitionist's hat.

Gus O'Toole says that there will be no picnics next Summer. Picnics were the aboriginal manner of dining outs says the report of the Sociological Committee of the Dodo Club.

Adam was the first Chauncey Depew. Abel was the first Sim Ford.

Picnickers, it is averred, will be subject to raids under the Eighteenth, the false tooth in the Constitution. Everything in bottles will be suspect. No Manhattanite can deport his home-made Red to the waterfalls of the Bronx River.

Prohibition has struck a deadly blow at dining out in its *al fresco* roots.

The little Sunday night dinner for six, with the cold bucket under the table, at Guglielmo's or the Hotel della Robberie is no more.

Eating out is now businesslike. Get to the charlotte russe and demi-tasse as noon as possible. Have it over with. There's a glass of nice filtered water for you as you go out, just off the coat-room, if you're athirst. Then rush your guests around to the "movie," where you can sleep off the water.

Eating out says Gus O'Toole, used to be a pleasure; now it is only an organic necessity.

Sic transit gloria. Saturday and Sunday—also the fascinating and lost art of "straightening out" on Monday.

Politeness! There are still vestiges of private politeness, says this veracious chronicle of our moral debacle, but public politeness in New York has given place to the frozen glare and, in public places, the brutal barber shop, "Next!"

The little courtesies of life have vanished. Nobody will make change for you any more. "Yes" or "No" are snapped at you from public servants. Everybody seems to be going around with a chip on his shoulder.

Everything grinds and creaks these days; the oil of politeness and smiling tolerance has disappeared. Even the genial buttinsky has vanished; his was a militant politeness at the most and a humorous politeness at the least.

Gus says the disappearance of this art is the most momentous of the lot. For, says he, where politeness ends black eyes begin.

Extravagance! People spend vast sums of money to-day, the Sociological Committee finds, but they are in reality tightwads. Extravagance in New York is one of the lost arts.

Twenty dollars for a pair of shoes or a bottle of rum is an expenditure of a vast sum for necessities; it is an extravagant price, but not an extravagant outlay. This subtle paradox is Gus's, not mine.

Extravagance was a famous Manhattan art. To save is human; to spend is divine, and we flung away money divinely in the old days.

Extravagance is the mother of all the arts, says Gus. All civilization and happiness are founded on it. To spend money well but not wisely kept the old town alive.

Gus says that "wasting money" is a contradiction in terms. How can any one "waste" money? Somebody else always gets it. Extravagance keeps alive millions of persons in superfluous occupations, which are better than none.

Every extravagant tip helps the children of a poor waiter. Manhattan used to put one hundred thousand dollars a night into drinks in the old Tenderloin—maybe it was a million—and this money was never lost. It bought furs and diamonds for the babies of the proprietors of the restaurants. Seems logical enough.

Extravagance is a formal altruism. If we were all Diamond Jim Brady's, the old town would be happy.

Imagination! With the extinction of the highball and the cocktail the Grand Style liar went out of existence.

Where are those marvelous romances that hubby used to invent over the 'phone at 6 P.M. from downtown to account for his delay while his wife toyed with the toast over the electric toaster?

Where are the perfect short stories about "lodge night," the one-reel scenarios about that "business deal" over in Brooklyn, or the saga about that sudden trip to Boston?

Imagination, thou art fled to sober breaths! says Gus.

The committee goes voluminously into the disappearance of the Art of Genial Lying in all its forms. The ouija board has taken the place of our brains. The Manhattanite's imagination being bankrupt; we have passed along lost powers to ghosts and "controls."

"To lie like a New Yorker," used to be our boast, says Gus. Now everybody tells the truth about himself and his business, going to the unheard of length of swearing to it before a notary.

Gus says that ginger ale and the income tax blank have destroyed the poetry of life in this 'burg.

Lending! This is a branch of Living, although the Sociological Committee has made of it a separate Lost Art. It goes into the rise, perihelion and disappearance of the "touch." It is rooted—this evanescence of a great social virtue—in the universal psychic grouch.

Manhattan suffers keenly from tight-waditis. Rates of interest are exorbitant, nothing less than radium or Jumbo lobsters will be accepted as collateral; and as for personal loans on the friendly terms of a Smeared cigarette—nothing doing. Gus knows.

Before the war, says Gus, everybody knew someone he could hit for a hundred in a pinch. Try it to-day. It is the only form in which the Art of Lying survives. Ask a man for a hundred and you'll revive his hair-trigger imagination all right.

Walking! The "morning constitutional" has disappeared. Legs

are used now for standing, kicking, corn-pounding in subways, stretching in bed or hurrying between a trolley car and the Mayor's Committee on Rent.

Where is the Manhattanite who now walks to business with a rosebud in his coat and the gleam of the midnight Scotch in his eye? Where are the old city-wide rambles? Even Bob Holliday uses a "car." Every vehicle is jammed to capacity.

Gus finds all energy has become introspective. Motion and emotion are gone out of our lives; everything is commotion and locomotion.

The Dodo Club's report on the Seven Lost Arts of Manhattan ends with this profound and portentous sentence:

"Life to-day in Manhattan is *sub rosa*."

The Campaign for Civility

IT was a year ago.

The wind was booming in from the Hudson like the voice of a Congressman from Poke-Stogie demanding a million dollar appropriation for a new ceiling in the Post Office.

The lady, well off in embonpoint which suggested more beer de beer than Vere de Vere, started to climb down from the top of the bus at the Tomb.

As she got halfway down, the wind, which is about the only thing left uncensored in the land on which the moonshine never sets, with a Prankish pirouette blew Madame Embonpoint's skirt up beyond the Plimsoll line set by the International Deform Bureau.

Woman will be woman, just as boys will be boys. The lady in question stood still, with a smile of obese coyness playing hanky-panky over her face, allowing ankles to be seen by the wide, wide world.

But the bus conductor had passed many Summers at Coney Island and many Winters in California as diving board director of Mack Sennett's Bathing Beauties. He was devoid of an esthetic complex. An Al Woods show would have had no more effect on his sensory apparatus than a glass of milk on the gullet of a bootlegger.

With his blunt fingertip on the "Go" button, he imprecated loudly "Step lively, madam! Legs ain't no treat to me."

The esthetic lady bawled out the conductor, and made a solemn promise to report him. I think she did, for I next saw him as a deckhand on a Coney Island boat.

Also about a year ago: I was riding late one night on the inside of a bus. I ordered the motorman to stop at my street by pressing the button. Thoughtlessly, I kept my hand on the button a second or two beyond the allotted time.

"Say, you, over there—what yer doin'—ringin' a fire alarm box? Dat man kin hear yer. He's got a headache from you button-pushers."

It was the conductor, who draped himself over me like a Parting tower. I blondly protested but he ragged me with voice and eye till I reached the sidewalk. He too, probably got in trouble before the week was out.

This was the beginning of the campaign of civility which the Fifth Avenue Coach Company inaugurated. There is now a Placard on every bus with the single word "Civility" stamped on it. That appeal is not only made to their employees, but it is made to you. August was Civility Month for both riders and employees of bus lines.

September is harvest month. What will the harvest be—in the matter of civility?

Anyhow, the coach operators deserve credit for starting something. It would be a good idea to keep that word Civility blazing on all the buses all the year round. The steady tick-tack of a word on the brain has been noted by all psychologists. If the word Mesopotamia had power to draw tears, why has not the single word Civility power to make us all polite?

For the last two years every one who goes round the town a good deal has noted an increase in grouch. Everybody you meet bristles like a military brush. Answers are short, faces are long. curses are deep. Taxes and prohibition, maybe. People are silent, morose, suspicious, and their voices in public places are like unto a rusty saw cutting ice.

Personally, I regret the demise of the bartenders. They were the most courteous public servants I ever met. "Keep smiling" Was ever their motto. The retort courteous was ever on their lips. Their affability spread among their patrons, high and low. They set the manners of an age that has gone with their "smiles " and "winks." Rarely comest thou now, Spirit of Delight. When the Taines of some future time shall come to study the decline of public civility in New York after the war, I believe they will lay it to the fall of the bar and the café table.

Who shall fathom tile disastrous effect on manners of the disappear ance of the expansive noontime beer lunch and the sleep-invok-ing night cap? As to civility among the proletariat—it is a question of the "growler" or the grouch?

To jack up a peevish humanity the bus people have got out a lit-tle pamphlet of Chesterfieldian manners in riding on their vehicles. To the midnight bus spooners and sparkers this little booklet will mean nothing. In fact, if the bus on which they are riding should collide with a cow or a comet, it would be indifferent to them: They are beyond civility and the accidents of this world; They traffic in imperceptibles.

"A pair of them spooners fell all the way down steps one night in a snowstorm," said a conductor to me, "but they never knew it was snowing or that they had fallen—there's civility for you?"

When civility spreads to the subways we may finally find a neces-sity converted into a pleasure.

Guards will be provided with whisk brooms to brush off the la-dies after leaving the cars during the 6 o'clock jam. All girders will be padded with velvet in case a door opens casually while your back is jammed up against it between stations.

Instead of the raucous "Watch yer step!" the man on the platform will announce, "Ladies and gentlemen, there is a slight abyss between the platform and the vehicle. I adjure you to circumspection."

In case of accident, guards will pass up the women's hats first through the exits. The gong that frazzles our nerves at the express stations will be replaced by harps that will play Lydian airs. News papers will be supplied by the guards to those rubbernecks who now read yours.

The Subway Sun will give out a free graphic section to all strap-sub-scribers on Wednesdays and Saturdays. Pickpockets will be requested to turn in their assets and freeholds at the "Found and Filched" win-dow at the end of route. Gunmen must be civil in boarding a pay-car.

I hope also to see the civility campaign reach the drivers of auto-mobiles in our public thoroughfares.

Good breeding should at least dictate the sounding of the horn before killing a pedestrian. In skidding, courtesy ought to demand of you that you try to hit a fire hydrant instead of a baby. Don't frighten people by running over his toes.

As no automobilist at the present time ever violates the speed law when passing a roadhouse, why can't this be applied to dry sections of a county as well?

When a policeman holds you up to examine what's under the gnat or in the thermos, pass him the time of day, and other addenda, courteously. He's human, remember, and a little hand-running appreciation of his services is never amiss.

If civility ever reaches the domain of copdom, I suppose the first thing that will be necessary will be for many of the force to find out what street they are walking on when they move.

The curious habit some of them have of grasping their clubs and tightening their jaws when you ask them in a perfectly blond voice where the nearest hospital is should be discarded. Uncouthness in suddenly dubbing babies and elderly women might be toned down with a few lectures at headquarters.

Flask raiding is distinctly churlish. A flask can be levitated with the same ease and regard for the, feelings of a flaskee as a gardener in Chautauqua lifts the tender shoot of a laburnum.

The policeman's social instinct should be developed. At present it is too narrow—it never seems to have got beyond the proprietor of the peanut stand and the ruddy-cheeked Riverside Drive maid.

But the most glaring instances of incivility in the metropolis to be noted lately are observable in the actions of the prohibition enforcement officers. Only the other day a man going home with a small jug of home-made wine under his coat was held up by an enforcement officer who demanded $500 from the unfortunate. Being refused; the officer of the law, devoid of all savoir faire, shot the jug hider.

A more civil procedure would have been to grab the jug and drink the contents, after which a blackjack blow or two it the base of the brain would have been sufficient.

Incivilities like these are helping to bring the popular Volstead law into more disrepute than it had to begin with.

In these trying times that try men's pocketbooks and gullets, Civility should be the slogan of New York. Life should move like pussy in a molasses factory.

Renaissance of the Masher and Swashbuckler

NEW YORK threatens to go on the loose for the next two years—in spite of our Volsteads and Crafts.

A perfect jamboree or romantic immorality is threatened. The leaden lid of "Thou Shalt Not" has been hammered dawn on us so tightly that the explosion of our suppressed healthy animality may become a classic example of Dr. Freud's dictum, the way to revitalize an instinct is to suppress it.

Don Juan, d'Artagnan and Blue-beard have invaded New York from beyond the artistic three-mile limit. I hear in film circles that there is talk of screening the life of that philanthropic highwayman, Robin Hood. It is also whispered that Gil Bias and Benvenuto Cellini may be glorified in celluloid.

Lord Byron, who once put a deep dent in the armor of British respectability, will soon land at the Battery in the shape of John Barrymore. In fact, it is said there will be two Lord Byrons in town this Winter. And Arnold Daly is in training for Rostand's "Don Juan." As there are fifty-seven varieties of the Don Juan legend, you may as well lay up for a hard and immoral Winter.

The movement of revolt against Things as They Are may go so far—they say—as to cause Lionel Barrymore to put on Falstaff, if someone will write a drama for him around that Old Soak. And what's the matter with Marie Dressler or Fannie Brice as Jezebel?

Henry VIII lately looked over the Old Town in a "movie" called *Deception*. Catherine The Great, with all her suppressed complexes aired, was given a private showing recently in the projection room of a large moving-picture concern. A scenario writer has retired to his bungalow in the Orange Mountains to do a Jesse James. An Italian film corporation is screening the life of Europe's "Huck" Finn, Gabriele d'Annunzio.

If there is anybody missing, I haven't heard of him. Satan? He lately passed this way in a personally conducted tour ciceroned by George Arliss.

It is rather portentous, not to say comic, this artistic renaissance of all the scoundrels, fire-eaters, rakes and Old Soaks of history. Reminds me of one of the climaxes in Flaubert's *The Temptation of St. Anthony*. That grand old ascetic, who lived in a desert worse than the Middle West or the South, thought he had Satan pretty well floored at the end of the seventh round and had, in fact, counted ten on him, when Little Old Nick looked up at Anthony with a naughty grin and said. "I'll come back through your imagination!"

Is America trying to play St. Anthony? It looks that way. But Nick is caning back through the back door of the Imagination. He smiles from the glittering point of Doug d'Artagnan's sword, he peeps from the feather in the bat of Don Tellegen, he winks from Bluebeard's whiskers (or mustache), he gambols in Gertie's garter. We shall soon see his fiery breath in *Ten Nights in a Barroom* (to be screened), where, as Joe Morgan, he may die but never resign.

It's a long way back to the psychological and problem drama. What the human race wants is not "truth" but romance. It may be that romance to the living breath of "truth." The demand for romance on the stage is in Inverse ratio to the supply of it in our daily lives. Digging for the rent hasn't much of the make-believe about It. Neither has ginger ale. At night we rush out to seek it—not ginger ale, but romance. Like sympathy, it is now to be found only in the dictionary—at least in America.

New York's own little idea of the Spirit of Adventure in the past had been founded on the idea of gayety. Now there can be no " Gay New York" (or gay anything or gay anywhere) without the presence at least of Bacchus and Gambrinus. When the cabarets, dances, cafés, saloons and seagoing hacks were in their flower the New Yorker found the Spirit of Adventure floating around every corner. After theatre he set sail for the great voyage across the sea of wine, beer, high balls, jazz, conversation (not the dead exchange of canned smiles and dreary commonplaces you hear now at tables), casual acquaintances and taxis that whirled him to some strange "little place" that some other fellow knew.

The sea is dried up. "Gay New York" has become a myth. The night, like the day, is cut and dried. A New Yorker now schedules his pleasures after dinner as he blueprints the cares that infest his day. The old devil-may-care spirit of New York is now rounded in a "movie." The romance of night life is gone.

Nothing happens. Whatever is is blight. Lewis Carroll's Alice one day, if you remember, stood on the mantelpiece and after looking at the large looking-glass intently it turned into mist. Alice walked right through it into Topsy-Turvy Land, where all sorts of strange adventures befell her.

A beautiful allegory of old New York before the renaissance of the romantic, swashbuckling "movie" and play. Hundreds of thousands of New Yorkers used to stand every evening with mystical potions; before them looking intently at a wall lined with mirrors. And, just as happened to little Alice, in a short while the mirror turned to mist and soon they had entered a country where all sorts of wild adventures began. *The Mirrors of Washington* and *The Mirrors of Downing Street* will not substitute for the mirrors of New York. They have become "movie" screens and stage settings. The shimmering veils of the cocktail and the wine bottle are rent. Doing the best we can in the circumstances, we work out our suppressed complexes vicariously—through the antics of the romantic daredevils and "vamps" of history.

So New York is going on the loose this Winter and next in the only way left to us—through the imagination. This reaction was bound to occur in a city where bandits and clubbing cops are the only ones -who enjoy any degree of liberty. Join a crime-wave or get on the force if you desire a little tang in your daily existence.

Of course the greatest outlet for the personal liberty complex is to get a job as a prohihition enforcement officer. But prosperity comes so quickly, so meteorically, so to speak, to this small surviving band of liberatarians that they do not live long enough to taste the fullness of their lives as d'Artagnans and Don Juans.

Returning to Art (sic), which is the only form of living that the Middle West, the South and Penn Yan have left to New York City, there is the case of *The Three Musketeers*. What is to be said (as Dr. Straton would say) of an American audience that will alt night after night and revel in thrills, shout its approval and listen unashamedly to the still small complex in its spine whisper, "That's the life!" to the doings of a half-soused crack-head who would run you through for a thimble of cognac?

Where are the days of Little Eva and the old oaken bucket?

Doug. Fairbanks's d'Artagnan is really a glorious and blood-thirsty bit of work. To look at it puts civilization back on its peaks.

You feel while sitting in your seat the density of the Dark Ages out on Forty-second Street. The Great White Lights are only jack lanterns for boys. Trolley cars, automobiles, telephones, railroads, "Pussyfoot" Johnson and all the other triumphs of civilization—Including Imperial Wizard Simmons and corn on the cob—what are they compared to the liberty of living in a time when every other building was a rathskeller, when maidens with the voice of the bulbul trilled in your ear when you fought a duel, when the wheel spun, the sword flashed, and the gendarmes paid you to stay off their beats?

It's a curious paradox that we approve of actions and characters on the stage and screen that we condemn In reality. The paradox is all the more greater when we remember that they are more "dangerous" when portrayed under forms of art than If they had a reality.

It is true, Europe has its d'Artagnen. His name is d'Annunzio. But in New York—or even in wild and wayward Harrisburg—a d'Artagnan or a d'Annunzio is as inconceivable as an original Idea in the House of Representatives.

At the opening night of *The Three Musketeers* I jammed my way into the box occupied by Doug. and Mary, Charlie Chaplin and Jack Dempsey—probably four of the most famous beings who are now do-ing sketches on the back of Old Mother Earth—and shot a question at Doug. which I had pinned in my hat while Charlie and Mary were tearing Ricardo's Theory of Rent to tatters:

"Mr. Doug., what do you think would happen to d'Artagnan if he landed at Ellis Island?"

"Under the present immigration law he'd be the last man over above and beyond the month's quota. But it would take a battleship to get him back to Gascony," replied the Gilbert K. Chesterton of the somersault and handspring.

Whether Lou Tellegen lasts or does not last in "Don Juan" it makes very little difference. As I indicated above, there are fifty-seven varieties of this famous masher on the way. The only actor I could discover who was not looking over a Don Juan part this year is Raymond Hitchcock.

"I am not a victim—and have never been—of suppressed corner ogling," he said to me haughtily, as he stalked toward a Nedick nectar.

Recondite, but pointed.

I wonder whether there are a few graybeards like myself that can remember the Don Juan of Richard Mansfield? It was a flat failure. There was a reason. In that time the American was free to live as he chose. Don Juan was looked on as a piker.

At that time I was a corner masher myself in Wilmington, Del. So, like the rest of the young men of the country, I saw nothing extraordinary in Mansfield's way with the gals. But time elapses and changes (as Hall Caine pithily says somewhere), and now in the Bored Republic we applaud anything on the stage or the screen that gives us a taste of the forbidden.

I asked Lou Tellegen—in my wanderings for sociological data—what would happen to the Don if he plied his ogle in New York to-day.

"The Morgue or Ludlow Street Jail," came back the sententious reply as he went back in the first act to teach one of his pupils in mashing to climb a leafy garden escalator.

That artistic times in America are most shamefully out of joint is proved by the revival of " Little Lord Fauntleroy " on the screen by Mary Pickford. While hubby Doug. cries "Back to Fee-Fi-Foo-Fum! " his gentle wife quietly points the way back to sanity. A house divided against itself—but still tiding over the income tax.

Fauntleroyism is the reigning legalism in America. But the Invisible Empire of the Instincts look on and approve of d'Artagnan, Don Juan and Bluebeard.

Watchman, what of the Blue-Law Night?

Brains Under the Barber Shears

WHATEVER is has a centre.

This is a mathematical axiom as famous and as unshatterable as that other mathematical dogma—two parallel lines can never meet; two parallel jags always do.

New York is a queer paradox. It is the only city in the country that has broken over and over the dogma of "whatever is has a centre."

New York has centres. It has perpetually moving centres. Its centres jazz and scamper all over the five boroughs, playing hide-and-seek with census enumerators between decade figgering.

The only centre that seems to be kept put and that resists all attempts to dislodge it is the financial centre. Broad and Wall and thereabout remain decade after decade the Empire City's Hub of the Cush.

Several attempts have been made to swing it from its moorings. Five-hundred-and-twenty-per-cent. Miller some years ago tried to carry the centre to Brooklyn. The result is well known.

Another attempt was lately made by a Boston Archimedes—Pond by name—to carry the centre of financial gravity bodily from this city. Failure marked him for her own.

All other centres in New York, however, keep moving.

The gambling centres move so quickly that they look like a straight line. These centres are pursued by plain clothes flying wedges.

The Great Whisky Centre In these days is having the time of its gay old life. This centre used to be around Forty-second Street. The rapid fall of the booze forts around these corners and the rise of the chocolate and soda centres on their ruins is a matter of near history.

176

No whisky centre now lasts more than a month. It moves with satchel and suitcase so fast to other points on the chessboard of the Big Town that half the time the thirsty have nowhere to plant their gullets. These centres are racing so rapidly in various directions that there are often collisions. Then comes the tug of graft.

The theatrical centre, being a slow body, moves with precision and somewhat ponderously. Its objective is due north. I remember when it was at Fourteenth Street and Broadway, with "Mike" Lyons's, at Bowery and Houston, for the midnight souse. The geographical centre is now at about Forty-third Street. In forty years it will reach Washington Heights with a revival of *The Old Homestead.*

The centre of population in the greater city has always been a matter of guesswork. It moves with the turning of the earth on its centre-pole. Five hundred thousand humans, more or less, clear out of the downtown districts before 6 P.M. to various parts of the urban compass. This causes a violent bobbination of the centre of population.

The centre of population might be at about Fourteenth Street at noon. Presto! at 8 P.M. it bobs up at Forty-second and Broadway.

In the ancient days we have often thought the centre of population of the city was looking at the Futurity. At night the centre of population could be placed at Shanley's, Rector's or "Jack's." During the war it moved to the Library steps.

Every lithe centre in New York has a meaning of its own.

Inquiring into the movements, whereabouts and psychological movements of the centre of New York life, I came to ask the question. Where is the Centre of Intelligence in New York?

Does the brain of New York move erratically like the rest of the organs of this Titan?

To speak of the centre of intellectual gravity in New York City would be a misnomer. One should speak of the centres of intellectual levity. And It is as inevitable as human thirst that these centres are always found in a cafe or a tavern.

In those days, so far away, when Washington Irving and Fitz-Greene Halleck lived, the centre of brain sparkle was far downtown. Literature was, literally, a floating population then. Poets seldom slept in their own beds—conceding they had one. Their wit often came out of a bottle. Intelligence often moved to the music of the beers. Canal Street drama probably shed a few sparks. Most books landed at the Battery from England. There were "salons" modeled on the Paris and London Institutions, and many times the cream of the centre of intelligence held its soirees (if cream can hold a soiree) in debtors' jail.

Old Greenwich Village had always been a centre of light unto itself. The light here was rather exclusive. It muzzled its rays, the skulls containing the sacred gleam meeting indoors around big wood fires. Walt Whitman, Edgar Allan Poe and the rest of the literary rowdies of these days were rigidly excluded. Clean linen and a spotless cravat—astounding to relate—were necessary in that circle.

At the time the Light centred in these Ninth Ward drawing rooms, a reading out of Sam Johnson was preceded by something on the zither, (allowed by Gray's "Elegy." Byron crept in in later years, when the Village began to crack under the poundings of the younger generation from Fourteenth Street who came knocking at the door.

To-day the 'Village is still a centre of intelligence. Its big beam is the clock tower of the Jefferson Market Police Court. It is a shabby-genteel, run-down centre, with light-shafts that need scrubbing. The Promethean spark down there is now imbedded in pea coal. The friction of a cop's club on a small sample of pea coal sometimes brings out the sacred spark in the shape of an epigram or a poeme rouge.

The Centre of Intelligence dragged its anchors of gravity about forty years ago and dropped into Gramercy Park. Some of the Light Inundated Eighteenth Street and Irving Place and broke violently against the bulkheads of Lüchow's bar, spraying Tammany Hall with some bubbles of intelligence.

The Light took to food in that quarter. It was the glorious era of the Pension, the free lunch and basement red ink. Much brains has been spilled around that section. They still point out the place where O. Henry and "Bob" Holliday first met and where James Huneker and Victor Herbert bad the row over Bach's inharmonious sixteenths in the dining room of Mme. Gros-Ventre's boarding house.

New York's intelligentsia at that time carried the banner along

Fourteenth Street. The centres of New York's brains? It was the very solar plexus! Irving Place, stretching from Gramercy Park to Fourteenth Street, was both a Mississippi and a Styx. How many travelers—poets, dreamers and mere writers—have started at the iron gates of Gramercy Park and headed toward the rathskellers on Fourteenth Street never to return! Some were washed over onto Third Avenue all the way down to the Bowery, where the alcoholic gravity was so strong that to this day they have never returned to their parent centre.

However, the National Arts Club and the Players still disperse some heaths, and these two clubs may still be called a Centre of Intelligence, for they as yet have no record of a McGraw Evening.

The Centres of Intelligence got pretty well shot up all over town after O. Henry died, Jo Davidson moved into the Hotel Crillon in Paris, and the disappearance of Huneker into darkest Flatbush.

At one time all brain-beams gravitated to Mouquin's, on Sixth Avenue. For some years it was a regular Midnight Sun of shimmering intelligence. Every problem on earth was settled there in the evening, and stayed settled until the next evening. Problems, political and aesthetic, have return tickets.

The uptown cafes were pullulating and ululating Centres of Intelligence for many years also. Most of the choice rays in the centre at Mouquin's used to trail their garments of glory up Sixth Avenue to "Jack's," where brains wagged till the dawn. Once Igoe Introduced a ukelele among the bearded Senators, and once Trotzky appeared on the arm of Corse Payton in the Councils of Intelligence: but both music and Bolshevism were quickly ruled out by Sir Jack on the ground that they disturbed the intellectual lighting system of New York.

Then came the check, the change, the pall. The war and the Eighteenth Amendment doused our intellectual glims for a while. Can brains meet around the soda water fountain? Is there a Pierian Spring hidden in the tealeaf? Is there an Old Prometheus in Young Hyson?

The Centres of Intelligence of New York no longer emigrated. They were smashed to embers. Where can we go now to hear Good Talk, to meet Brains, to see our fire-carriers incinerating a score of Ephesian domes of an evening?

Answer: In the barber shops.

Slowly but surely the lost Centres of intelligence or New York are coagulating again around the bay rum bottle. The popular barber shop has now become the life of the city—that part of the city that wishes to spend several hours of the evening in give-and-take and mauling out the intellectual, artistic and serial problems of the day. Hair cuts are 50 cents, but opinions may be had for the asking.

"Let us go around and have a haircut" has taken the place of the old invitation to have a drink. Lady poets are having their hair bobbed in order to be in the barber shop brain push. Poets are running to clippers. Uneasy ties the mane that has an idea to exude. Over to Tony's with it. Many a short story is now mentally exfoliated from under a hot towel.

The Bronx may soon be the centre of population of the planet, but that Assembly district that has the greatest number of barber shops is now the Centre of Intelligence of New York.

Fancy Dress Revels

*New Yorks All-Night Balls—How Prohibition Doesn't Prohibit—
The Flapper in All Her Pertness and Disguises*

IF winter comes—can the pagan revels be far behind?

By "pagan revels" I do not mean the grand old open-air picnics, rodeos and Bacchic barbecues that were regular Saturday-to-Monday affairs when Rome and Greece were tottering toward the Anti-Saloonitarian Era.

The pagan revels that I know are those series of routs, balls, parties, dances, masquerades and flask-jigs that are just now drawing to a close in New York. It has been a brilliant season, so brilliant that I—throwing my life-long pose of being a serious, commonplace workingman to the winds—bought a costume and felt unashamed. I have danced and jigged and reveled at various hotels and balls until dawn—well, about twenty times since last November. That's pretty good for my first season "out." In fact, a record, I think, for an evening-dress debutante.

It was the afternoon after the Kit Kat ball at Palm Garden—one of the gayest and most joyously wet events of the season—that I read in a newspaper Mrs. Margot Asquith's now famous declaration of independence against the Anti-Saloon League and the other Neros of Morality that rule us free-born (please don't query that word, Mr. Proofreader) Americans.

She had just returned from a lecture tour through the West in the United States of Bootleggers and declared she had heard everywhere of the great amount of drinking from flasks, vanity cases, walking sticks, piped hatbands and the fennel-rods of lorgnettes that was being done publicly in private and privately in public. She had heard of the flask-habit of young men and women at bails and parties. Asked if she had seen this personally, she replied that she had not. Her information had come front those who had attended these soirees de hip and through her secretary, who had seen these things with her own eyes.

The colossal thought entered my head that I would invite Mrs. Asquith to one of these balls in New York—taking her there personally, and letting her behold—what she would have beheld. She might have given me three thousand words of racy comment in her virile English that would have set America by the ears. It is a pity, by the way, that we have to rely on foreigners to lash us for our hypocrisies and faults; but if we Americans continue to take orders in the spineless, docile way which is our outstanding national weakness and go around with a padlock on our lips, mumbling curses in our beards and groveling when the Seven Solid Mahogany Virtues of rural America tweak us by the nose—well, we've got to let the foreign visitors do our talking.

Be that as it may, I laid my plan before Mrs. Asquith with all the verbal wiles that are my well-known stock in trade. I particularized. I would have a box for her, say, at Barney Gallant's the Ball of a Thousand and One Nights on the evening of March 17. She should see how at least one element of New York's population enjoyed itself under the blessed aegis of the Eighteenth Amendment, or I would lead her to the dancing party of the Fakirs, or the high-jinks of the Independent Artists, or any one of a dozen other similar joyous entertainments.

From her box she would see the aura of prohibition. At any fancy dress ball in New York now, I explained, she could see the newest American dances—dances of which Europe never heard.

There is the Minuet of Passing the Bottle. There is the Sarabande of the One Glass that Does for Five. There is the famous Hip-Pocket Jig, led by Ethyl and Methyl. There is a Mazurka of the Bulging Coat. There is the Side-Swipe Crash, very fashionable when the dance floor is packed. There is the Want Alcohol Reel, a rare dance on these occasions, despite the organized warnings of the dry rulers. There are, besides, the Ballet of Bootleggers, the Synthetic Shimmy, the Prune Juice Buck and Wing, and, finally, the Promiscuous Swig Breakdown.

All these curious dances, born in the ultra-violet rays, of the Volstead act, Mrs. Asquith might have seen in the Winter's indoor revels here. But it was not to be. Mrs. Asquith had lecture engagements out of town, and the sociological data that she is gathering here for a book on us will be minus the interesting reflections and analyses of these dances. More's the pity, for it becomes more and more apparent that if we are ever to have any relief from the tyranny of the national Poison Phalanx we must get it from the reaction of European opinion and ridicule on our curious post-war customs.

At the big events given this Winter in the hotels and dance halls for charitable purposes Mrs. Asquith would no doubt have pondered on the disastrous effect of prohibition on the receipts, for at none of these affairs is liquor to be purchased—at least openly, immense sums have been lost in this way to the hospitals and the poor generally.

Before prohibition planted itself upon us great sums were collected at balls and entertainments by the sale of wines, beers and pure liquors. Couldn't the ban be lifted on these occasions tor Sweet Charity's sake? Gibbons was lately knocked out at Madison Square Garden for the sake of charity. Why can't they knock out the Volstead Law at costume balls and dances for the same purpose? There's a reason. Ask the dry rulers and the bootleggers—they know.

Look over the list of some of the Winter's "bohemian" events. There was the Pagan Rout at Webster Hall. Here Mrs. Asquith would have beheld the American flapper in all her pertness and disguises. And the male flapper, too. The flapper and the flask are one. You may see a flask without a "flapper" attachment, but nowadays at fancy dress balls there are few flappers without flask attachments.

The Beaux Arts affair at the Hotel Astor was a dream of color and light. This is an annual affair of the aristocrats of the art world—fashionable portrait painters who have a villa on the Riviera, and lady sculptors who always dress at this ball like Cleopatra or Semiramis or Bernhardt as Hamlet, Here Mrs. Asquith would have noted drinking done decorously. Imported stuff! The cocktails in thermos bottles. Flappers, of course, in full disarray.

Ah! That Kit-Kat affair at Palm Garden! It lasted until the milkman's goods had been consumed by the school children. The last thing I saw as I left the Kit-Kat ball was a certain staid professor of mathematics seated on a chair with a well-known caricaturist, both weeping because there were no more flasks to conquer. The professor of differential calculus was dressed as a cadi, and the caricaturist had on a nightgown and red socks.

On the night of St. Patrick's Day, at Barney's ball of a Thousand and One Nights, I had a box reserved for Mrs. Asquith. This was a Greenwich Village affair. It was my desire that Mrs. Asquith should see our Village in action. There was action—also the joy that made Horace immortal and Dan Webster talk. From the boxes the floor at 2 A.M. was a chromatic crazy quilt. Mrs. Asquith would have noted the new customs of dry America at their extreme. Excepting for a thousand or two, I did not see many persons drinking.

The season is not over. I may still succeed in getting Mrs. Asquith to attend one of the revels, so that on her return to England she can report as and our lost cause aright, and the way we make shift for hilarity in the land on which the moonshine never sets.

Roughing It
In The Big Town

IT was in the Metropolitan Opera House—the Pantheon of Parsifal and Tristan and the vocal cinderpath of Jeritza's top note.

My friend from the West was sitting in the Diamond Horseshoe smoking his corncob pipe.

I sat next to him throwing a barrage of cigarette smoke toward the lowered curtain.

It was Morning (not by Grieg, but by Einstein's bent-light).

We had the vast place to ourselves, except for the musicians who were tuning up for a rehearsal of *The Crimson-Nosed Mujik*, the latest Russian operatic bomb.

Having been an opera habitué since the days when Milka Ternina hurled to the floor the dose of wood alcohol secretly prepared for her by Brangaene in the grand old operetta of *Tristan and Isolde*, I knew that the Diamond Horseshoe was just the place to talk. It is an ideal spot for an interview, a conversation or an argument.

Well, my friend from the West and I were there to compare notes on roughing it in New York. Our city has been advertised throughout the country as a winter resort, a summer resort, a sanitarium for the over-healthy, the wickedest city in the world, the nuttiest city in the world, the city of magnificent tips, the green meadow of the Golden Calf, the Heartless Thing, the suburb of Greenwich Village, the fat pork chops of the Tammany Tiger, the Hang-Over Gardens of Babylon, and too many other appellations too true (happily) to mention.

But my friend, a son of an old Forty-niner, and himself a Klondiker, had come to New York to "rough it." Unique, I thought, in the history of the eight thousand and one reasons why anybody leaves America or Philadelphia to come to our wonderful town. Here was a man who had come from the gold fields of Nevada to New York city because, he said, he felt the "call of the wild" in his blood. Could anything be more paradoxical? Could anything be more hieroglyphical or more *je ne sais quoi?* Not on your income tax oath! So I got him to unfuss his meaning in an interview.

"You see," he said, with a blast of smoke-suds toward the upper tier of boxes, "I came from a quiet mining town in Nevada where nothing happens. Everything is push-button. Civilization out there has reached its final perfection—sleep. There is nothing to do but dig gold and patronize the circulating library. We read Barrie, Wells, Ibanez and Karl Marx during the lunch hour. There are no crimes in town except in the 'movies.' I got tired of all this, and fed up on all the New York newspapers and what the Chicago and Milwaukee papers said about your city.

"I got excited. My father was a Forty-niner and I was a Klondiker—did Alaska with Jack London and all that. Memories and ancestral calls got stirred up by what I read of your town. I began to feel the old gambler in me calling 'Take a chance!' I love the rough stuff, and I thought New York was the one place left in America where I could find it.

"Roughing it! Why, I've only been here a month and I have had a rougher time in one day than I ever had in those old gold-seeking days in Alaska and the Tonopahs, or even in Mexico. where a man knows what to expect and is seldom disappointed.

"When I landed at your Grand Central Station my first thought was to stake off a little apartment somewhere. While I was looking at that lovely picture on the ceiling five men with badges crushed me, ripped my bags from my hands, while a sixth propelled me from in back toward a 'lower level'—so the sign in the mine was marked—when I gave up my change to all of them.

"I had my 'dope' in my head, and made for what you call the shuttle on an upper shaft to Times Square. It was 6 o'clock at night.

"Well, young fellow, I've been in a battle royal at a public land grab in the old Indian Territory with 100,000 homesteaders; I've stood off at the points of two guns a hundred men in a gold claim in Alaska, but I must admit that that game down under your Grand Central shafts beat them both for excitement. I didn't dare stop with all that luggage in my hands. I was smashed, kicked, nicked, scratched, and finally ground into a cage with a puffing, sweating, clawing gang of River Drift beings. When I landed at your Times Square my watch was gone and my wallet had been carved out of my hip pocket by some rustlers.

"I longed for those quiet, lonesome evenings when I sat by my fire in the Alaskan wilds looking at the kindly eyes of the wolves shining in the dark.

"Three somersaults up the steps to Broadway, where I tried to cross the street just as one of your traffic cops whistled 'Go'! to a long line of automobiles coming my way. When I reached the other curb my trousers were smeared with wheel prints, one of my bags had been crushed, and the Scotch was dribbling out. Three chauffeurs and two cops were leaning in my ear calling me names.

"Then I set out in earnest to hunt for my little three-room furnished apartment, with tile bath, electricity, hot and cold running water, steam heat, in the central part of the White Lights. My limit was fifty dollars a month. Of course, I didn't know. I paid four bonuses to two janitors in three hours, and was told to go to hell by all of them. One place near Fifth Avenue charged me admission to look at an apartment which turned out to be five hundred dollars a month without gas burners. Looking like a hobo and feeling like a bar-rag in a wood alcohol den, I bunked at the Mills Hotel that night. I hadn't eaten a thing and was too tired to feel hungry.

"The next day, feeling tired and suffering from New York crowd-damp, I did not get out until noon, and then I began roughing it in the Sixth Avenue restaurants for breakfast. A scramble for a gold pocket was nothing in comparison—take it from me. Between 12 and 2 o'clock a seat in a restaurant seems to be as precious as the insides of a bottle of 1910 Bass. I have grub-staked many a man out in my country, but it cannot be done in New York at the noon hour. In one restaurant I stood in a bunch of five persons in back of a man who was finishing his charlotte russe with one hand and his other holding onto his fur overcoat hanging into the soup of the man next to him.

"The five of us were after that man's chair, and we all held our watches on him. I understood then and there the cannibal. Also the murderer—not to speak of anything so gentle and human as a thief. The high civilization of the mining camp—its courtesy and stoicism, its delicacy—disappeared in me entirely. I wanted to beat my four hungry chair competitors to a pulp, murder the fat guy suavely eating his charlotte russe, and pinch all the food in sight. Thus will twenty hours of life in New York set back the delicate hands in the culture clock of a simple miner's soul.

"I visited eight restaurants before I got a seat, from which I rose without a hat. Some one had left me a golf cap. But I was being atavised rapidly—atavised, young man, is coined from atavism; it means the return of man to the brass-knuckle stage of his evolution. So when I was held up in a Seeing New York car at 4 o'clock that afternoon under Trinity Church together with about fifty other guests of the city, I was not only surprised but delighted. It recalled my boyhood days, and I felt young again.

"I rushed to a theatrical box office for a ticket that night. Famous show on—*Between the Lounge and the Bed*, by Gussie Eclair, translated from the English into Broadway. I was on the twenty-yard line in the crowd, with a ten-spot in my hand, when a ticket speculator, who whispered out of his ear something about 'two in the family circle,' grabbed the note and shoved two subway tickets into my hand.

"He disappeared and was lost amid a bunch of cops. I fought my way back to the street minus my keyring, my pipe, and my Elks button.

"I'm going back to Mexico for a quiet time. I'm too old to rough it any more."

The curtain had gone up for the dress rehearsal. My friend's corn-cob had gone out. I tiptoed lightly out of the box just as the bowl of his pipe rolled down into the orchestra.

But, making a fair wager, it's a trunkful of radium to a ringworm that my Western friend will turn up in New York within a year, itching for the old flying wedge. It's a long lane that doesn't lead back to Manhattan.

A Midsummer Night's Scream

NERO fiddled while Rome burned. If that aesthetic pyromaniac were living in New York in the summertime and took it into his cracked cranium to stage such a show, he would probably insert his *Marcheta* record in his Dinrola No. 37, open all the windows and the door to the dumbwaiter and squat on the fire escape, where he could watch the flames from the Aquarium jazz toward the Hall of Fame.

You see what I mean—or you can hear what I mean any morning, noon or night in this little island of Manhattan, built with a strict eye to the transmission of sound.

In the spring a New Yorker's fancy lightly (cerebrally speaking) turns to thoughts of new phonograph records and cracked trombones.

The skunk cabbage and the horseradish—those first floral heralds of spring—have been saluted by a fanfare of cacophonic caterwauling rarely, if ever (as the cub "best seller" writer would say), equaled.

Tenors, sopranos and basso-bluffos issue their bleats and high-geared gargles with the coming of the milkman and cease only upon the midnight hour, when the Cats' *Ninth Symphony* begins and trombones give up their last dead note.

Flats and apartments in New York used to be places to live in or be kicked out of. Now they are five and six-holed musical boxes.

The needle used to point to the north. It now points to your tympanum.

As I write this it is 8 o'clock, and you'd naturally think that the shades of night would be falling fast. It is falling lento—for to the left of me there is *Silver Threads Among the Gold*, to the right of me

189

Aase's Death and somewhere above me *The Rosary*.

In the back of me they have turned the radiators into music boxes for the summer. The steam pipes have been holed for flutes. The fire escapes are being strung by experienced harpists, and the clotheslines when not in use tinkle nightly and merrily like aeolian lyres of Far Eastern design that are guaranteed to keep evil spirits away; I will vouch for the truth of this, for I wasn't able to hit any of 'em.

The window screens do not escape, for the flies have caught the music mania and their Gatti Casazzas rehearse the Horsefly Anvil Chorus in the dumbwaiter shaft.

Spring has had a habit of telescoping itself into summer from the time when the memory of robins and ex-bock beer runneth not to the contrary, but now the telescoping is being done not under the auspices of the robin or Fritz von Bock, but under the auspices of Calliope, who used to be one of the highbrow double sextette from Parnassus, but who is now the new Muse of Noise in our musical flats.

Prohibition and the high cost of amusements and human addenda like clothing have been the main causes of this hurricane of jazz that hovers over the million or so silence-wooers who still remain in the big city.

Remember the good old summertime? Halcyon and vociferous days of gloamings and honeymoons, pretzels and beer. The memory of these ancient days are all put to music now, for the human soul driven in on itself turns to music. When Liberty sails away to Havana or the Continent, those of us who are left (a goodly company) turn sadly to our inner resources and call from their deeps the flautist, harpist, fiddler, piper, trumpeter, fifer, drummer or minstrel that is latent in our beings,

Prohibition! What crimes against our ears are committed in thy name!

The opera season only closes in the Spring in a Pickwickian sense. There is a postscript season in every apartment house in Manhattan. Caruso, Galli-Curci, Bonci have only moved; they never quit. Their voices never die or resign. Every open window is a stadium.

Thrum and Strum have taken the places of Mike and Andy of corner saloon fame. All the old barflies and highball nosegays have put their winter savings into Pandean pipes, bassoons, bugles, concertinas, hummingtops, zithers, jew's-harps, mandolins and Chinese gongs.

Sir Toby Belch is studying record catalogues. Falstaff is studying the xylophone. The old Bacchanalian Chorus at Mouquin's and the Hennessy Hail Morning! Society at "Jack's" are studying parts in the Chocolate Sundae Choral (if the proofreader passes this *Chloral* there'll be no kick).

Lo! the poor child that practices on the piano three hours every morning! With the windows down and buttoned 'gainst the coming of Jimmy Valentine we had a little peace. But with the windows up in summer we shall scale—not to say gamut—the depths of nerve-rack, for on the prophetic soul of one of our musical uncles we have it in cold minion that "the child who practices on the piano has returned."

Oh, for those good old days when the neighborhood mutt used to race up and down our block every morning with a tin can tied to its tail! We can still see with our ancient mind's eye the Holy Roller face of Zeph Baker on the can as it bounced from brick to brick, for Zeph Baker's corn was famous among housewives in those days. But this Symphonic Tincantine was as sweet as 6 percent beer to a mummy's gullet compared to the horror that lies before us—"the child who practices on the piano has returned."

Then there is the kermess of the apartment courts. The Little German Band is for reasons best known to the ex-Kaiser no more (and, to give up the truth without any violent suffering, I confess that that little band awakens tender and happy memories—memories of a sentimental and humorous Germany that is no more).

At the very hour in the morning that you sit down to begin to manufacture your five best epigrams for the day, while the pajamas of the neighborhood are taking their siestas on the clothesline, a bunch of Neapolitan Nightingales line up under your window and begin to glut the air with those Italian songs of love, stilettos and wine that lull you into a fantastic doze and destroy all possibilities of your earning a check for that day.

As the summer wears on dance parties are organized ex tempore on the appearance of these ex-Chianti waiters in our courts. Let the kids have their fun. You can flee to silence in the Woolworth Tower.

Our Board of Aldermen should get busy on a musical zone law. Why not segregate the melomaniacs? A section of the city could be roped off at certain hours for these devotees of mellifluous hullabaloo. Why not plant them all in the vacant lots under tents between certain hours of the day and pass a Sullivan law prohibiting any of these deadly musical instruments in a house or on the person outside of the segregated districts?

If music hath charms to soothe the savage breast, it also hath potencies to awaken it.

The Beethovens of Babel and the Wagners of jazz are playing with deadly weapons—the infra-violet musical vibrations.

If a single sustained note can make a man commit a crime, what will be the result on our instinctive natures and our Freudian complexes when we become chock-full (around the mutt days of mid-August) of the musical bellow, blare, yowl, grunt, bleat, ululation, woodnote, shimmy-twist, drone, gurgle, hiss, blatter, croak, squeak, pule, Ethiopian apotheosis, jingle wheeze and tintinnabular tesseract?

I dreamed that the fish tanks in the Aquarium had all become music boxes and the fish were all dancing the "Tarantella" and the "Whatthehella."

The tops of the Singer, Woolworth and Metropolitan towers had giant self-playing pianos installed on their balconies. They could be heard within a radius of fifty miles.

The clock on the Metropolitan Tower was a giant record that revolved day and night to the tune of "The Mulligan Guards."

All the press-buttons on the surface car lines played an air when a passenger pressed them. The giant dynamos in the electric power-houses were calliopes. All the electric lights in New York gave out kilowatt music.

The tonneaus of all automobiles rolled along to the tune of any old thing the chauffeur wanted.

All the dumbwaiters in New York rolled up or down on musical cords.

All the faucets when turned on played municipal music.

The summers glare we need not fear, but the summer's blare is here, is here!

A Midsummer Night's Steam

WHENEVER you are "up against it" take a boat for Staten Island. Whenever you have a problem to solve or a debt that you can't pay or a next chapter to work out in that novel that is going to make Rex Beach look like a penny stamp, get on one of those boats. In summer time especially it is the Trip Magnificent. You can go 'round and 'round for a little more than nothing. And presto! everything begins to unravel.

There are gnomes on those boats. They may come out of the water. Maybe they are born of the air, or of those shores that glitter at you like a vast being, a Sphinx with a thousand-thousand eyes.

Anyhow, I met my gnome on my fourth trip around on a glorious summer night. I sat on one of the seats surrounding the cabin rubbing the back of my ear—like Aladdin rubbing his lamp. My mind was harping on the Destiny-of-Things-in-General. Why do I rub the back of my ear when trying to dope out What-It's-All-About? I do not know; but since that night I have discovered in an old tome that the bone in back of the ear is really the subway to the Invisible Domains.

While I was rubbing, gently rubbing at this chamber-door to Magic Land some one tapped me lightly on the knee (it was my tenth rub, I think). I looked around negligently, expecting a "touch" and I beheld the queerest-looking person I have laid my eyes on this side of Washington.

A rather fat boy, dressed in blue serge, a standup collar, flaring red tie, from which shone a green-stone pin; patent leather boots, and in his hand a little walking stick—something like a wand—gold-tipped with a ferrule of opal. His hat was grotesque, for it was an old style low plug, such as some equestriennes affect.

I recognized Robin Goodfellow—just as I had seen him in a faded print years before in an old Sussex tavern. This was, indeed, a midsummer's night steam!

"You rubbed your ear ten times, and here I am. It's my cue. You are worried over Things-in-General, hey? Well, I am not, and I know a deal more than you.

"I am the Comic Spirit of Things. Laughter is my religion and the Absurd is my recreation.

"I differ from my cousin, Jack Mephistopheles—the old rascal—in not being cruel. I *do* play pranks with you earthlings—for the mere joy of joking. I am the Imp of Topsy-Turvy Land—the Charley Chaplin of old Mother Earth. If you mortals were not so serious you would not have so much trouble. An absence of humor is the beginning of all tragedies."

"Then you are the veritable Play-Boy of the World?" I asked him, not doubting for a moment that I had gone insane.

"Precisely," ejaculated the Urchin of Laughter, flourishing his cane, from which flew into the night air thousands of little faces wreathed with laughter and smiles. "I am the little God of Circumstance who slyly strews your path with banana peels and puts into your pocket purses filled with sawdust.

"Ah, you do not see me as I really am. The trouble with the times is that you have lost your real eye—all of you—the Imagination. Where is your statue to Mark Twain in this country—hey?

"Too much business—not enough humor and imagination—that's what's the matter with the whole bunch of you humans. You have forsaken me—Bob Goodfellow—and are running after strange and ugly gods."

And he whirled his cane—or wand—around in the air thrice as if pronouncing a comic anathema on civilization, squat there before us in the night with its thousand eyes of artificial light.

"I have wings. And you could have them, too, if you had more humor and imagination. Laughter and imagination, they are your wings given to you by me at your birth. What have you sold them for? Now look at the scrape you are in!

"Eugenists, prohibitionists, birth-controllists, puritans, sentimental landlubbers, war-lords, suffra-this and suffra-that, trade-lords and heaven only knows what have taken possession of the planet, and my kingdom is in the dust. Laughter, like good red wine, will soon be extinct if you don't brace up and see the funny side of the fine thing that life really is.

"Too much rote and reason," he continued, kicking a carpenter's rule lying on the deck into the bay. "Too much common sense and not enough uncommon sense, which is a little sane carelessness about things. Efficiency! Pah! I wouldn't get on a boat if I didn't think it stood a chance of being wrecked. I wouldn't aviate if I thought it was a safe sport." (I took a hurried look toward the life-preservers.)

Picking out my room in the psychopathic ward, I ventured to ask whether His Highness of the Quintessinal Giggle thought the world would ever be ruled by laughter, whether the humorists would some day rule the world.

"Without a doubt," he chuckled. "But not until my cousin—old Jack Mephistopheles—has finished putting ears on you all and you have looked full-faced into my mirror."

"Your mirror?" I asked, hoping for a nice, soft keeper in the booby-hutch. "What is that—your mirror?"

And I heard, for answer, a laugh so silvery, so space-enveloping, so sewn with health, gladness and sanity that the lights of the Jersey shore and Brooklyn seemed to be drowned in a finer essence than light itself.

Bump!

"Last trip—you can't sleep here!" some one bending over me said.

It was a cop.

BOOZE

Apologia Pro Vita Souse.

All the good conversation I ever heard was
    after the cocktail.
The best jokes I ever heard were from the
    lips of rounders.
The only democratic institution that was
    unalloyed was the barroom.
All the spontaneous guffaws I ever heard
    were alcoholic.
The most beautiful human faces I have ever
    seen were those that were lit up.
The wittiest men I ever met were bartenders.
The most generous human beings I ever met
    were intoxicated.
The only time I evar heard the truth was in
    a drinking bout.
The only good fellows I ever met I were
    drinkers.
The politest men I ever met were jagged.
The few friends who lasted a lifetime I first
    met in cafés while drinking.

Polemic Against Sobriety

MAN, whether biologically, mentally, morally, historically or æthetically conceived, is not fundamentally a sober or a peaceable animal. Nature made him drink-loving, war-loving, and libidinous. He is born an anarchist. He hates—he will always hate—civilization, restraint, all laws whatsoever and discipline of any kind, the smug-mug Utopians and peddlers of Mansions in the Skies to the contrary notwithstanding. If he follows economic and religious saviors, it is only because they give him a new kind of emotional souse. He must have some sort of relief from the hells of sobriety, reason, peace and boredom.

At the psychological bottom of all promises of redemption, national glory and economic freedom lies the souse-wish. Anything that takes man out of the Gehenna of sour sanity is welcomed: drink, war, women, laughter, holy-rolling, bullfighting, prize-fighting, hog-calling, spitting marathons. Books of history repeat in sing-song fashion, "And now a period of peace and good-will ensued, and there is nothing of importance to record." Our nerves, our brains, our spines, our flesh, our "souls" seem to be manned by gay and tragic Furies. Sensation, frenzy, irrationality, illusion, madness, however sublimated, are the normal cravings of all human beings.

We all await the Mystic Trumpeter of some great Saturnalia. The mystical *Tag* in America, for which millions of us secretly pray, is the repeal overnight of the Eighteenth Amendment and the Volstead Act. If such a thing could happen by fiat it would make Armistice Day look like a soda-water festival in Westerville, Ohio. The human race is, in fact, always awaiting the sudden and miraculous repeal of some form of enforced sobriety. The hydro-pot has no more permanent human validity than a middle-aged virgin. The miracle at Cana has suddenly made Jesus one of the most popular of We Boys. The Vatican and the Church of England will never go dry—God be praised! The Methodist Crô-Magnons and the Baptist Neanderthalii of the South and West know that their peoples are secretly crying for the coming of King Swizzlenick. The bootlegger and the failure of Prohibition in Turkey, Russia, Norway, Sweden and America are the triumphs of biology over transcendental psychopathic hooey.

There must be a reason for this perpetual and health-generating will-to-unreason. There is a logic of the illogical and a *rationale* for all forms of the irrational; and the irrational is the soul of human evolution. The biological reason, that all organic matter aspires to frenzied sensation and violent extroversion of its smothered potentialities, is not sufficient. There is something more. The human being has an ineradicable instinct to surpass himself, as Nietzsche says. He must lift himself by his own bootstraps periodically, if not continually. He seeks the miracle of levitation. Every day he hopes in some way to transcend Routine, Sanity, Sobriety.

Nature, benign and cruel, satanic and merciful, has herself given him the means of thus surpassing himself, for if her two primal laws are Life and Death, she has yet a third for us to curtain the ills of one and shut out the terrors of the other. It is Fermentation. She is the primal distiller. She is Bacchic, Dionysian, alcoholic. She is the preestablished and pre-ordained Barroom. All the cells of our bodies are Houston street cellars. It was not an uninspired hand that wrote the sacred phrase, "the vineyards of the Lord." And while the lilies of the field may not toil nor yet spin, still, in due time they will, in sheer static repose, ferment and make alcohol. That is the sacred unreason of Nature herself, and all the Snoopers' Sodalities, Meddle Mollies, Poke-Noses, Blue Bromides and Seraphim of Sanctity cannot put asunder what Nature bath joined together: Man and his Gargantuan thirst.

II

Having demonstrated the biological, moral, imaginative, religious and naturalistic bases of the legitimacy of Drink, I shall now disclose some of the secrets of the Alcoholic Dimension (mainly for the purpose of converting the Boy Scouts of the Piltdown and Crô-Magnon areas to a biological and æsthetic view of drink) before I venture upon an anatomy of sobriety—for sobriety is one of the great evils of the present day in America, due mainly to the high prices and deleterious nature of our booze. Indeed, sobriety is now the curse of our working classes. It is an aid to brooding thought and unrest, it lowers production, and it tends to Bolshevism.

A hydropot can never extricate himself from the trap of the three platitudinous dimensions. He may seek escape by going on prolonged lawn-tennis bats, movie stews, chess-and-checkers jags, or crossword puzzle brannigans, but they will not lift him for a moment out of his sulks. Inject some soda-water, unfermented grape-juice or even the fruit of the Nedick into the hide of a sincere hydropot, and you have merely succeeded in making a sedentary mummy walk—which, as far as I know, may be the Methodist alcoholic dimension, for we were lately told by the Great Omslopogas of the Westerville Neanderthalii that walking was to be the only amusement permitted hereafter on Sunday (which day is, by the way, the nethermost rung in the hell of sobriety in thousands of small towns of the Grimaldi belts of our unhappy country).

I invite you merely to look at the generality of faces of our anti-drink crusaders. Lips like split daggers, ice-water eyes, the pinched nose of a corpse in the Sahara. You will see such faces in Dore's illustrations of Dante's "Inferno." They are paying, O my gay raddlers and soshers, for their sin against the Holy Ghost of Biology and their heresy *in re* the miracle at Cana. The sober, non-alcoholic face is recognizable instantly even among lay-drys: hard-boiled, parched, arid, bloodless, embittered, turned in when not hatchet-shaped. Compare this anti-Bacchic mug with the mugs of the pro-Bacchic, those who have uttered Yes to the eternal law of cellular fermentation: exultant animalism, florid fecundity, Homeric laughter, jovial foolishness, unbuttoned complexes, a New Year's glint even on Yom Kippur.

To be concrete, and to snap a common pose illustrating the passage of the soul from Death Valley to the Venusberg, I give a dinner for eight. They squat around on divans and chairs, after the usual cold-mitt introductions, in sacks of solitude and sobriety. Each one eyes the other suspiciously. When they utter some common- place their voices—hark! hark! a sound from the tombs! Twenty pairs of ears are strained and ten brains are centred on the emergence of one sound from the diningroom—the crash of ice against a metal con- tainer. Hark! Hark! the lark! I am shaking the cocktails! A secret prayer all around from my guests: Thank God, sobriety is come to an end! I put into their mouths that which steals away their pains. With three rounds of nullification water the wedge into the delight- ful dimension of absurdity and unreason has been driven. Brains un- lace, hearts uncorset, throats unbutton. My guest who was the most reticent and dignified is now running his hands merrily through the wild-waving bob of the lady who thirty minutes before looked as hopelessly unapproachable as Parsifal's first wife.

There should be courses in all our public-schools, including our Sunday-schools and Boy Scout lodges, on the beneficence, the gran- deur and the mysteries of the Alcoholic Dimension. Physiology and psychology should be taught with a view to pointing out the evils, the biological and psychological pitfalls, of lifelong sobriety: the harden- ing of the human emotions, the arteriosclerosis of the laughter-glands, the danger of Schopenhauerean ptomaines, the constriction of gen- erosity, the imminence of the epicene uplifting germ that lurks in perpetually arid gizzards, the warding off of the Upton Sinclair dis- ease, swifter and more harmful in its ravages on the imagination and the Comic View than all the absinthe ever swilled by Verlaine; the terrible inroads of the cancers of cruelty, busybodyism and masoch- ism—with charts showing our boys and girls the hideous results of lifelong sobriety on human subjects taken from the cowpen, hayrick and pig-trough areas of the South and West, the frightful livers and kidneys that only half function in Kansas, Indiana, Mississippi and Nebraska, where corn-mule and home-made gins are secretly used by apostates to sobriety in their pitiful attempts to get away from their hells of workaday reality; together with a photograph of Billy Sunday and John Roach Straton with their faces screwed up to the nightmare grimaces of the Medusa Sisters while their parched tongues hiss out from arid throats their blasphemies against Bacchus, Gambrinus and the sublime home-vintner of Cana.

Follow this up with warnings as to the dreadful effect of a sober life on literary style, with samples from the flat-breasted poetry of Eddie Guest and the glandless prose of Calvin Coolidge, while, on the other hand, pointing out that Kit Carson, Edgar Allan Poe, O. Henry, General Grant, Lord Byron, Napoleon Bonaparte, Daniel Boone and Algernon Charles Swinburne were not only conscientious drinkers but did almost all their best work while swizzled or, at least, on the jouncing, bouncing, heaven-lifting hang-over.

My own experience is that sobriety is only of value as a background, a negative state in order the better to get the full epicurean flavors of a Dionysian souse. As darkness is to light, as work is to play, as duty is to irresponsibility, so is sobriety to intoxication. Sobriety, work, calculating sanity I regard only as a seeding-time, a power-house, a charging battery the better to let fly. Aren't we always planning, hurrying, cleaning-up the work for the next party, the next razz, the next explosion of our real selves? Jazz-dancing is a good way of getting drunk. It is strictly biological and natural. But it doesn't last. Nothing since the dawn of life on the planet has been found to take the place of alcohol as a release from the futilities, inanities, stupidities and immeasurable yawns of reality.

So the great secret of the Alcoholic Dimension, my dear Boy Scouts, is, like the magic feat of Alice who walked through a mirror into Wonderland, the miracle of metabolistic and ethical transubstantiation. And, let me whisper into your ears, that is the reason the Blue Snouts of Sobriety are afraid of it. Alcohol transvalues all values. It wrecks the home, the church, the workshop and all the other sacred founts of that Heaven-anointed Christian civilization which lately culminated in thirty millions of sober men bayonetting one another through the bowels and plashing through one another's brains—to make the world safe for Mussolini, Leninism and the Anti-Saloon League.

Another magic of the Alcoholic Dimension is the obliteration of my everyday, cautious, prudent, polite personality and the birth of a boasting, egotistic, sublimbofoghorn personality. Get drunk and announce yourself! Give your Napoleon, your Caruso, your Jack Dempsey, your Keats an airing! The alcoholic swill-to-grandeur is of divine origin (see Plato or any Bible). All real prophets are either drunk or doped. You will kick stories of marvel out of your very shoes and out of your Stetson you will drag Iliads and grotesque versions of *Yes, We Have No Bananas To-day*. The sober-lifer must carry his one stale, changeless, moth-eaten personality from the cradle to the grave unless the good Lord puts him out of his misery by suddenly having him go coocoo.

III

But lower yet in my estimation than the sober soul is the drinker who boasts that "I have never yet lost myself," "I just know how far to go," "They say I'm always a gentleman," "I know how to carry my load," "I remember all I do or say." He doesn't belong, as Yank the Hairy Ape would say. He is a spy, peeping into both dimensions, a go-between, a Philip drunk and a Philip sober simultaneously. I say unto the Boy Scouts, verily when ye grow up, be a regular on whichever side of the liquor question you stand, but for Bacchus' sake don't be one of those squibs who are afraid to get cock-eyed!

I suppose every sound and round bottle man knows the exquisite sensation of the first touch of wine in the stomach after a prolonged siege of the demon Sobriety, that first gentle flutter of the black veil of sanity, its complete rending and disappearance on the second bottle, and the final ascension and abiding in the Land o'Prester John. When *Mater Tenebrarum* opens her black parasol in my brain and goes a-promenading through my soul, I possess the magic that will turn the parasol into a heaven painted by a Renoir and that will transform Our Lady of Shadows into an Aphroditic wench. That magic, that witch's broth, that alchemic substance is Rum.

Here is a concrete instance of mash- magic. For some weeks I had been condemned to the hells of total abstinence. I've forgotten now whether the trouble was gastrocele or just a light case of lipostomy. However, I got on a Madison avenue car. My face was set like a Chinese Buddha looking at a portrait of John Roach Straton. The rest of the men and women in the car had faces cast the same way. The teetotal megrims. This man looked as if he were riding to escape the idea of murder. That woman looked as if she had a huge tumor on her flank. That fellow over there, I am sure, was going to commit suicide at about Ninety-sixth street. *That* man in the corner was *going* to be dispossessed tomorrow. And so we rocked, jolted, swayed along the avenue in this trolley-tumbril, each of us rotting in his own private sober Hell. Why doesn't a mail-truck smash us all up? I thought.

But, instead, at Fiftieth street, three young fellows corned to the panache got on. Their faces were three round, grinning rubber moons. They sang, they danced, they batted quip and quiddity up and down the car; they laughed with that titanic laugh of Danton when they told him he was conspiring against the Republic, the laugh that smashed up the session of the Tribunal. And that is what those three alcoholic dimensionals did for us. They busted the Tribunal of Sober Introverts in that car. We began to *giggle* and eye-nod one another. It was like the sudden breaking up of the Yukon Winter under a tidal wave of hot Scotches. Even the conductor leaned over his nickel-coop and split asunder. Blessed be the honest bootlegger who hash done this thing, was the silent prayer of each of us.

Another magical property of alcohol is its power to abolish the time-sense. Under the influence of the Good Stuff past and future are obliterated. Intoxicated, we live in Emerson's Eternal Now. There is a veritable hypostatic union with I Am, I being the Am, and the Am being myself. A pox on Einstein! He says Time is relative.

Well, he was never sashed, else he would know that Time is Absolute, and that, as the Absolute and Nothing are as one according to Hegel, Time does not exist. This I can prove by millions of spirituous aviators. Space still exists as long as you can navigate. But Space also cashes in if you prolong the ecstasy to the dawn.

The sincere Dry-Bellies of the West and South, fearing to take their first drink lest they would never be able to remember taking their last, have in days gone by made pitiful attempts to clamber out of their Tophets. There were Peruna, Duffy's Pure Malt Whiskey, Jamaica ginger and a thousand other alcoholic medicines for what they called their "puny spells." Many of these solaces are now denied them, so they fall back on horse liniment, hair tonic and other concoctions made of skunk-essence.

This is in line with the whole anti-naturalistic, anti-biological course of American life and history. The European nations are tragic effigies of the Christian idealogies; but America is their caricature. Comic masochism is a national trait. The American is the greatest counterfeiter and perverter of all normal, natural and biological values that the world has ever known. He parades a cheap, wet-varnish soul before the world. His religions, his wars, his visions, his business, his culture, his face lack quality. His instinct is to adulterate, debase and poison whatever is healthy, normal, natural and earth-valid.

War is valid in itself; but we turn it into a vast enterprise of redemptive fiddle-faddle. The sex act is legitimate in itself under most conditions, but we glaze it with a sentimental sacrosanctity and hedge it around with the blah-blah of a Mann Act. The right of the artist, either of the brush or pen, to absolute freedom of expression is a biological and mental necessity in the creation of a cultural class, but we geld him and his work in the name of Home, Health and the puke about Purity. Drinking and intoxication are the immemorial escapes of the body and mind from the beasts of routine and prudence, but we make it a crime in the name of Uplift, which is our ethnic abracadabra to mask our instinct for sadistic snooping and our instinct-to-graft. The Englishman is naturally and legitimately a hypocrite. It becomes him like a virtue, in the elder Roman sense of the word. It is innate, biological, ethnic. But the hypocrisy of the American is a steady deterioration from innate hypocrisy to lying and make-believe. He now only apes the Englishman.

IV

I could never understand certain traits in the American character until I was compelled not so long ago to remain drinkless for about eight months (thank God, the doctor decreed the Restoration in full alcoholic regalia just before the late joyous Yuletide). A careful physical, psychical and mental daily notation of myself disclosed unto me the why and wherefore, and even the malign legitimacy, of those anti-social, anti-natural and anti-pagan monsters that root and roar in the bodily hells of the sobersides of the West and the South. A diary of those eight months when my periodical souse was denied me would be a valuable contribution to the study of demonology, misanthropy and Scroogism. Cutting it short, I developed during my alcoholic Yom Kippur sadistic tendencies, bad manners, ill-humor, sour-vision, envy, evil-dreams, murderous maledictions, the John Roach Straton lip, a desire to get even with everything and everybody in general, suicidal melancholia, a craving for dope, chocolates, lady-fingers and angel cake, a tendency to look through keyholes in hotel-rooms, an uncontrollable desire to drop the janitor's babies down the dumbwaiter, and, above all, and, I may say, below all, a desire to enter politics.

Yes, my dear Jonathan Edwards, I now believe in Hell. It is perpetual sobriety.

That Last Night Of King Alcohol

Hilarity and Gloom Vied with Each Other as New York Said a Hesitant Farewell to J. Barlycorn—Broadway's Queerest Celebration

WAS last Monday night the funeral of old John Barleycorn or the wedding night of Bacchus and the chemical blonde daughter of Gambrinus?

It was both. There was a wake over a corpse that may only be playing 'possum, and there were merry village bells over the union of Mild Wine and Meek Beer.

And thereby hangs a strange tale that New York will tell till the last swan sits on the ruins of the Casino in Central Park and squawks its last squawk at the tottering towers of lil' ol' Mana-hatta-by-the-Battery.

The purely psychological panic that preceded the edict of the Department of Justice leaving in doubt the fate of beer culminated in one of the most amazing, paradoxical, and puzzling nights that had ever been seen in New York. Nothing happened, yet most tremendous things were taking place. New York simply refused to take prohibition seriously. When was there ever such a crazy-patch of humor, pathos, thanks-giving, cursing, threats, expectation, denunciation, singing, sneering, put on exhibition before? Good-natured assent to the decree that sent John Barleycorn to a perhaps brief interment—until the wand of the Prospero in Washington should call him again from the vasty deeps—looked into eyes that spelled social TNT. The brandied hiccough met the Hooligan howl of the highball. The cork that has popped since the birth of the Adam of Omar Khayyams sounded to some like a far-off call to arms of all the Red Ink Guards of revolt. To others it was the beginning of a new era, when the whisky agent ceases from butting in and John Barleycorn lies at rest.

Monday night proved that New York was a very sober city. It takes more than one prohibition act to get it "soused."

Everybody looked during the afternoon as if he stood at some new kind of Armageddon. It was the boozers' Marne without a Joffre in sight. It was the Ginmillennium. To millions, 1919 A.D. was the year with two New Year's Days. Tuesday, July 1, was the beginning of the year 1919 ½. Monday was the end of the great razzle-dazzle in New York.

People went about their business maunderingly sober. Expectation, rumor, innuendo, were as rife as maggots in a trench. Little old New York, that had never taken water, literally, figuratively or constitutionally, had the Katzenjammer of fear and disillusion on its soul.

The old town had got over many "a morning after"; but here was, for many, mentally, a "morning after" before the shades of night had begun to sop up the daylight. The Peace Treaty, the League of Nations, old Doc Wilkins, the Lusk Committee, the baseball score, were matters of no earthly consequence. What would it profit a man to gain the knowledge of the day's "extras" if he lost his suitcase of joy-water?

All roads led to the booze store. In spite of the fact that hundreds of saloons had handed it out straight that they would not be "canned," the lines of pilgrims, *en auto*, afoot, in ancient seagoing rigs, and even pushing heel and go-carts, improvised New York a home-made Mecca. If all the bottles of whisky, wine, and beer that were pur chased in the twelve hours preceding midnight of last Monday could have been piled on top of one another in City Hall Park they would have made the Woolworth Tower look like a coalbin in the house of an ant.

The strangest of all phenomena of this strangest of all days in the city's history was the way thousands clambered down off the water wagon and thousands who had been in every condition of inebriety, from the merely "lit up" stage to the daily "I won't go home until morning" condition, began as far back in the past as last Saturday to clean up, taper off, wash out, and take all the other measures to clamber on top of the orange cart.

Old rounders and young rounders, who had disappeared for

months and years from the hotel bars, the late restaurants, the jazz houses, and the common garden variety of ginmill, crawled out of their somnolent respectability and made their way back to the scenes of their ancient chinfests, and went to it with a grim determination to have "one last good one" before the whistle blew. At the corner of the Rue de Booze and the Great Wine Way, which the initiate will recognize as Forty-second and Broadway, early Monday afternoon the writer counted seven men of his acquaintance who had come forth on this Last Day to materialize their vision of that "fine old souse that's coming to me yet" that every ex-tank carries pocketed deep down in the cells of his brain. Never had any prodigal son such greeting as those who returned to the fold. They seemed like heralds and avant couriers of the immortality of John Barleycorn & Co.

It was, per contra, the vision of pink elephants, green nannygoats, and the flying snakes of the Apocalyptic dry dawns at the end of the week that drove others to sobriety. These latter exhibited their "will power" in public like a Houdini doing the handcuff trick on the street corner or a Sandow, growing decrepit, who could still lift a barroom on his shoulder with a smile. They had beat the time clock to it. They not only helped put up the shutters on the Palace of Revels run by Bacchus, Barleycorn, Lim., but they actually got down and began to clean up the "mess of their lives," as one of these perverse citizens put it, as he dropped an eighth-of-an-inch quinine shell into his system to jazz along the depression into a smile.

But as the shades of night began falling fairly fast along about 8 o'clock Dry Face waned and Rye-Face waxed. The "uxtries" on the street flouting the staccato type that wine and beer were to be allowed to hold carnival on the coffin of old J. B. and Five Stars were like a sudden message from Mars, and the newsboys were, literally, Mercuries bearing tidings from the gods—from at least two of them anyhow, Bacchus an Gambrinus.

But nothing can hold back a New York crowd that has made up its mind long beforehand to celebrate something or other. The great Booze Cantata was on in earnest, and all the cops' horses and all the cops' men couldn't put curfew together again. Double-deck dinners were eaten early, for on this solid foundation of food there was to be erected an abiding pousse café of wine, beer, brandy, whisky, and gin that would reach to the eyes and keep the brain swimming and bobinating till Nox bowed them in sleep.

Some laid a firm foundation of porter house for the fuming chimney of drink; others laid foundations of lobster and chicken and spaghetti; others tessellated their interior groundwork with the plain and simple bean and carpeted it with veal and corned-beef hash. A few ate not at all, declaring food was *persona non grata* in such a court.

Between 11 and 12 the well-known alcohol igloos from Forty-second Street to Fifty-ninth were lined ten deep. It was the final bargain sale. Outside street vendors sold a march called "The Death of Personal Liberty." Nobody believed it.

The lobster palaces and the dance halls made a big noise, but over many of the parties there was the air of reminiscence—of the days when every night was New Year's Eve, when whisky was taken as a chaser, when no one went home until Pete Dailey had officially announced at the old Metropole that "Broadway was closed for the night," which meant the milkman was getting sunburned outside.

After 12 o'clock the diners and drinkers abandoned wine and beer, and until 1 A.M. drank whisky and brandy, where they were to be had, and grinned at one another like boys who had stolen apples.

At "Jack's," where the highball has been king for thirty years, Old John Barleycorn died a slow, agonizing death, and his final rattle was not heard until a wee' sma' hour. In the Room of a Thousand and One Jags the Old Gang held forth against the wrath to come behind great trenches of Scotch and rye purchased before that fatal hour when J. B. emerged from the death house and tottered to the chair. Papa John Dunstan sat calmly in the corner talking to Grandpêre "Jim" Wakely about Cycles of Virtue and Spasms of Humility. Rising at 1 A.M. he sang, as has been his custom for many years, "McCarthy's Daughter," ordered the curtains drawn, and pronounced with dignity a benediction and valedictory on the late J. B. The Old Gang then formed in line and sang *For He's a Jolly Good Fellow*, but whether he was Sir John Dunstan or ex-Mogul John Barleycorn has not been learned at this writing.

Down in Greenwich Village, where the poetic proletariat wages war with the bourgeoisie landlords, nothing of interest happened. Nothing can disturb your true Olympian. They who dwell in the eternal, like Harry Kemp and Jack MacGrath, wot not of current events. July 1 awoke only a languid interest in the nut-cellar of the Brevoort and the Turkish corners of Polly's. The denizens of the former and the inmates of the latter rooms rattled on as usual on their favorite airy-fairy themes, knowing that the bouncer would turn up as usual at midnight. Besides, beer and red ink had been preserved to them, at least for a while.

It was at Mouquin's, at Twenty-eighth Street and Sixth Avenue, famous rendezvous of artists and painters, that the strangest of sights was to be seen on this strangest of strange nights. The cafe was deserted at midnight, probably because John Barleycorn had meant nothing at this place. Deserted by all but one customer, a famous sketch artist, who stood upon a table making furious speeches in French and Pennsylvania Dutch on the iniquities of prohibition, while his friends stood outside peering through the glass at him. The waiters were all asleep.

It was early in the morning of July 1. The dawn was coming up a fiery John Barleycorn red in the northeast. A well-known ten-twenty-thirty actor was leaning against a "wet paint" sign at Seventh Avenue and Forty-third Street. His straw hat was rimless, his eyes were glazed.

"T'day's glor'us day," he muttered. "Sits July Firs'—r'turn of the penny postcard—d'partur'f whiskee. S' law of comp'nsation!"

There is something in this. The return of the penny postcard seemed to interest New York more than "making a night of it."

Postscript.—As everybody knows, Monday night did not really end all sales of strong drink in the big town, and he who knows how can get whisky or gin just as easily as "light" wine or 2.75 beer. It's just a question of winking at the bartender in many places. But the procedure since July 1 has been too complicated for open celebrations, and perhaps genuine prohibition is descending upon us gradually, after all.

Queer Phantasies of the Alcoholic Dimension

That Super-Plane of "White Magic," Into Which John Barleycorn
Introduces His Devotees, Discussed by a Group of Those Who Know

"I NEVER knew until lately how much real tragedy was concealed in that old saw, 'Birds of a feather flock together,'" said the ex-All-Nighter at the Club of Worried Good Fellows as he drained slowly and with reminiscent gurgles his "dry" pousse café.

"And it isn't so much because the feathers are the same as it is that the birds, have the same habits. Did you ever hear of a man who was a steady drinker, who lined up every morning for his cocktail—I mean, of course, before the dawn of the great bone-dry age—who took his wine or his beer and his brandy with his dinner and supper, who delighted in the midnight highball or the rickey, and who always went to bed generous of heart and lit up of face—did you ever hear of a man like this who had as a chum a man who never drank, who couldn't drink, who wouldn't drink, or who dared not drink?

"No, Sir, boys; the souse and the non-souse do not mix. And no one regrets this more than I, who have punished the stuff for twenty-five years. One of my closest friends, the man whom I regard most among all the men I have ever met, the man whose bank account was interchangeable with mine, the man who would go to hell or Philadelphia for me and for whom I would have performed the same little stunt, the man in whose eyes I could do no wrong, and the same here—well, that man and myself could never dine together. I drank and he did not.

"We have tried it. When my tongue would start to loosen up and the joints of my mind begin to crackle and thaw over the good stuff he didn't go along with me. To me his face got more and more sewed up, his line of conversation more and more stupid, his gestures more and more buttoned up as my ego began to unlimber. I'd begin to fidget; so would he. My hilarity began to wear on his dignity, and his dignity began to eat into and corrode my hilarity. By the time I had topped off my brandy and he had begun to puff his cigarette with the mechanical gestures of a man playing chess we were not really enemies, but temperamental antagonists. I could see a sneer, a mock, a contemptuous turn in all his features; while no doubt he could see the same in mine. We sat like Medusa facing Falstaff.

"It always ended the same way. I left him for another table where the thirsty birds, with or without feathers, were flocking together, and he beat it abruptly for his corner in the club library, where he could study the latest solid utterance of some hopelessly dry-bone mind in a magazine that hadn't a lead in its printer's office.

"I tell you," he concluded mournfully, throwing in a chaser of 2.75 beer served in a fancy coal scuttle, "that the drinker and the non-drinker, no matter how high their regard for one another, exist in a different worlds as—"

"Just it," cut in Dr. Rounder, the child psycho-analyst and poet emeritus of thousand White Way cozy corners. "The drinker and the non-drinker, the souse and the teetotaller, the bonvivant and the food-and-drink Yogi live in different worlds. They can no more mix than fire and water or a Bolshevik and a bath. They are beings that differ not in degree but in kind. They exist on different planes; walk, think, talk and act in different worlds. I would go so far as say that they live in different dimensions.

"There is," said the doctor, tossing off a very "dry" Martini, "an Alcoholic Dimension."

"Something like the Fourth Dimension, about which we read so many blurbs nowadays, maybe?" quelled one of us.

"Not quite, but not so far away, either, as you may think," resumed the Doctor. "The Alcoholic Dimension is about, generally, the third-and-a-half dimension. It is a little dimension all by itself. Length, breadth and thickness are as every high school boy knows, the elements of the three dimensional world in which we live—if we don't get filmed—and move and have our being. It is the dimension of the sane, reasonable, sober, rule-of-thumb man. The Fourth Dimension is still only a hypothesis. It is at most a brilliantly conceived negation of the third.

"Those fellows on the fourth floor of the world are said to walk right through the rest of the house without coining down any staircase as we know it. They step through walls, pass through you and me, much as we pass through a fog or sunlight. There is nothing miraculous about it, the sharps tell us; but they simply live in another sphere where the laws of matter and motion and mechanics are different from ours.

"Now, what I call the Alcoholic Dimension lie between the two—the third and the fourth. It is a dimension of the improbable, the fantastic, and Dutch courage. The man who lives in this dimension, and you all know him—"

"We *do!*" yelped the Bunch.

"The man who lives in this dimension lives in the domain of the unreasonable, the absurd, the paradoxical, the seemingly uncaused, the queer, the curious. It is topsy-turvy land, with a law of sequence and a woven network of circumstance all its own. Charlie Chaplin, Fatty Arbuckle, and the rest of the actors in those movie comics that send millions of people into hysterical laughter have parodied these laws and actions.

"Our own actions—our sober, sane, three-dimensional actions—no matter how commonplace, may seem to an eye and a brain of a creature in the Fourth Dimension as ridiculous and as comic as an intoxicated man or the antics of a Charlie Chaplin seem to us. It is all a matter of perspective, physical construction, and brain visualization.

"Your real intoxicated men walk through the walls of Routine, step right out of their daily lives' into an enchanted land where the Unforeseen meets them at every step and puts a nutgic day between two stupid es. They get rid for a while of their unbearable sanity and blow caution to the winds.

"*In vino veritas* we have repeated mechanically for ages. There may be a deeper meaning in this saying than appears on the surface. It generally means that the intoxicated man will spill the beans, will give up, will let the cat out of the bag—in a word, will tell the truth.

But there is something more than verbal meant here. as in all pro-verbial phrases. In the wine state—the Alcoholic Dimension—there may be a prefiguration of a still higher state of man than is attainable in his three dimensional jacket and pajamas. *In vino veritas* may have meant that intoxication is itself a truth of a higher order, and that the extraordinary adventures and vicissitudes of the souse are the materialization and manifestation of a subconscious personality that is profounder, deeper, and surer of itself than the prudent, cautious, reticent beings that we are when we are ourselves, as they say."

"Literally, Doctor, a submerged personality come to the bar of the world—hey?" asked the Kidder, nibbling at his parched mustache.

" Maybe," continued the Doctor. "But generally the creature who acts in the Alcoholic Dimension is never brought to judgment; at the worst, he is jugged till he comes back to the regular two-by-four di-mension, and then he must answer, and generally, too, he can't, be-cause he was otherwhere—literally, out of his mind and out of his body. He was in the dimension where all laws are nearly reversed, which is worse than if they had been wholly reversed.

"Jack London, in 'John Barleycorn,' that little known book of his wherein he describes his ascent into chimeraland and his plunges into goblin town under the influence of the 'jingle,' calls this other dimension White Magic. Sir Gilbert Parker, in a book whose title I've forgotten, makes of his hero, who is an average lawyer, politician, or something akin, but anyhow as mediocre as a prohibition Con-gressman, rise under the influence of drink to godlike flights of elo-quence; a perfect Ajax of courage; a tremendous and vital personality.

"When Watts-Dunton took the brandy bottle away from Swin-burne his genius left him. Gertrude Atherton has made a novel out of it. Genius itself is a form of ecstasy, and Plato tells us that a sane poet is no poet. But when the genii no longer dominate the souls of poets they call them from the vasty deep with alcohol—Swinburne, Ver-laine, Poe, Baudelaire are classic examples of this advance upon the between-state by the did of alcoholic stimulation. It is the mezzanine floor between the third and fourth dimensions."

"Going up!" sang out one of the crowd. as he winked the waiter for a camouflaged ginger ale and whisky, which is now known as a "red rug, with yellow tassels."

"The elevator that runs to the mezzanine also has a bad habit of sometimes falling into the cellar," remarked the Doctor.

"But it does create—that is, alcohol—a world all of itself, whether we call that world the Land of White Magic or the Land of Purple Nights. The brain of man is a kind of Aladdin's lamp; when John Barleycorn rubs it we kick adventures out of our shoes, walk on velvet and hit the trail to parts of the city where we never would have ventured in a sober state with no other Baedeker than instinct, willfulness, or somnambulistic memory. Obstacles seem to fall down at our touch as the Red Sea parted at the approach of Moses.

"The most curious thing about the whole matter is that we can watch this passing from absolute reasonableness and staid sobriety into the alcoholic dimension—actually see the man after each fresh drink pass into his super-state, which may, sure enough, soon become his stupor state.

"There's Pudgy Pullet. All of us have sat and watched the gradual transformation of his every facial muscle as highball falls on highball into his stomach. We have, literally, been present at a birth. How his eyes begin to dilate and electricize! How his features crash into a song of happiness! How his chest rises like an organ as his alcoholic ego begins to fill his arteries! How there come to him plans of the most remarkable adventures, which he works out—as we all know—into the strangest nights of our lives. His whole being is dithyrambic. But the next day he knows nothing about that. He has crossed his Lethe and got back, a glummer but not a wiser man.

"I knew a famous writer who after his second day out on an alcoholic tour of the city imagined himself to be a clever crook. He would appear before the desk Sergeant in the old Tenderloin Police Station and insist that he was a burglar and that tons—more or less—of loot could be found in his cellar. Old Sig Freud would deny that he was the inhabitant just then of another near-dimension. He would have laid his bogus confession of burglary to a subcellar wish in the psychical house of the subject which alcohol jazzed into a personality.

"Have you noticed how easy it is to get away with things when we are cornered? There is an assurance, a conviction, an audacity about the well lit-up man that carries all before him. He inspires a kind of awe.

"The drunken man's luck is proverbial. There isn't a drinker who could not narrate escapes from physical disaster while he was alcoholized that border on the miraculous. The guardian angels of the Alcoholic Dimension walk with him where traffic cops would fear to tread. He passes through the crash of bottles and the wreck of saloons like one who has a charmed life. He falls down the steps of the Washington Monument, and rises whole-skinned and cherubic faced. He walks off a wharf with a preordained certainty of falling into the featherbed of a police river patrol boat. He sometimes has his roll pinched when the janitors of his special dimension are off guard, but more often he will arrive home with more than he started with."

"Well, now that Uncle Sam has closed the Alcoholic Dimension during the Summer, what is there left for us to do? " asked the ex-All-Nighter, who had started the whole wheeze.

"Why, we'll have to worry along with the old three," replied the Doctor, " unless we can wink our way back occasionally into the merry mezzanine."

All-Night New York in the Dry Season of 1919

Bakery and Chop Suey Parlor and Sidewalk Dispensary
of Orangeade as Refuges of Evicted Round-the-Clock Revellers

IF the person who told us that "night hath a thousand eyes and the day but one" were to rebody himself just now and lay around New York City for a week or two he would observe that, no matter how many eyes the day in New York has, its nights have received about a thousand black eyes since July 1, and the New York of after hours has only two eyes—the coffee house and the chop suey feed store.

Stepping from high-grade metaphor to the lowly poetry of the Great White Way, "the old town is on the blink"—so completely "on the blink" that if there are any "blind tigers" to be found at 3 A.M., the jungles that the thirsty traveler has got to hack through to reach them are not worth the greeting he gets. Before 1 o'clock one gets around from cafe to cafe by a series of esoteric winks—and a wink is as good as a "smile" in many places. In the lobster cathedrals and dance mosques, and even in the straightout "stag" restaurants, you must belong to the Bacchic Signal Corps to procure a thirst reducer with a "kick." "Whisper to me only with thine eyes," the head waiter tells you when you are introduced.

The new all-night New York was born during the war—and patriotic New York acquiesced; but the new all-day New York and the new after-theatre New York are things untellably unreal. It awes, stuns, stupefies the oldest inhabitant and the younger blood of O. Henry's Bagdad-on-the-Subway; while the out-of-town buyer and pleasure seeker—who will quite often go back home and vote the prohibition ticke—says "Aw, you're kiddin' me; give me a Scotch. New York dry! Can't happen. I can carry it all right" If he has a prosperous looking

219

gargoyle on his shoulders and a "safe" look about the girth he may get "something for his stomach." He pays, pays, pays, concludes the game isn't worth the whisper, and the next night at the same table orders "real ginger ale," which nobody believes he's drinking.

If he is an old-timer he gets to ruminating and reminiscing. The evolution and decline of night life in New York will be the theme over which he will drowse as the hands of his watch travel toward 1 A.M. with the inexorable fatality of the rush of the sun and its string of planetary fish toward Vega in Lyra. One A.M.—why, in the "palmy days" things were just "opening up." It was the hour when the Grand March began in the incandescent ballroom of Gotham. It was the hour of bubble, bubble, without toil or trouble. It was the hour when the red spots began to glow on the cheek of Merriment, when the eye became the blazing caravansary of a thousand curiously tinted lights, when the feet began to walk on velvet and the harps and violins sounded like the invitation to some Oriental carnival. The millinery of the ladies—bless 'em!—seated roundabout, began to look like the magic domes and minarets of some enchanted city builded of mirrors. The head waiter actually began to look like a man born of woman, and the primrose path of dalliance slid away toward 6 A.M., at which time the dawn came up or did not come like thunder. Who cared?

The old-timer's memory might run as far back as Harry Hill and his gilded dance hall, where the cream of the sporting and political blood of the nation whiled the night away; or to John Morrissey's house, or to The Allen's, or Kit Burns's "cockpit for gentlemen," 'way downtown, where you could have anything from a battle royal to a bullfight at any time of the night if you had the where-withal. And there was old "Mike" Lyons's, on the Bowery—the "Delmanico" of the Bowery—that never closed its doors for many and many a year; old "Mike's," which was the centre of fashionable night life when the opera was at the old Academy of Music. In those now unbelievable days the "seagoing hack" was the blimp of fashion and Second Avenue was the Great Gas Way. This was only the other day if you are not very old, and yet it is a New York as ancient as The Hague Peace Conference and as dead as the year 1913.

Then all-night New York moved up-town by slow degrees. There were Rector's, Shanley's, "Jack's," the Haymarket, the old Royal Gardens, the "rath-skellers," the great gambling palaces of the "rooming Forties," the "back room" with its little negro string quartet, which never got tuned up until 3 A.M.; Akron's Tivoli, Mouquin's, where the Muses washed their feet in rich, red wine till the day squad of sculptors and canvas defacers arrived for breakfast; the all-night licensed barroom, where high hats elbowed pickpockets and boiled dress shirts bumped glasses with the tired printer, who had just sallied forth for " his evening." Twenty-eighth Street never closed in those days until the last waiter sitting on the ruins of the end table counted the final roll he had pinched.

Where Is the New York of yesteryear?
Why, it's all awash In 2.75 beer!

That New York, like Sergeant Majors, in Ol' Bill's refrain, never died; it simply passed away. And now there is another all-night New York. And this is the essence of our story, for there is another all-night Manhattan, and it is like unto the old one as the old Paris of the Moulin Rouge and the Hill is like Philadelphia on Sunday. The guns at Liege began the job; the prohibitionists finished it.

At 1:30 A.M. upper Broadway presents a curious sight. The late diners have literally been locked out of their restaurants. New York is officially closed. But there are great crowds on the streets where the white lights begin their final blink. They loiter, stand around in knots, and wear an expectant air generally as if waiting for a miracle to happen. In Palm Beach suits, in top hats, in business attire, in the slap-dash fake negligee of the young fellows who "Summer" on the recreation piers they congregate in Times Square and the adjacent streets looking up into the heavens for a Gabriel who, from the top of a blimp, will announce the resurrection of the wide-open all-night town. Their mental state is "stick around—you never can tell what's going to be doing."

They expect, it would seem, a magical Marathon runner to dart out of Union Square, and, running up Broadway, utter his "Open Sesame." Bat there is no Gabriel on a blimp and there is no "Open Sesame" magician. There are instead wild honk-honks from the Cimmerian depths south of Greeley Square, which means the big touring cars from the island are coming back to their stations. They unload their patrons, who look wistfully around at the faces of the evicted thin-gin merrymakers; and all line up at the new all-night bars.

Yes, New York has its new all-night bars; and they are right on the street There is all the scenery of the real bar except the brass rail, alcoholic drinks, and the pyramidal domes of many-colored glass. There is the white-aproned bartender, to be sure; and for 7 cents he will reach into the vasty deeps and bring you up a cool drink of what is labeled on the walls "orange drink," a reincarnation of "circus lemonade" of ancient and nauseous memory. There are dozens of these new "bars" scattered around the White Light district, and the ex-fizz water experts line up at them with the gambler whose roll is not working and the tired clubman. They all look at one another sheepishly, their eyes saying, "And who'd a-thought it?"

The centre of night life now after hours is, however, in the coffee houses. On the ruins of the all-night bar the Danish and French and Vienna bakeries rear their pasty (or Pastry) heads. Lady Nicotine and King Caffeine picnic on the grave of old John Barleycorn. These "bakeries" have come into being by the dozen. They are packed from 1 until 3 o'clock in the morning by all sorts of humanity—mostly the evicted tenants of hotel tables and jazz houses, who go to these "bakeries" and coffee house to bury just one more lobster or punish another rabbit. They are merry parties mostly, some of them bringing in with them neat little packages of tabooed joy. Those who still insist on "making a night of it" will take a taxi from the coffee house to some chop suey parlor, where one can grow hilarious on tea and view the gilded carvings of the lattice work. It's a great night if you don't weaken.

By 4 A.M. the streets are swept clean of pedestrians. The old nighthawk is secreted somewhere in a "back room," where a bartender creeps under the bar, draws a beer and creeps back on all fours and whispers in the inky darkness, "Put out that cigarette, you boob!" An actor lingers in the recesses of a "bakery" to discuss the ethics of Kant or the chances of our invading Mexico, or the greatness of Edwin Booth. A sleepy newsboy sits on his pile of morning papers. A cop looks over "To-day's Entries" under a drug store are light. The "shuttle" drones its weary way between Times Square and the Grand Central. New York is in bed as it never was before in its life.

"Gay New York" has passed. O. Henry's Bagdad-on-the-Subway has become a Bagdad à la Kokomo.

Life, Liberty and the Pursuit of Unhappiness

Now That Our Bronze Goddess Enlightens the World With
Wood Alcohol, the Inalienable Right to Decline a Drink is Alienated

ALL stories of current interest should now start with a date. A new law of some kind takes effect almost every day. You may write a story this week and it may be seditious the next. Our manners, morals and traditions are changing so quickly in the hard-working crucible of Be It Enacted that what you thought at 6 o'clock last night was a long peep into the future may be old fashioned at 12 noon the next day or an indictable guess before 8 o'clock in the morning.

Americans (I mean those antiquated and absurd souls who believe in the Fifth Amendment to the Constitution, the radical libertarianism of Thomas Jefferson and the archaic concept of personal interpretations of their life, their liberty and their pursuit of unhappiness) used to make that paleolithic date July 4, 1776, a starting point in their calendar.

Later, by a sudden transvaluation of national ideals and a miraculous ukase from the Invisible Powers that work through the enchanting formulas of House Bill No. 00023 or 000½ of 1H20, our dead reckoning began with July 1, 1919.

"Of course, that was before the first of July," one heard everywhere. Men winked at you in the street and whispered that "was before the first of July." Children in the schools are taught ancient and modern American history now. Our ancient history was pre-July. Our modern history was post-July. Our laughter subsided into a whisper. We used to speak of Uncle Sam. Now lave speak in awesome tones of his successor, Geoffrey Bootleg. We used to take our friends from Michigan down to Coney on the boat and point with pride to the big lady in the harbor. Now we rush them to the other side of the boat and point out to them the architectural splendors of the Bush Terminal docks.

Old Lady Liberty is still there, but she wears gumshoes and her torch is lighted with inflammable wood alcohol; in her other hand she holds a ouija board. It's the power of dates.

Another era set in on Jan. 16, 1920. This was the date, as all good school children should know, when the Lusitania Constitution was submarined by an Eighteenth Amendment. No lives lost, but everybody in water up to his lifebelt and the alcohol chests gone irretrievably to Davy Jones's gullet. It was the date of the New Freedom—for the blackmailer and the blind pig.

'Twas the evening, then, of Jan. 15 at the bar of the Psycho-Aqua Club. The Minute Men of the Brass Rail—a laughter-bound organization within the Psycho-Aqua Club—had gathered to watch the old beer out. Not even a pony stirred, not even a V. O. P. It was a 100 percent American crowd being tested to the very limit of their Star-Spangled Bannerism. Not, of course, that they cared about drink particularly, but their divine fiat of refusing one had been taken from them. They were covertly and whisperingly sore at the triumph of Kansas forordination over Gotham free will. Their eyes were as clear as Bryan's, but their hearts and their throats were as flint.

"Have you ever studied the rise and fall of democracies?" asked Dr. Lowrail as he bit off a mouthful of suds. Do you know that when the barroom goes democracy goes with it? Under the Caesars and Cromwell there were no bars. The bar parlor, the wine room, the cantina, the barroom flourish in direct ratio to the quantity and quality of the freedom that exists in a country. All Bastiles are undermined by the music of clinking glasses in public places. All Bastiles rise also to the pump of hidden stills.

"The American barroom abolished caste. The proletariat, the bourgeoisie, and the patrician got together over the bar rail. All men were created free and equal before a white apron. In the barroom race, color or present condition of servitude melted into universal good-fellowship. Liquor was the eternal democrat. Laughter and drink leveled all humanity before the big mirror. There was, in the good old barrooms, a continual interlocking of classes. A high hat was no better than a pair of overalls in the sight of John Barleycorn and Bacchus, not to speak of Fritz Gambrinus.

"When I entered a barroom, whether it was on the Bowery or Broadway, I felt I had entered the democratic heart of America. A bartender, like a cat, could look like a King. Awe, bunk, dignity, and fake standards of conduct were shed at the door. You had to be a man—whether you were talking to a poet, a bum, an automobile manufacturer, or a retired plumber.

"The barroom," flew on the Doc as the crowd grew denser around him, "was the place of the universal showdown. Clear-headed second-story men and brace game artists had no use for a barroom, for here the cat always got out of the bag. It has kept many a 'bad man' on the level, and dilated the generous instincts of many a tightwad. It put pleasure before business which reduced the number of profiteers. It kept money in circulation which otherwise would have been lavished on bank directors.

"The American barroom democratized ideas. It was the emporium of brains and wit. No one of us would ever buy a drink for a stupid man—not two drinks, anyhow. No such forum had ever been in existence in the history of humanity. It was a vineyard of idea, a hothouse of curious dreams, a clearing house of grouches, a magical trick bag of talk, a department store of brains, an undiscovered America, where every than was a Columbus, a"——

Angel Abe, the Kelley pool expert of the club, rammed the idea end of the Thing on His Hip into the mouth of our eloquent psychologist. He drank long and gurglingly. He emerged pop-eyed and radiant.

"The evils that barrooms have done live after them, but the good is interred"——

"In us!" broke in Yogee Maginnis, Chairman of the Ouija Board Committee.

"In us! Right-o!" thundered the Doc. And the barroom crushed to suds shall rise again! For the barroom was the materialization of a need. It was the safety valve of the man with a dangerous idea in his mind. Three whiskies with the bunch ironed out his anarchy and exploded his anger-bomb into a series of idiotic but human grins. Boys, if ever we have real trouble in our country it will come from the sane and sober hunch—the teetotaller anarchist, the smileless, cold-water

Bolshevik. They have abolished the great American soapbox, the tribune of the people the barroom; the time machine will take the place of the soapbox.

"Young man, go West!" said Horace Greeley many tears ago. Rot! Young mart, stay at home in New York and get your education in a barroom, I would have said.

The barroom was the limousine of the workingman—and we are all workingmen, except the Kaiser and Bryan. After a long day's work do you think the workingman wants to read Herbert Spencer, Ralph Waldo Trine, play with the ouija board or snore in a movie? Not on your Old Adam! He wants to evict a few inhibitions, indulge in a little hum-bug, stand on his head, hear a good story. If he gets a black eye once in a while, all the better. As between a black eye and a sissy's lisp—well, Abe, where's that hip-wagon? "

The Doc leaned heavily on the bar in the grand old Delsartean manner of the days that are no more. Don Conde stroked his goatee mnemonically. Yogee Magginnis drew esoteric arabesques on the suds-weeping bar. Angel Abe wiped off the Battery end of his bottle.

"Again," said the Doe, "did you boys ever stop to think that if the world goes dry—which Bacchus forbid!—it will decrease the production of laughter 50 percent? Laughter is a form of cell-combustion, and the coaling process of the cells, in the brain and in the heart, will suffer through the lockout of Bacchus, John Barleycorn, and Gambrinus. In wine and beer especially there were laugh bubbles. Whenever three troubles met over a seidel or a glass of port laughter had the final word. Where there is no laughter there is no democracy.

"As things go to-day we are threatened with a calamity—a decrease in the laughter output. Alcohol created a million laughs where it made one black eye. As Don Condé says somewhere, Exit Falstaff; enter Falseface.

"Boys, democracy and laughter fare their Armageddon in the disappearance of the bar rag."

Nox caught the good old Doc and laid his head gently in the suds.

It was 12 o'clock, Jan. 16, 1920. The tail of the Constitution had begun to wag its superb head.

Angel Abe tossed his hip-pocrisy out of the window. It was as empty as life in 1920.

The Booze Venice

I HAD a dream that was not at all a bad dream. It was a dream such as only Anatole France or the earlier H. G. Wells could do literary justice to. The gorgeous word-stuffs of Victor Hugo might have treated it adequately.

It was such a dream that all thirsty New Yorkers upon reading this will hunt up a chicken bone and make a wish that it might come true.

My dream might be entitled "The Booze Venice of the Atlantic," "The City of Joyful Night," or "The Mansion of a Thousand Barrooms."

You may have heard of Venice. It's a large body of water entirely surrounded by gondolas. There are a lot of palaces that thrust their heads out of the water here and there which would float away into the sunset if they weren't moored to one another by little bridges.

In my dream I had a vision of such a gorgeous Venice that rose out of the sea about fourteen miles out from Sandy Hook as the Old Crow flies.

It was the unique city of the world. It was a Venice of barks, brigs, schooners, clippers, luggers, houseboats, ferryboats, towboats, catamarans, whalers, sloops, colliers, retired liners, Grand Republics and Mary Powells.

They were anchored there till Doomsday.

This sea city had a permanent population of about 300,000 souls. On Sundays and holidays visitors swelled the population to half a million. The population might be described as a floating population.

The municipal officials of this Booze Venice all wore white

aprons. The Mayor was called the *Maitre de Bar*. Its motto was *Nil Desperandum*. Its coat of arms was a bottle of Scotch and Burgundy regnant, with a green snake couchant on a milk-punch white background. Its flag was a wine-red piece of cloth, with oak-colored bars running horizontally across, in the middle of which were five stars. The flag was called the Five Stars and Bars.

The national air of this little country was "Keep the Firewater Burning!" Its constitution had a provision against any form of sobriety after 8 P.M., under penalty of being deported within the twelve-mile limit, which was equivalent to capital punishment in this benign sea city.

The weapon of the police, whose duty it was to preserve a reasonable degree of intoxication among the inhabitants, was a brass rail. This weapon was to the inhabitants what the mace is in the House of Representatives or the appearance of a piece of lead pipe in a Ninth Avenue saloon.

Nothing more magnificent in any dream than was the vision of this city in ship dress, especially in the sunset of a Saturday evening, when the boats rocked, when all decks were awash and when the bands played *Half-Seas Over*.

At night everything was lit up. The lights—hundreds of thousands of them—rocked and danced and cavorted like mad things of life. No light was less than 200 booze power, and the dynamos that supplied them were hidden in great wine vats and whiskey barrels in the hulks of the boats.

Every floating iceberg in the North Atlantic had been corralled for cold-storage purposes. They were anchored for miles in every direction except toward the twelve-mile limit.

It was an hallucinatingly beautiful sight to see millions of bottles of cognacs, Scotches, Burgundies and Bass ale encased in these icebergs. The sunken gardens of Catalina were bourgeois in comparison. The gold and silver labels sparkled in the moonlight, and ships for hundreds of miles out took their bearings from their beams.

The North Star paled its ineffectual fires.

Naturally, the chief industry of the citizens of Booze Venice was importation, exportation and deglutination. It was the center of a vast traffic. It was the ocean clearing house for the vineyards of Europe and the breweries of England and Germany.

Submarines disappeared every day under the waves, bound from Booze Venice to points of interest on the eastern seaboard of the Verboten Republic. There was a Hollywood Express among the submarines, which went loaded to the periscope with the stuff that puts a joy in your heart to steal away your gloom.

The tortures of Tantalus were merely a game of tag in comparison to the physical and mental anguish suffered by thousands of persons in the great arid belts of the West and South when they beheld in the heavens a mirage of Booze Venice.

The mirage appeared with greater regularity than most mirages. There was something diabolical in the jest. I could see in this portion of my vision that on the days when the mirage appeared to the inhabitants of the alcoholic Saharas of the West and South there was little work done.

Opera glasses and telescopes were leveled at the mirage, which in many cases brought gin rickeys, foaming beakers of beer and sparkling wines so close to the lips of the gazers that many went mad. Others attempted impossible feats of levitation.

On the days of the booze mirage the giant telescope at the Lick Observatory was the objective of a ceaseless pilgrimage. Street telescope men did a circus trade. Photographs of the Lost American Art were taken for posterity.

Congress passed a law prohibiting the showing of a "movie" of the mirages of Booze Venice on the ground that it tended to the spread of Bolshevistic principles and was deleterious to the gullet.

Whether they were actual mirages or a collective vision projected by thousands of secret desires—see Freud—the scientific jacks of the day never agreed. But many were the words spilled over the matter. Einstein was forgotten in the visions of another stein, not relative, but actual—but alas! so far away from the inhabitants of the great areas of desiccation.

At the corner of the Grand Republic and the Mary Powell—the Times Square of Booze Venice—all the glad old faces could be seen again. Lying in hammocks, spread out in steamer chairs, standing at the palatial open-air bars, was the old Forty-second Street Country Club—redivivus.

Their slogan was still, as of erst and of yore, "We shall die facing our enemy!"

A lane of boats stretched away north and south for miles from the aquatic Times Square. It was known as the Great Tight Way of the Seas. Bridges were thrown across from boat to boat, and one passed down a street which at night outdid Paris for light and gayety.

Little old Broadway in its palmiest days was never so completely and impenitently open. There were even booze automats.

Some of the boats I noticed had roof gardens. They were extended crows' nests and lookouts. Revolving and glaringly lighted at night, they turned to the laughing music of the beers.

When the constellations warmed up overhead the old summer gardens of blessed memory came back. They were situated on top of the cold-storage icebergs.

Waiters rushed around on skates over the glisten-. ing floors serving the 10 percent foamy while the band blared the latest song of the day, *The Bimini Navy Never Will Disarm*, written by the Sousa of the Seas.

In these summer gardens there were basket parties from Boston, New York, Philadelphia and Corona. The antique art of laughter had been revived. The only rule was that in family parties in the summer gardens no child under twelve was permitted to drink over six seidels of beer at a sitting.

Near the Times Square of Booze Venice a battleship had been cleared for action. On it had been built a replica, somewhat reduced, of the Knickerbocker Hotel with its cacophonic bar. The famous free lunch in the middle of the floor wagged its tongue in delight at Maxfield Parrish's *Old King Cole*, back on the wall to the delight of the Old Gang, who assembled there each evening at 6 o'clock and exchanged *vers libre* to the sosh-sosh of the gentle waves against the sides of the big boat.

Rathskellars had been dug out of the icebergs, where around the old pine tables could be sung the old ditties that used to be sung in the cellars of the Café Boulevard, down on Second Avenue.

The currency of Booze Venice was called Case Notes. They were notes issued on the old reserve stocks. The value of the notes rose and fell with the number of cases stowed in the bergs. Any one could have a note cancelled in bottles of Scotch or rye on call.

There was a law that the Great Brandy Berg should never fall below one hundred thousand quart bottles. This berg was the ultimate resource of this little nation. The currency chief of Booze Venice was known as the Secretary of the Cases.

A Board of Estimate and Apportionment, who sat (or stood or swayed) with the Secretary, was exactly what its name implied. They estimated the capacity, on the law of capacity and averages, of each permanent resident of the country (or city or continent, or whatever you'd choose to call it) and apportioned his drinks accordingly.

Booze Venice might float away, but it could not sink. The copper-riveted stomachs of its inhabitants insured the country against marine disaster. A water-logged boat was inconceivable.

Art and alcohol have always run tandem. It was a marriage made in leaven. Art had not gone blue-y in Booze Venice, as it had in the land where Comstocks never cease from troubling and the beery lie at rest.

I could see in the vistas of my vision of this only Armada in history that had ever been bottled up on the high seas statues erected on various boats to the famous Saints of Soak.

There, of course, was "Jack" Falstaff, with a foaming bumper in his hand, his great eyes sparkling like deep flagons.

There was Dick Swiveller, pickled in bronze, with his glass at his lips.

Omar Khayyam stood on the Grand Republic, jugged to the scuppers. He drank out of an Inverted Bowl.

Anacreon, covered with vine-leaves, seemed to be chanting one of his odes to grog.

And at the Battery of Booze Venice there was a giant group of three—Bacchus, Gambrinus and John Barleycorn—arm in arm, who chanted from music boxes placed in their giant throats "We care not who makes a nation's laws if we can drink its booze!"

My dream slowly faded into the light of common day as I heard dying away in the sea winds, "Water, water everywhere, and not a drop we'll drink!"

Lost Booze-Trails

WHILE prohibition lasts Bohemian New York has no tomorrow. All roads lead to yesterday.

Volstead killed the grape that laid the golden jag, and the mellow suns that shone in seidels have sunk to rest in a sea of soda slops.

Those magic barroom casements that glimmered on perilous corners on fairy trails are quite forlorn.

The Great Booze Trails of Manhattan have been almost obliterated. There are still relay stations for the Stanleys that know their darkest Gotham, but the caravans that sang and laughed and roistered as they made their way over the routes made sacred by Gambrinus and Bacchus have melted away like a tale that is told.

Drinking in New York was once an art. To-day it is only a delightful crime. Boozing was an art in those days—the Periclean and Augustan age of guzzle—that was practised by the chosen with a fervor and zeal that were religious.

Men moulded their daily thirst with the love and ardor of a Rodin moulding a Cupid and Psyche.

Bacchus was the tenth Muse—the only male (a deep-throated basso) in that heavenly choir. Gullets and palates and nerves were exquisite lyres that were kept in daily repair in order to evoke wonder jingles just as the sun went down or just as the sun sped west from Cognac, France, to the claret valleys of California.

The booze artists—creatures of infinite breath and fancy, joyful toilers whose laughter sounded like a symphony of joy at the Ginmillennium—have gone to join in the toxic air of the Soda Oblivion those devotees of the other arts that have died out of time and date and of which circumstance hath not left one wheeze behind.

The great lost booze artists had their independent guilds. There were the workers in rye metallic voices; masters of subtly equilibrated forms poised on glistening bar-rails; great brush workers who did marvelous Titian reds on the nostril; rare engravers of words long soaked in seidels of brandy; Maestros of suds who could conjure up smiles on the plastic flesh that made Da Vinci's *Mona Lisa* smile look like God-forsaken grief; chisellers in ale; artisans of grotesque absinthe gargoyles; Scotch realists and creme de menthe romantics; sinister etchers in mara schino; kings of the Burgundian dithyramb; Curacao impressionists; giant masters of *vers libre* cocktails; mint julep classicists; Tom and Jerry virtuosi; toddy imagists; wassail-bowl illuminators; punch-work stylists; stingo cubists; Bacardi Vulcans and solid woodcarvers in Bowery beer.

These great artists and their guilds have been blown to the four winds of Volstead, where they sit withering in eternal hope at the end of the rainbow —the symbolic rainbow!—for is not the rainbow a marvelous pousse café built by the celestial mixer of the elements?

They—like all of us—lie asleep in the dark ages awaiting the coming of a Lorenzo the Magnificent, who shall put a golden megaphone to his lips and announce the great Rum Renaissance. And the walls of Volstead shall fall down at its blasts and the rum fleet that launched a million bottles shall disappear like a whisky down the throat of a cop.

The old Alabaster Stomach Club that used to begin its daily sessions in "Jack's" at 3 A.M. lately foregathered in Aunt Tabitha's rum parlor on Forty-eighth Street for a talk on the Great Lost Booze Trails of Manhattan. The Alabaster Stomach Club was the holding company, so to speak, of the above named guilds.

Many of those who are now resting on their oars will recall our genial president, Bert Igoe, who introduced the only orchestra ever heard in "Jack's"—his own ukulele. Bert could twang music out of that instrument that would have brought envy to a lark on a souse. The cook kept it hidden from him in the fishbin; but one day "Jack," looking for a dozen cold eels for his breakfast, discovered it—but that's another story, as Tom Geraghty says.

Aunt Tabitha, having spread the cloth and served the éclairs and gin, the remnant of the old guard of the Alabaster Stomach Club—who never go dry and who never will resign—began reminiscing.

There were present, however, the Stanleys, the Livingstones, the Shackletons and the Kit Carsons of the old blazed trails. What tales these ancient mariners and Bronx booze pioneers had to tell of midnight suns, false dawns, pigmies that had fallen by the wayside, strange Tenth Avenue tribes and bleached bones!

The Grand Trunk Line, as Julius Fireman calls it, was of course up Broadway, starting from the Bat tery and ending at the point where it was necessary to take a sea-going hack.

Although the North and South Poles have been conquered and the Northwest Passage negotiated, there was one feat that defied all human endeavor—the Grand Trunk Line of Booze, stretching along Broadway from the Battery to Van Cortlandt Park, had never been conquered by a single pedestrian. Nor was it ever taxied or cabbed.

The farthest north ever reached was Times Square by an exploring party headed by myself and Carlo de Fornaro one summer afternoon in 1913.

We started at 11 o'clock in the morning—five of us—from the bar of the old hotel at South Ferry (the Tropic of Capricorn) equipped with a solid steak foundation.

Two of the party went into winter quarters at the Hoffman House (75 degrees north) after passing the equator (Fourteenth Street) successfully; another was rescued by a search party from the West Thirtieth Street police station at Thirty-fourth Street (85 degrees north).

Carlo and I alone reached the Arctic Circle (Times Square) at half-past four the following morning. We put into the Igloo de Jack, where it registered way below zero on Jim Moran's face when we showed up.

The shortest and most interesting of the old booze trails in the days that have gone up the spout was at Thirty-sixth Street and Sixth Avenue.

This corner was a trail in itself—a tiny miniature of the Lincoln Highway. Men have started from the Herald Building on the southwest corner at 4 P.M., crossed the street to Eisman's canteen, on the southeast corner, emerged heavily accoutred at 7 P.M., crossed the street to Tim Shine's pump room on the northeast corner, emerged at 1:30 the next morning and got back into the Herald Building with brains afire for work just as the second edition was going to press.

This trail was nicknamed Multum in Parvo.

There was the all-scenic booze trail which began under Maxwell Parrish's Old King Cole at the Knickerbocker bar. From there to the Waldorf roof (if it was summer) was a short hike. Here there were mint juleps and starlight, a Strauss waltz and a pousse café. Thence to the gargoyle room in the Hofbrau House, where one's gullet could swim in Culmbacher. Art, music, nature and booze—a lost trail whose disappearance makes me pessimistic as to the cultural future of my people.

Staten Island was in those days the great alkali desert. But there was a trail for hardy stomachs down along the waterfront starting from St. George. This hike could be done once only in every ten years if you desired to live and do your daily dozen.

There was a favorite night trail in the elder, olden days when newspaper life centered on Park Row. The explorers would meet at 2 A.M. in Andy Horn's inglenook and after laying in a store of red monkey glands would trek next door to Furthman's for a final internal hot towel. Then up through the Grand Canyon of Park Row and the Bowery to Pat Farley's dovecote at Bowery and Canal.

In Pat's one could find hardy travelers strewn around like emeralds in the path of Peggy Joyce. Here these hardy heralds of the dawn would lap up a small keg of beer and depart for Mike Lyons' snuggery de luxe at Bowery and Houston.

Mike Lyons!—the Delmonico of the Bowery, the Brillat-Savarin of the east side. There was no bar in Mike's. Many sat down; few arose. Mike's, like Bryan's mouth, was always open.

There is an old lost trail between the Academy of Music when the opera reigned there and Mike's. Every one went to Mike's after the curtain had fallen on Patti's last note. That was a trail before my time—but many living Manhattan graybeards have gone over it.

There are a thousand and one other trails which we go over again and again every night in Aunt Tabitha's sittingroom—but the trails themselves are obliterated.

On these great adventures we used to be led by John Barleycorn, Bacchus and Gambrinus. Now we are chaperoned over the soda water trails by Little Eva, Little Lord Fauntleroy and Pollyanna.

Quelle bull!

Gentlemanly Sleuths of Prohibition

IT will be remembered that when last Jan. 17 was due to blow in on Time's whirligig the Internal Revenue Department gave it out that we were to have a brand-new set of sleuths in New York to enforce the Ex-Vee-Triple-Eye Amendment to the Federal Constitution.

The impenitent, anarchistic, beer-loving millions of New York City were threatened with the bogie man from the mountains of Kentucky and Tennessee.

Look out! The Fearless Ferrets of the secret stills in Moonshine Land cannot be fooled, we were told. These men are trained to scent home brew as the needle of the compass was trained by Noah to point to the Pole. They are the Rough Necks of Law and Order, one official expounded to the city editor of *The Subway Sun*.

And the knees of the Angostura bitter-enders here in New York creaked and sagged and the pale 6 percent froth of fear came to the lips of Homo Malto as they remembered the newspaper reports from time to time of the mighty deeds of these enemies of Uncle Uric. For is It not known of all men from New Dorp to Getty Square how these men after 100 years of effort have put the mountain stills of the South completely out of business?

Goes without saying.

And it was no bluff. The amendment had not had on its working clothes for more than five days than a crowd of these sturdy gin-snoopers from the South descended on a bar-room in the West Thirties or Forties, drew their guns on an alleged bar-tender and all fired at once. Their shots got lodged in the legs of some pedestrians in the street while the alleged bartender cried, "If you gentlemen don't quit making a noise I'll not serve you."

Excuses were made from Washing-ton about the aimlessness of this gun play—unpreparedness, poor drilling, the absence of a Platts-burg for revenue officers, &c. They were called off and the 5,650,178 drunkards in New York resumed the even tenor of their transgressions.

Then there was an interregnum, a regular hiatus, for awhile, in which the trans-Appalachian molders of morals lay low. It was apparent that New York would not stand having scrambled gingeraleries and demi-tasseries rushed like a Common Kentucky mountain rat-gutterie.

The wrecking crew was switched to the background and a brand-new kind of rum-pointer was put out on the market.

He is the very opposite of the very first sample. He is clean in manner and of tongue. He is of slight build. His trousers are always creased. He has a smile that coos at you like friend Bryan or Hoover. He often wears a barbed-wire pompadour. There is no display of Memphis jewelry. He wears oxfords, eats peas with a fork and leaves a bit of his asparagus stalk on the plate.

He is the Beau Brummell of Hawkshaws. He gets $5 a day and expenses and a clean handkerchief every other day from his chief. He never makes an arrest—he takes people into custody. He never "pinches" a bartender or a cafe proprietor—he whispers aside to them that it is unfortunate, &c., but, my dear Sir—

This new detective in New York, whose duty it is to sleuth out the places where liquor is sold for other than sacramental, cooking or medicinal purposes, is part of the general' attempt of the law-defying and law-I enforcing classes to get away from the rough stuff.

Manners are softening, and thieves, murderers, counterfeiters, bond collectors, booze-mixers and detectives are softening with them. Handcuffs are only seen in the "movies" now. When one of us gets arrested he hires a touring car, says "After you" to the detective when he opens the door, and both roll to Headquarters discussing the box score over a perfecto.

I was invited recently by one of these new gentlemen detectives to spend the evening with him on a "clean up."

He is a friend of mine, a man who can tell a Rembrandt from a Rudy Dirks, an epicure who can tell the difference in a single whiff between H20 and C. y C. He is a graduate of a famous Sixth Avenue university. He has all the social accomplishments and owns a small music box. His prize possession is the first "Dardanella" record out of the factory. His reading is extensive—Homer, Fanny Hill and Louis Brandeis being his favorites.

He took me to his duplex apartment in Macdougal Street to put on his "disguise," as he called it. So he fixed himself up to look like a gentleman. He took a light walking stick out of the bathtub, presented to him by Frank O'Malley after the latter discovered that nothing could be broken over my friend's head.

Under his arm he put a volume of Ezra Pound's poetry.

"A book," said my friend, "renders you immune from all suspicion. You can pass for a boob anywhere with a book under your arm."

The expense account running freely that night, we hired a large touring car with compartments for "seized stuff."

The first place we stopped at was a dance hall in the Village. My friend laid his book of poems ostentatiously on the table, pushed up his horn-rimmed spectacles (plain bottle glass variety) and ordered two bottles of imported ginger ale, stressing the word "imported."

The bottles were placed before us, opened by the waiter and their contents poured into two large glasses filled with ice.

We drank. I recognized the "imported" flavor immediately. This ginger ale had just been imported out of bond. I domesticated another bottle immediately, while my friend arose and said to the proprietor, "May I have a word with you in the back?"

"But I have a wholesaler's license," replied the proprietor with a smile. He hadn't stirred an inch or batted a lash.

"But we are not buying by the wholesale, and I insist that you come with—"

"Your friend over there, I insist," broke in the proprietor, "is buying it and consuming It by the wholesale."

True enough. I was on my fifth bottle. It was part of my friend's expense account. I should chafe!

However, there was a conference in the back room, loud words and things were passed, and we left the place—just the two of us.

This was about what happened in five places in many parts of the town that night. My friend was never questioned. The routine was always the same. At 1 A.M. we sang our own version of "The Mikado" to a full house in a chop suey restaurant around Columbus Circle and were retired down the steps by the Oriental Flying Wedge.

The new prohibition sleuth, always now of this highbrow type, sometimes has a woman with him, sometimes several. No restaurateur will ever refuse to serve a gentleman with implicated ginger ale or even the straight frumenti when he has a lady with him. The proprietor is "pinched," and sometimes "stung," but the dance and the joy go on unconfined as before; there are smiles all around, and the price of something in the restaurant goes up a dime the next day.

Those who play must pay.

The late Mayor Gaynor was wise in his many ways. His theory was that nothing could be suppressed, but it was advisable to suppress the facts about their non-suppression.

The new prohibition sleuth is a gentleman. The Eighteenth Amendment has done one public service at least—it has raised the sartorial level of the federal "bulls."

Coney Island in the Desert

CONEY ISLAND is as dry as a prohibitionist lost in the Sahara Desert.

This is not a fact, but an emotion. The emotion is founded on the total depravity of the beer for sale there.

Even the water down there is dry and warm. The few cakes of ice that are exposed on the soft drink stands melt into tears under stress of internal combustion and memories.

A camel walking from Brighton Beach to Surf Avenue across the parched sands would find nothing but salt water to load up on.

The bartenders still make their thirty-second degree passes over tumblers of suds, but there is a decayed smile on their faces.

Even the famous Coney Island bar-flies have departed for Havana. They waited around in great clusters near the Steeplechase Pier until the Supreme Court put Hope Deferred on the Kill galley.

"Well, that's the limit!" exclaimed the main mahogany 4 percent lush from Stanch's.

"Well, the limit's only three miles. And beyond the Lightship lies Havana. Pick up your wings and fly with me!" shouted the leader of the pine-board sappers, Diptera Dypso, the leader of the gang.

They flew:

And for that reason any Coney Islander will tell you that there are fewer flies in Coney Island this Summer than at any time in the history of the resort.

It took several vast fortunes to clean out the mosquito along New York City's coastline, but a simple "Be it enacted" in the mouth of Mr.

Volstead drove the flies thither.

"When the flies come back again" has taken the place of "When the swallows nest again" in the ironical vernacular of Coney Island.

For this is really Coney Island's first dry Summer. Last Summer the five million or more persons that visited that most curious of islands were pitching and tossing on the crest of 2.75 beer, which, if not quite intoxicating in the sense that a bottle of sparkling Burgundy or an absinthe frappé is, was nevertheless sufficient in exhilarating power to make one feel that because Frozen Face, Ariz., had voted for Virtue it did not follow that cakes and ale should no longer season the pagan gullets of New Yorkers.

If one freuded out for any length of time any of the 2.75 that swam around the tables in the beer gardens off Surf Avenue last Summer, one was sure to come up against the alcoholic complex in the saffron solution topped with a wilted soft collar. And there was famous "Marble Alike," the white wings behind the long oak of one of the big hotels at the end of Ocean Parkway, who always had a "dash of something" to go into the glass that made a gentleman feel at home with himself. "Marble Mike" no more this Summer. He is running a bath-house at Rockaway. When he gets enough of the coin, he says, bell be off for Havana, for, says Mike, "What's the difference where yer born as long as you can die in Havana?"

Trolling along with our Freudian nomenclature, we assert that Coney Island has always been, until this Summer, the suppressed desires of Father Knickerbocker and Grandma Brooklyn on parade. The invader always left his spiritual janitor at home. The journey represented dash into freedom. It was an adventure in noise, humbug and booze. When the boat or train landed at the Island one got into his psychic pajamas, and his instincts ran around barefoot like the late Huckleberry Finn.

Coney Island was the "Kur" of the greater city. We went there in the old days to "take the waters"—as a "chaser." To be foolish in Coney Island was as necessary as being a wise man in Athens. We went there to give the low-brow in us an airing.

Beer ran like a Niagara, and we all went over in barrels, and floundered out of the rapids Monday morning. The roller coasters were greased by the great god Gambrinus. "Hot dogs" were dipped in seidels. Grave professors fresh from the deciphering of Babylonian bricks were seen to poise steins on their left ears after 9 A.M. Good Taste abandoned all hope at the entrance to the Bowery. To swallow sea water while in bathing was lèse Barleycorn. Every band played *There'll Be a Hot Time in the Isle Tonight!* One went down there Saturday night as thin as a "movie" plot and re-turned Sunday night with a corporation whose overhead charges were only a headache—only that and nothing more.

Happy vulgarians (which most of us are at bottom)! Wise swamis of the Golden Grail! Pitted yogis of the unswabbed table! Where be your quips and quirks and katzen-jammer now? Quite crestfallen, you take your bath and make a quick dive foie the trolley to find excitement in Joe Conrad's latest sea tale ensconced beside your pitcher of lemonade.

One feels the new atmosphere of Coney Island begin to impregnate the nervous fluid when one boards the boat—those Coney Island boats that no ocean has the heart to sink and that no fog has the power to hide! Once on board, down the old parched gangplank, one spies to the left the "bar"—empty of customers.

Sleeping on a soap box behind the settling bar board is a figure that once was a bartender. Over his head tower, in memoriam, shelves loaded down with bottles of "sass," ginger ale and Bryan beer. A seagull whirls in at the window, peeps around and beats it out to the three-mile limit, where he can hear that glad old-time yowl, "Bar's op-n, genmen!" Let the gum-and-suds Ganymede sleep. He sleeps the sleep of Budweiser. *Pax vobeerum!*

On deck, where we used to sit on campstools, with our bottles on the floor, all is quiescent. The three fiddlers from Mulberry Street are playing *Jerusalem*. We look at Mme. Liberty with lack-lustre eye. A big boat is going out to sea. Beyond the Hook lies—ah, but what's the use?

We used to bump into Coney Island. Now we just warp in in a weary manner. The crowd lands and makes its way Nedickward. The old Mint Julep Squad are wearily taking high dives into a kickless swimming pool. The faraway din of the barkers cm Surf Avenue as-sidle your ears—*din lento*.

Surf Avenue, as usual, is lined with candidates making front-porch campaigns for the dime or quarter that goes without saying. But the "pep" has gone out of their speeches. The beady eye and the well-oiled tongue are not in evidence when one listens to these barkers this Summer. Careful psychologists of the Island would report "decreased vitality of the larynx." There is no coal in the ovens of their erstwhile o'erheated imaginations. They invite and invite, and few enter in. Sobriety has put an enem to their pockets in their mouths.

And the crowds are not so easily lured this year without a beer or two to salt their curiosity. Still, the Bradstreet's of Coney Island has not reported any failures up to date. But if you have a freak or two to exhibit that is anywhere higher in the social rank than the usual skeleton in the closet, .you will find the housing facilities excellent.

This is caused by the number of cafés, restaurants and beer gardens that have passed into the grandeur that was rum and the glory that was rickey. A Hole in the Wall or an Ableptic Pig may still be seen right off the main thoroughfare if you have the trained Philadelphia Sunday eye for such things and the delicately nuanced olfactory centres that are indigenous to a long residence in the swinging door district of the Roaring Forties—whose roar has now become a Nedick Lisp. But these subcutaneous Island facts are only for the candy cognoscenti. The pullulating public are disbarred.

The crowds in the big amusement parks, except on Saturdays and holidays, are not as large as in former wet years. Many thousands in the Empire City, whose capital is now Lincoln, Neb., prefer to stay at home and test the fireside brew from hour to hour while the latest musical bull-bull chants from its tired throat shut up in the corner music box, and the children reverse the table for the big afternoon and evening poker game.

Prohibition has brought the bar parlor and the gambling mania right into the home. In time it will reach the little Red Schoolhouse on the Hill. Charity, which used to begin at home, has abdicated in favor of the Kitty and the Keg. Sweet are the uses of the Volstead adversity! In America nowadays, if you want to go to the devil, stay at home. Bad runt, bad music and poker riots! We are bringing up our children on the American Plan with a vengeance!

Tacking to leeward on this superfluous sociological observation, let us return to the amusement parks and such at Coney. The crowds still go through a dirty Venice, roll down a pasteboard Alps, watch the yogi from Brownsville hypnotize the slim Princess from Eighth Avenue, and take their trips to the paper moon; but the gayer laughter is gone, and the rollicking feeling that Eva Tanguay invented in her celebrated epic entitled *I Don't Dare!* is gone.

Maybe it was the war, maybe it is taxes, maybe it is the dispossess in the pocket, maybe it is the Memphis crime wave that has come to New York that is doing it. But a wise observer will say it is the absence of beer and wine. An immoral theory that—but human nature at Coney Island always was immoral and orderly. Now it is strictly moral and psychically quasi-Red.

Stand outside of a tintype factory and watch the people having their pictures taken on submarines, flying machines and the observation platforms of Pullmans diving into calico Grand Canyons. I couldn't see a smile on Their faces in spite of the wild orders of the bulb squeezer.

There was one man, however, sitting in a chair in a photograph gallery at the bottom (or top) of Surf Avenue who was smiling uproariously while the camera clicked.

I peeped in to get a line on the unusual phenomenon. Wise little Daguerro who was running that face factory! The walls of the booth were papered with Old Crow labels.

The rifle galleries, however, are packed. I soon discovered the reason. Every shot is aimed at an imaginative "dry" Congressman. Just a little way we Americans have of taking it out innocently on some one who boobs us along!

As I turned into the old Bowery a familiar face greeted me. The said f. f. grinned at me from behind the board of a bazaar.

In was Fritzschentzen von MacRyan, ex-head bartender of one of the oldest beer gardens in the Island. A man who had served humanity well in the days that are whilom.

He was selling rag dolls and teething rings!

I took the last boat back to the Battery. The old-time sparkers sat decently apart, some discussing the Einstein theory; others deep in the question as to why the silk industry in Brabant disappeared during the Middle Ages.

"Wet" Parade Mottoes

Other High Eights in Prose Song of an
Anti-Prohibition Marcher

NAPOLEON said an army walked on its stomach. The Anti-Prohibition Parade of July 4 will march on an arid gullet.

The parade may be the thing wherein we'll catch the consciences of our Kings!

On that first 4th of July which the calendar sat up and took notice of we Easterners (mark that! we Easterners) blew a fare-ye-well to England because we were taxed without representation. Well, just 145 years afterward we Thirteen Staters have got the taxes still with us, lack of representation has given place to super-representation from the South and West our cries for home rule and personal liberty are black-balled as old American superstitions by the Congressional Country Club—and we Declaration of Independencers (as overwhelmingly wet on a show-down as the signers of the document in Philadelphia) have got to get out on Fifth Avenue and demonstrate our inalienable right to life, liberty and the pursuit of wine and beer by a thirst that will be heard around the world! (Yes, our thirst can be heard!)

I think that the great Anti-Prohibition Parade will mean more ultimately than merely appears on the surface. It doesn't mean that we all want to drink, but it means that we do not want to be told we shall not drink if we want to. It is also a protest against certain lobbyists, sectarians, paid moralists, bootleggers, uniformed housebreakers, stool-pigeons and cold-water Nancies with seraphic mugs.

The Anti-Prohibition Parade will be Unique in the history of parades in New York City—city of great and historic parades of the past, and the prohibi tionists are organizing one of their own for the Saturday following. Someone has referred to these two parades as the Antis versus the Aunties.

It will be straightout Americanism versus Bolshevism. (In Russia to-day drinking is a capital offense.)

Under which banner—Pickwick or Squeers?—Mark Twain or William Jennings Bryan—Abe Lincoln or T. S. Arthur?

I am told by the Director General of the Anti-Prohibition Parade that thou sands of men and Women will march Who have assured him that They have never taken a drink of intoxicating liquors—not even beer. The most bitter opponent of the Eighteenth Amendment and the Volstead-Mullen-Gage trailers is a man of my acquaintance who has never taken a drink.

"I sum up," he says, "the prohibition question by quoting Judge Cullen's smashing bit: '"A doesn't think that B can handle his drink; therefore A decrees that C, D and E shall not have it.'"

This would be a good banner to hoist at the head of the Division of Inexorable Logicians of the parade as illustrating the muddled reasoning of the Neros of Righteousness and the Tiberiuses of Reform.

If Puck should become ruler of the world for a month and in his infinite Wisdom should cause all the drinking water on the planet to ferment, the rulers of the Invisible Empire of Prohibition would decree the drinking of sea water, although it would kill us all. This kind of people may -die, but they never resign.

A banner I should suggest would be:

> A drunkard is a person afraid to take his last drink—
> A prohibitionist is a person afraid to take his first one.

These two undesirable citizens are parallel lines that meet at the point of moral cowardice.

Another banner might run to this effect:

> Wine is a sacred symbol in every language—
> Water the most commonplace.

Another, that will appeal to those who are most concerned:

> I care not who makes a nation dry—
> If I can forge the booze permits.

This may be considered lightly anarchistic by those who care not who make a country's Constitution if they can gumshoe through the amendments.

There should be a float in the parade showing a tableau of the National Association of Revenooers in session in Independence Hall at work on a sliding scale.

And why not the Statue of Liberty in 1923—become a bootleggers' nest?

Heading the Satiric Division there might be a float representing Little Eva and Little Rollo ducking Sir John Falstaff and Dick Swiveller under the town pump of Fresh Water, Kansas.

Or, Columbus sighting Dry Land—and turning back.

Or, Washington at Valley Forge pass ing around a flask of Delaware River aqua to his cold-bitten men.

Or, Daniel Webster and Henry Clay arm in arm at an orange juice booth.

Or, Benjamin Franklin drinking the health of France to the tinkle of the mineral water flagons.

Or, Abraham Lincoln uttering a decree, "If Grant drinks, I'll fire him and dig up a prohibitionist Commander-in-Chief!"

Turning away from cheap satire and getting down to bona fide facts, I suggest banners inscribed with some of the thoughts of great men on the question of drinking. For instance:

CONFUCIUS—We tried prohibition in China, and a man invented opium to counteract its effects.

TENNYSON—Water is the death of poetry; but that's probably why it is so popular in America.

THOMAS JEFFERSON—*Lèse Liberté.*

NAPOLEON—Prohibition is all right for the dead; but I got away with Austerlitz on brandy.

RABELAIS—Abandon hope, all ye who enter the grapejuicery.

BYRON—I wrote *Don Juan* on a hundred bottles of Burgundy. The water drinkers tried to answer it—but who were they, anyway?

DANIEL WEBSTER—Prohibition is a sign of national decadence. A country that is too cowardly to drink is on the tobog.

"BOBBY" BURNS—I should prohibit the use of alcohol in the arts and sciences, but not otherwise.

MARK TWAIN—I would have lived to be 140 if I had only substituted wine for work.

First and foremost, of course, in the Big Parade should be a giant image of Pegasus, the mount of all the poets of the ages. As Peg thundered on the air in his flight toward the Empyrean his hoofs shot forth hippocrene, a hooch 200 proof, which made of that immortal horse-bird the great hooflegger. Bacchus and Gambrinus should hold his bridle on either side: Squat on his back I should suggest either Shakespeare or Rabelais—prophets of "Live and Let Live!"

Following there should be, in costume, on foot, that illustrious and immortal line of poets and vagabonds from Anac reon to Edgar Allan Poe, with the Allellujah chorus from Jack's Blue Room (nights of sacred memory!).

What a crush of those who loved the Grail and Cheers!—Tom Shadwell, Ben Jonson, Johnny Oldham, Tom Ravenscroft, Bill Congreve, Dick Sheridan, Tommy Peacock, Torn' Dekker, Sir Jack Suckling, Oliver Goldsmith, Lord Byron, Percy Shelley, John Keats, Ben Cellini, Frank Villon, Walter Scott, Bob Herrick, Johnny Gay, Gil Chesterton, Bill Maginn, John Masefield, Bill Thackeray, Charles Dickens, Vic Hugo, Dick Wagner, Chris North, Omar Khayyam, Mark Twain, Steve Crane, Nat Hawthorne, Old Walt, Jim Riley. Gene Field, Syd Porter—but it would be a planet directory of immortals to go on.

The Mouquin Light Wine Division should be headed by Happy Harry Lea, the Haroun Al Raschid of a million and one nights, now safe housed in the inns of Provence. Pity he's not with us!

The Brevoort-Lafayette Division of Bubbling Burgundian will be marshaled by Carlo de Fornaro.

The Ancient and Honorable Artillery of Scotch Dissenters will be lined up by Don Marquis, in whose brain was first of all conceived the idea of this parade.

The ladies will be there in their own division under the banners, "I Never Raised My Boy to Be a Booby," "Keep the Home Brew Churning," and " Take the Grouch Off Papa's Mug."

Mr. Drake will not forget the bartenders, in their immaculate white aprons, their cheery word and human touch. This much-maligned guild will sing its swan song up Fifth Avenue, but they will not sing it to the swirl and purl of H20.

The saloon will go, but the Raines law sandwich will return.

Who will characterize Falstaff and Rip Van Winkle? It is whispered that Phil Goodman and H. L. Mencken will handle these two delightful bon vivants.

As 500,000 persons from all points in Original America have asked to march on the Fourth, it may be necessary to clear Fifth Avenue for a week.

At one end of the route is the Washington Arch and at the other General Sherman. Neither Washington nor Sherman ever wrote odes to water. In fact, the first never stopped anywhere else except at an inn. And didn't the latter say "Thirst is hell"?

The Anti-Prohibition Parade should be remembered as the second Boston Tea Party—and you know what that crowd did to tea.

Hopes Of The "Wets"

Forecast of an Anti-Prohibitionist Who
Counts on Nation-wide Reaction

THE "wet" tide is steadily rising.

Movement is not receding. There is no doubt of the anti-prohibition crusaders' activity. Whether their campaign will break in bubbles and one-half of one percent suds and disperse itself in hot air or crash with a regular Jack Dempsey wallop against the solid mahogany bulkheads that protect the Volstead law remains to be seen.

Even the "drys," many of them, concede that prohibition, like immortality, the discovery of the North Pole and the sanity of Hamlet, is still very much of an open question. The "wets," the personal libertarians, the Seventeen-Seventy-Sixers and a few old fogy individualists say the question of getting what the guild wants when it wants it is so open that they propose to consolidate all the scattered anti-dry and anti-blue law organizations in the country into one militant organization for the purpose of repealing the Volstead law and putting the Eighteenth Amendment on a local option basis.

These "wet" propagandists declare the day for sentiment and mere talk is over. They propose a national political movement with a showdown in every Congressional district in the country. They say they will fight lobby with lobby. Business methods, they say, put the amendment and the Volstead-Mullin-Gage laws through. Only business methods can destroy them.

"Dollar for dollar" they announce as their slogan—and organizations and mass meetings in every city and town in the country, directed by a national Congressional committee and district Assembly committees.

The "drys" will fight, it is conceded, to the last ditch of poisoned whisky. The "wets" do not prophesy they will achieve a 100 percent victory, but they assert that they will achieve a wine and beer compromise. They say it was not the wet parade on the Fourth of July up Fifth Avenue—a broiling day that sent every human being out of town who could possibly get away—that was so impressive, but they insist that the spirit of the men who toiled for weeks to organize it indicates the strength of their movement. One had but to be associated, as I was, with Frank Drake, the originator and director general of the demonstration, and his committee to feel that same fanatical spirit restoring personal liberty that actuates those who have been undermining it. These men, like the men who organized the Association Against the Prohibition Amendment and the 1776 Society, are not poets, sentimentalists or political and economic theorists, but business men, men of the world, men with practical brains, with a punch all over them, physically and psychically.

When Mr. Drake first called for a meeting at the Hotel Astor two months ago he did not know a single man present. They did not know one another. They came with their sleeves rolled up for work. Their testimonials, if they had produced any, would have been American through and through. Colonel Warren Shaw Fisher, President of the United War Veterans, of Revolutionary stock, was there. And—But there's no need of a list.

The anti-prohibition parade is now a matter of history, or rather of the "movies," for there were at least ten different "movie" cameras turned on us as we went up the avenue. And this last fact constitutes the influence of the parade. It will be shown in moving-picture houses throughout the country. The "wets" are sure it will reflect the spirit of the East on constitutional prohibition. (Be it said here and now that the right to local option has never been attacked by the "wets.")

The parade in itself may have been nothing. But that there was such a parade in this country aimed as a pro test at part of the Constitution of the country and reviewed by the Mayor of the largest city in the world is a fact of significance. If the parade had only contained five hundred men it would have been unique in America, where we swallow what the lawmakers give us without holding our breath—so easy going are we Americans.

Having shown that the spirit of public protest against prohibition laws as they stand is alive in the East, Mr. Drake and Colonel Fisher say that steps will be taken at once by the Personal Liberties League, Inc., of New York to get in touch with the Association. Against the Prohibition Amendment, whose permanent headquarters are in Washington. This latter association, they say, will be the nucleus of the national political personal liberty party.

The National Association against the Prohibition Amendment is a business organization, and it has been fighting the Anti-Saloon League crowd at the national capital. Among those on its rolls are R. L. Agassiz, General Felix Agnus, Willard Parker Butler, Brig. Gen. Charles T. Cresswell, J. Clarence Davies, Warren Delano, Edward Everett, Stuyvesant Fish, Dr. Austin Flint, William Barton French, Robert A. Grannie and John A. Roebling. The men and women who belong to the organization, but who for one reason or another do not care to have their names made public, would make a tremendous list.

"I believe," said Mr. Drake to me the other day, "that there are enough voters in this country opposed to constitutional prohibition and the Volstead law to swing a wet Congress if all the various scattered energies in this country can be welded into one single concrete national organization along political lines. Make no mistake about what we have to do. We have got to swing a political club in the hands of hard-boiled master politicians. There is no other way. Essays and poems will not do. We are fighting an enemy that gives no quarter and that does not fight in the open."

With the fight under way, it does not take half a prophet to see that the next Congressional election in many districts will be fought on "wet or dry" lines.

New York's Day of Dupes (A Memory)

JANUARY 17, 1920! And thereby hangs a strange tale that New York will tell till the last swan sits on the ruins of the Casino in Central Park and squawks its last squawk at the tottering towers of lir ol' Manhattan-by-the-Battery.

The purely psychological panic that preceded the Great Edict culminated in one of the most amazing, paradoxical and puzzling nights that had ever been seen in New York. Nothing happened, yet most tremendous things were taking place.

New York simply refused to take prohibition seriously. When was there ever such a crazy-patch of humor, pathos, thanksgiving, cursing, threats, expectation, denunciation, singing, sneering, put on exhibition before?

The brandied hiccough met the Hooligan howl of the highball. The cork that has popped since the birth of the Adam of Omar Khayyams sounded to some like a far-off call to arms of all the Red Ink Guards of revolt.

Everybody looked during the afternoon of the 17th as if he stood at some new kind of Armageddon. It was the boozers' Marne without a Joffre in sight. It was the Ginmillennium.

People went about their business maunderingly sober. Expectation, rumor, innuendo were as rife as maggots in a trench. Little old New York, that had never taken water literally, figuratively or constitutionally, felt the katzenjammer of fear and disillusion invade its soul.

The old town had got over many "a morning after"; but here was for many mentally a "morning after" before the shades of night had begun to sop up the daylight. The Peace Treaty, the League of Nations were matters of no earthly consequence. What would it profit a man to gain the knowledge of the day's "extras" if he lost his suitcase of joy-water?

All roads led to the booze store. In spite of the fact that hundreds of saloons had handed it out straight that they would not be "canned," the lines of pilgrims en auto, afoot, in ancient seagoing rigs, and even pushing wheelbarrows and go-carts improvised New York into a home-made Mecca. If all the bottles of whisky, wine, and beer that were pur chased in the twelve hours preceding midnight of the 17th could have been piled on top of one another in City Hall Park they would have made the Woolworth Tower look like a coalbin in the house of an ant.

The strangest of all phenomena of this strangest of all days in the city's history was the way thousands clamored down off the water wagon and thousands who had been in every condition of inebriety from the merely "lit up" stage to the daily "I won't go home until morning" condition began far back in the past to clean up, taper off, wash out and take all the other measures to clamber on top of the orange cart.

Old rounders and young rounders who had disappeared for months and years from the hotel bars, the late restaurants, the jazz houses and the common garden variety of ginmill crawled out of their somnolent respectability and made their way back to the scenes of their ancient chinfests, and went to it with a grim determination to have "one last good one" before the whistle blew. At the corner of the Rue de Booze and the Great Wine Way, which the initiate will recognize as Forty-second Street and Broadway, the writer counted seven men of his acquaintance who had come forth on this Last Day to materialize their vision of that "fine old souse that's coming to me yet" that every ex-tank carries pocketed deep down in the cells of his brain. Never had any prodigal son such greeting as those who returned to the fold. They seemed like heralds of the immortality of John Barleycorn & Co.

It was, per contra, the vision of pink elephants, green nannygoats and the flying snakes of the Apocalyptic dry dawn that drove others to sobriety. These latter exhibited their "will power" in public like a Houdini doing the handcuff trick on the street corner or a Sandow, growing decrepit, who could still lift a barroom on his shoulder with a smile. They had beat the time clock to it. They not only helped put up the shutters on the Palace of Revels run by Bacchus, Barleycorn, Lim., but they actually got down and began to clean up the "mess of their lives," as one of these perverse citizens put it as he dropped an eighth-of-an-inch quinine shell into his system to jazz along the depression into a smile.

But as the shades of night began falling fairly fast along about 8 o'clock Dry-Face waned and Rye-Face waxed. The "uxtries" on the street flouting the staccato type that wine and beer were to be allowed to hold carnival on the coffin of old J. B. and Five Stars were like a sudden message from Mars, and the newsboys were, literally, Mercuries bearing tidings from the gods—from at least two of them anyhow, Bacchus and Gambrinus.

But nothing can hold back a New York crowd that has made up its mind long beforehand to celebrate something or other. The great Booze Cantata was on in earnest and all the cops' horses and all the cops' men couldn't put curfew together again. Double-deck dinners were eaten early, for on this solid foundation of food there was to be erected an abiding pousse café of wine, beer, brandy, whiskey and gin that would reach to the eyes and keep the brain swimming till Nox bowed them in sleep.

Some laid a firm foundation of porterhouse for the fuming chimney of drink; others laid foundations of lobster and chicken and spaghetti; others tessellated their interior groundwork with the plain and simple bean and carpeted it with veal and corned-beef hash. A few ate not at all, declaring food was *persona non grata* in such a court.

Between 11 and 12 the well-known alcohol igloos from Forty-second to Fifty-ninth Street were lined ten deep. It was the final bargain sale. Outside street vendors sold a march called "The Death of Personal Liberty." Nobody believed it.

The lobster palaces and the dance halls made a big noise, but over many of the parties there was the air of reminiscence—of the days when every night was New Year's Eve, when whiskey was taken as a chaser, when no one went home until Pete Dailey had officially announced at the old Metro-pole that "Broadway was closed for the night," which meant the milkman was getting sunburned outside.

After 12 o'clock the diners and drinkers abandoned wine and beer, and until 1 A.M. drank whiskey and brandy where they were to be had and grinned at one another like boys who had stolen apples.

At "Jack's," where the highball had been king for thirty years, Old John Barleycorn died a slow, agonizing death, and his final rattle was not heard until a wee sma' hour. In the Room of a Thousand and One Jags the Old Gang held forth against the wrath to come behind great trenches of Scotch and rye purchased before that fatal hour when J. B. emerged from the death house and tottered to the chair. Papa John Dunston sat calmly in the corner talking to Grandpère "Jim" Wakely about Cycles of Virtue and Spasms of Humility. Rising at 1 A.M., he sang, as has been his custom for many years, "McCarthy's Daughter," ordered the curtains drawn, and pronounced with dignity a benediction and valedictory on the late J. B. The Old Gang then formed in line and sang "For He's a Jolly Good Fellow," but whether *he* was Sir John Dunston or ex-Mogul John Barleycorn has not been learned even unto this day.

Down in Greenwich Village, where the poetic proletariat wages war with the bourgeois landlords, nothing of interest happened. Nothing can disturb your true Olympian. They who dwell in the Eternal wot not of current events. January 17-18 awoke only a languid interest in the nut-cellar of the Brevoort and the Turkish corners of Polly's. The denizens of the former and the inmates of the latter rooms rattled on as usual on their favorite airy-fairy themes.

It was at Mouquin's, at Twenty-eighth Street and Sixth Avenue, famous rendezvous of artists and painters, that the strangest of sights was to be seen on this strangest of strange nights. The café was deserted at midnight, probably because John Barleycorn had meant nothing at this place. Deserted by all but one customer, a famous sketch artist, who stood upon a table making furious speeches in French and Pennsylvania Dutch on the iniquities of prohibition, while his friends stood outside peering through the glass at him. The waiters were all asleep.

In was early on the morning of January 18. The dawn was coming up a fiery John Barleycorn red in the northeast. A well-known ten-twenty-thirty actor was leaning against a "wet paint" sign at Seventh Avenue and Forty-third Street. His straw hat was rimless, his eyes were glazed.

"T' day's glo'us day," he muttered. "Sits January Eighteens—r'turn of the penny postcard—d'partur' f whiskee. S' law of comp'nsation!"

And out of the Dreadful Night of the 17th of January, 1920, was born New York's Day of Dupes!

Spring Festival
—Model 1924

IN the days before the black Puritan locusts descended on New York and when drinking was an incident to eating, dinner parties at home were as decorous and respectable as the faces of the Smith brothers.

The evening passed with a little music, a few highballs and the passing of the chocolate caramels.

Now a dinner party is the greatest indoor sport in America. What used to be a feast of reason and a flow of soul is now a feast of unreason and a flow of bowl.

The mental compass of the diners points sousesouse-east.

And after dinner the billiard room remains dark, the jazz records are put on the phonograph and one is caught in a cyclone of Scotch. Tune in and catch the alcoholic waves.

The rooms become madhouses. There is instead of "talk," a bacchanalian revel where we all become nymphs, satyrs, fauns and dancing dervishes.

The kitchen is gutted for Scotch. The drinking tables look like Saturday night shambles in a Philadelphia speak-easy.

Dignity crawls on the floor at midnight and howls like a hyena. There is communism in drinking glasses. Somebody drops a bit of ice down your wife's neck.

Hidden complexes uncoil themselves from their vasty depths. The cop comes in off his beat and loads the six barrels of his shooter with gin.

It is a dinner party in which no one remembers the dinner. It is an evening in which no one remembers the evening.

And now it is the blessed springtime—and the indoor revels are at their height.

The gin buds are opening. The pinch bottles are blooming in Bimini. Shy labels come out of their hiding places in Rum Row. The Scotch sward is a-greening.

The song of the little yellow Bacardi is in the air. The juniper sings its synthetic lay by the side of the glycerine brook.

That which has been bottled up all winter bursts its corks and o'erflows the genial gullet. The vales of Canada waft their malty essences to our nostrils. Gentle showers of home brew rinse the mind.

All things are being born again—and behold!—the rye that was not yesterday is born unto us to-day, a green little thing nursed by the tender care of the good fairy Bootleg.

I had attended a half dozen of the newer dinner parties since the sun staggered over the line on Mardi 21 and given a few myself.

All of them, without exception, were half-nude studies in ultimate democracy.

If the saloon doesn't come back soon, "Home, Sweet Home" will become as extinct as brains in the skull of a Congressman.

A home is now a series of rooms surrounding a bottle closet. A dinner party is the shortest route between two given jags.

In ancient Greece and Rome spring used to be the great unveiling. In these spring Volstead dinner parties I have noted a recurrence of the ancient fashion. It is mostly psychological, of course, whereas the ancient myth was interpreted literally.

The talk is as loose as it used to be at "Jack's." Beneath the tuxedo there beats many a barroom soul.

Don't judge a man these days by his white shirtfront. It may conceal a booze thief.

The poet blows in. He is known for his metaphysical free-verse rhymes. I had always pictured him as dignified, hard-boiled, with a professional air.

Or maybe he would have tolstois hanging from his face, wield a heavy oaken stick and announce his views in a deep "Let there be light!" voice.

Nothing of the kind. He blossomed in at this particular dinner party with a bound, threw his hat and coat over the bed and his round, cherubic face opened with "Fix me up two right away, will you, old man?"

Before midnight the free-verse metaphysician had his coat off and he was doing a flip-flop backward the length of the floor in order to prove to H. L. Mencken that arteriosclerosis had not yet set in.

His conversation ran exclusively on the seven ways of testing bootleg gin.

All dinner parties, now that the dawn has resumed its yearly habit of breaking away from the night at an early hour, last till breakfast. This is a master stroke of efficiency in sleep-saving.

Some hardened diners-out during the current Volstead Reformation never appear for dinner in evening dress because they go straight from their host's to the office the next morning. Night navigation is dangerous these days when the seas are running high; and taxis are not always to be had.

The new Volstead apartment is under way by up-to-date builders. The walls are seven feet thick. Booze safes are being built into walls with combination locks.

Stationary dining tables with steel legs built into the floors and compressed air tubes that shoot bottles to immovable or collapsible guests in all the rooms are being considered.

I have noted also that food is rapidly disappearing from the tables of these dinner parties. After the soup nothing more is known.

Rare cases of consciousness may demand a sandwich at midnight.

Throw your chicken legs into the court. Wings may be deposited behind the couch.

On the night of June 24, 1916, at 11:30, I slept in my steak at "Jack's."

I was precursor. I had imagination. I was the father of our great indoor sport.

Genius never knows what tremendous things it is doing. Coming events had cast their Benjamins before.

Now steak-sleepers at supper parties are quite common.

Carlo de Fornaro, the charlotte russe yogi, grand inquisitor of the Brahmanic yawp, says that in the springtime a yogi's fancy lightly turns to thoughts of blood-cleansers.

Carlo attends every dinner and supper party given within a twenty-five mile radius of City Hall. He lives exclusively on charlotte russes and Pluto water in the springtime. He is the only diner-out who preserves his hidden complexes intact.

"The saloon must go!" was the slogan of the prohibitionists.

I can quite conceive that their next slogan will be "The dinner party at home must go!"

It is undermining the health of moving picture executives and city editors.

It is ruining the efficiency of free-lance writers and book reviewers.

It is destroying the confidence of the steady drinker in the value of food.

If the Uplift wants something to work on let it take a shy at the dinner parties.

We all need lifting up after midnight during the term of these Spring festivals.

The Coming Great Booze War

IF the final decision of the courts upholds the ruling of Attorney General Daugherty that all foreign ships entering American ports must come in loaded to the waterline only, will not another War Cloud loom on the horizon?

This War Cloud will be filled with something besides water. Political meteorologists say it will be a bootleg cloud, preceded by a fine Scotch mist, The five stars of Hennessy will be fighting in their courses on the side of the Wets. The Drys claim that the stars (as Billy Blake predicted) will throw down their spears and water heaven and earth with their non-alcoholic tears—if they are beaten.

A war over the question of prohibition would be a unique war on a planet already gutted, drenched and gashed by wars on every conceivable subject. It would be such a novelty in wars that it would cause the first dry smile on the face of Bacchus and amaze Mars— who is always shopping in the department stores of human motives for old reasons for new wars and new reasons for old wars.

The human race 'since that little affair between Cain and Abel over whose lamb stew was most fragrant has found many reasons for intra-racial throat-slitting and land-swiping.

The countries that spoil the landscapes of earth and the trillions of human beings whose presence has interfered with the progress of plant and animal life have exterminated one another heretofore for good. sound business reasons.

All wars up to date have been ethical. Their bases have been rooted In the profoundest of all instincts—property rights. The wars for human liberty themselves are based on Property rights. Even the wars between kings and robber barons were fought for material reasons—hence ethical reasons.

Swag, Loot and Land—the bloody competition for these has created civilizations.

Among these conflicts the Great Booze War will be unique. It opens a new vista of blood-letting on purely idealistic—almost spiritual—grounds. Only the American people—the most fertile in inventive genius—could have conceived of it. A great world war over a sense as metaphysical as taste, over an organ as delicate as the gullet, over a substance as evanescent as champagne and as transparent as whisky—does not this stir the souls of our SheHeys, Chopins and Blakes?

The country that gave the world the steamboat, the telephone, the telegraph, the electric light and the magical cocktail now comes to the very apotheosis of its inventive genius in proposing a war to make the world safe for H2O. We only need the word from the purple heights of the highest courts and every Anti-Saloon Leaguer will be at his post behind his mouth hurling American anti-booze conscripts on the vineyards of France and the ale-vats of England.

And in that conscription there will be no slackers!

"On to Munich!" "On to Pilsen!" "On to Champagne!" "On to Burgundy!" are slogans that will send a million to Europe, where "On to Berlin!" got a thousand.

In that war to dry up Europe, who will bother about uniforms? Who will care about gas masks and trench knives? We will go panoplied in thirst. Attacked by the Wets over there in Macedonian phalanx, we will throw up our hands and shriek "Kamarad!" Would this be base desertion of the United States of Bootleggers? No Simply a physiological fact—the triumph of instinct over Anderson.

Seriously, though, an astrologer who studies the five stars nightly told me that a war with Europe over prohibition was coming. Aquarius was in the ascendant. Aquarius, he says, Is the symbol of the United States,_and the sign of the Crab and the Bull are its most dominant forces. When these two meet in the "reigning house," Aquarius—the water-boy —is tossed on the horns of a very direful dilemma.

A conjunction—or, rather, a collision—with Mars is imminent.

Privately, I think there is a great deal of Taurus in my friend's astrological knowledge, but I do agree with him that if the Volstead act Is not quickly amended there is every possibility of a war with every nation on earth whose boats come into our ports.

If all foreign boats that come to this shore have got to dump their liquid treasures at the three-mile limit, under penalty of seizure on crossing the equatorial booze line, the first act of retaliation will be by England. She will refuse admission to any British port of a professed American prohibitionist, just as we keep out professed Bolshevik.

Why should England permit a "Pussyfoot" Johnson, for instance, to bawl up and down her empire for the destruction of one of her greatest and oldest industries—glorified in Shakespeare and Chesterton? England bounced the Puritans once for propaganda. Why not again? Would we permit a rabid English "wet" to come here and begin a propaganda for the overthrow of the Eighteenth Amendment? Not on your K. K. K.

England's first move, therefore, will be to deport every American "dry" in her empire. And jolly well right she will be! Keep our fanatics, like your idiots and family skeletons, at home.

The French Parliament will pass a retaliatory law compelling every American boat that leaves her ports to carry stores of her wines and cognacs. She has as much right to protect her home industries as we have with a Fordney-McCumber tariff. In France, brandies and wines are natural products. They are her baseball.

Brazil will pass a law providing that no American boat shall leave her ports unless she carry a full quota of Indians to he educated in the College of the City of New York.

Holland will pass a law compelling all American boats that leave her shores to carry nothing but her cheeses.

Italy can retaliate by a law holding every American trader in port until her crew is made up entirely of men drawn from the Fascisti.

Mexico will have her say. No American boat in the harbors of Vera Cruz and Tampico shall feed to its crew anything else but chili con carne and no boat shall acme those ports whose crews are not dead drunk on pulque.

China and Japan will retaliate in kind.

We will then be compelled to declare war on all the world to uphold the principles of the Anti-Saloon League and its 2,000,000 hardworking bootleggers. There will be no American pacifists in that war—for here is a conflict holier than the lately projected war of the Children of Sweetness and Light against the Turk in order to make the Sultan's realm safe for the anti-Koran missionaries.

Its slogan will be, *Make the seas safe for the international bootleggers!*

Sad to relate (?), we will be licked to a frazzle in that war against the combined navies and breaths of the world. The far-flung alcoholic aura of Bacchus will triumph over the cirrhosis-faced drys and the prune-juice auras of the American bootleggers. The world will be made safe for laughter and likker.

In that war, sad to relate (?), many of us Americans will be compelled to be traitors. Not that we love America less, but rather because we love it more.. We must take the side of the wets In that war because we are followers of Washington, Hamilton, Jefferson, Paine and Andrew Jackson. Our slogan will he, "The booze of the Fathers!" Anderson may pen us up by the million in detention camps, but our Thirst will go marching on.

The decisive sea battle, I believe, will he fought off Curacao. Bryan and Anderson will be in full command of the Drys, and Admiral Cognac and Lord Bass in command of the Wets.

There will be an Armnistic Day throughout the world in which Dverybody will participate except Mr. Bryan, Mr. Anderson, Dr. Crane and Lady Astor—the four die-hards.

The Peace Commissioners of the Great Booze War will meet in some neutral city like Munich or Pilsen. The whole world will be declared wet forever and forever to the human race and its astral assigns in the Versailles Treaty of Booze.

Some of the Fourteen Point in the treaty we can forecast : America must dedicate at least one day a Year to the worship of Bacchus in the form of a public Saturnalia.

All moonshine liquor and stores of wood alcohol, private stills and home-brew utensils shall be surrendered within sixty days to the international Booze Tribunal, sitting at Pilsen, to be destroyed.

An indemnity of $2,000,000,000 shall he paid to the various nations of the world for loss of liquor trade during the dry era in the United States.

Chronic drunkenness and chronic sobriety In the United States shall be declared misdemeanors.

Manufacture of all liquors and beers shall be under the rigid supervision of life-long drinkers.

The illicit manufacture of alcoholic beverages shall carry the same penalties as counterfeiting or manslaughter.

Beer gardens, rathskellers and wine parlors shall be legally declared public utilities by act of Congress.

An Amendment to the Constitution of the United States shall prohibit the manufacture, sale or transportation of any alcoholic beverage containing less than 7 percent alcohol.

In all invoices and hills of lading alcoholic beverages Shall be billed as food.

Propaganda of any kind against any form of thirst or gourmandizing shall he unlawful in any part of the world.

The United States shall become a member in full standing of the League of Drinking Nations, subscribing allegiance to its motto of Life, Liberty, and the Pursuit of Joy.

And after this war is all over let us put an electric sign over Old Lady Liberty In the harbor, reading:

> "Shoot, if you must, this old gray head,
>   But spare our country's thirst!" she said.

The Golden Elixir

ALTHOUGH beer has been used for over three thousand years as a beverage and anesthetic, it remained for my wife and myself to discover at least a dozen other uses to which it can be put. We have a secret laboratory rigged up on top of our penthouse, and we are now giving to the world for the first time the results of some of our experiments.

For a shampoo: Fill a big earthenware mixing-bowl with beer and beat to a foam with an egg-beater. You will soon have a superb lather. Rub it through your hair vigorously. For a goat-curl use bock beer.

For typewriters: Our typewriter had arthritis in the key-joints. Most of the letters suffered from low visibility. The ribbon was anemic. The space-bar had muscular trouble. We put the machine in a foot-tub of beer overnight. In the morning we hardly recognized our little portable. It was swollen to the dimensions of a real machine and was rarin' to go.

Beer Flapjacks: Make a heavy batter of dough. Wrap it around a cold bottle of beer. Place it in a red-hot oven for ten minutes. The great heat will crack and dissolve the glass and thicken the beer in the dough, which will be cooked to a delicious brown. Cut into twelve slices—one bottle makes about twelve flapjacks. Pick out the glass with an oyster-fork and cat hot or cold.

For old razor blades: I had collected about five hundred razor blades in the course of five years. I had tried all kinds of patent sharpeners and found them of no value. Now I will not have to buy a new blade for years to come. I dumped the five hundred in a keg of real beer. I let them soak for a week. The dullness dropped off them like an old skin. They are now as sharp as an hyena's tooth.

Bald heads: I have been bald-headed since the Harding administration. Although I voted for Al Smith in 1928, my hair continued to fall out. While moseying around our laboratory an idea broke up the morning static. Knowing the chemical affinity between the brain and alcohol, I doused a sponge in beer and tied it to my head, using a chin-strap. In less than a month I developed what I call hop-hair, for it seems literally to effervesce through the scalp.

Beer-dumplings: Make a large apple-dumpling without the apple. Make a hole the size of an egg in the dough-ball. Pour into it all the lukewarm beer it will hold. Boil the dumplings in a kettle for at least fifteen minutes. Serve hot with mustard and horse-radish. Eat with a knife.

Cleaning watches: Same process as cleaning typewriters, with this difference: soak only the works in beer overnight, removing the case. If the watch was a Christmas present and the case has begun to turn green, soak it in ale and throw the works away.

For developing photographs: Soak your negatives in a sink full of beer. This process develops the most extraordinary effects. It not only brings out the face and features with preternatural clarity but also develops nimbuses and auras.

BARS

Elegy in a Malty Mood

NEW YORK mourns its lost beer-trails. Wines, brandies, gins, whiskeys it has in quantities—and qualities—to make the stomach sick. Its face and neck are sicklied o'er with the red cast of methylated boils. But its beer is gone. Gambrinus has taken to using the needle. A bottle of needle-beer sells for from fifty to seventy-five cents. Six bottles will efface all memory of God, honor, family and buttoned-up decency in otherwise lovable and loyal souls. And the stuff that is not needled is draught slops that lie like a dead weight on the dear kidneys, which bark and yelp for help. Home brew? It is made in dirty crocks in dark cellars and darker tenement rooms, and drunk while still green; every bottle means you are one hour nearer the end of your insurance premiums. Gins and Scotches, as bad as they are, are better bets than most of the beer now to be had in New York. I speak as a *maestro,* not as an amateur. Volstead killed the brew that laid the golden souse, and the mellow suns that shone in seidels have sunk in a sea of poison and pollution.

Make no mistake—New York wants the old-fashioned saloon back. It wants the mirror wherein it can watch the slow transformation of its poker face to wreathed smiles and wanton jests. It is bent on getting Louis and Gus and their white aprons out of the speakeasy trenches, if not before this Christmas, then before some other Christmas. It dreams, talks and thinks of planting its belly once again against good old American timber, as they used to say in the Pigs' Knuckles Era. Its right leg has generations of cell-memories enshrined in it of being hoisted joyously on to a shining rail. Every

273

beer-lover is conscious of that atavistic leg habit and of its fierce, hidden rage at being balked. He wants to see once more the little swinging-doors, so like B. V. D. drawers—eternal symbol to him of the vocal and mental undress beyond. He wants the sand on the floor, the cheese and *Leberwurst* at the end of the bar, and the little round pretzel-bowl to nibble from and re-whet his dying thirst. And the dirty old bar-rag—more beautiful now in memory's hollow halls than the white plume of Henry of Navarre. Now he consults the calendar or feels out the weather to find when Spring has come; but in the grand days of the saloon he knew it by the appearance on a sudden miraculous day of four words flashed from thousands of magic casements: "Bock Beer" and "May Wine."

The hypocritical sop that the wets have thrown to the drys, "The saloon is gone forever," is heard by New York beer-lovers, the Kit Carsons and Stanleys of the great beer-trails of Manhattan, with tongue in cheek, if not finger to nose. No beer-buddy believes it for a moment. He's for Al Smith first, last and all the time; but if Al should be nominated for the Presidency and pussyfoot on beer (full-strength, domestic and imported beer, drawn from the wood!) he will lose New York. The beer-thirsty of that town do not care a hair on the head of a baldheaded eagle what Al thinks about the international debts, the Russian boycott, the theory of evolution, or the pitiful cry of the hog and wheat interests of the Dakotas. What interests them is release from Prohibition, which means, concretely and down to cases, domestic and imported beers in corner beer saloons, the disappearance of which was coeval with the final collapse of democracy and the rise of boils. The near-beer of to-day bears about the same resemblance to what the millions of beer drinkers of New York want as a melted horsehair sofa does to a gushing barrel of Kulmbacher. The old-time saloon was a crime-dissolver, an idea-exchange, a public confessional. Ask Gus and Louis, priests of a million secrets that were absolved in "Have one on the house."

II

The gin-mill and the beer saloon—of which there were about fifteen thousand in the greater city before the invasion of the Goths and Vandals from the swamps, hayricks and cow-pens of the West and South—the gin-mill and the beer saloon belonged to two entirely different genera. The gin-mill was an evil-looking, cheerless, bare boozing-ken, wherein a pair of slit-eyes and cyclopean haymakers stood between a bar and a mirror which looked like the public comfort station of all the flies in the world. Beer was seldom drunk in such places. They were the clearing houses of rot-gut. They survive today in New York, multiplied a hundred-fold, as speak-easies. The old German beer saloon was the antithesis of a gin-mill. The bartender's face was a fat beam of light. His mirrors were chalked with delectable ten-cent dishes. There were often tall stools for the beer-buddies. The bar was lined from end to end with goblets filled with amber gullet-washes, their tops encircled with immaculate, evanescent collars of foam. Home and mother were never like that! New York was always beer-conscious, is so yet, and it will always be. To Bryan and Wheeler and their visible and invisible abettors the town was always, and still remains, the beer and wine Anti-Christ, if not the Scotch and rye Beast of the Apocalypse.

Then there were the great beer-halls, rathskellers and open-air beer gardens. Lüchow's!—magic word! Merely to pronounce it now before a beer-loving New Yorker causes an auroral suffusion of his face and a blush of pleasure to his gizzards. Lüchow's immortalized in song and story, for it was Lüchow's great beer emporium in Fourteenth street—Irving place begins at Gramercy Park and ends at Lüchow's, not only the end of a street, but once upon a time the dock for all beer-going souls who sailed and sailed and sailed in boats of glass and stone—it was Lüchow's of which the poet sang the crashing song that fired the beer drinkers of the whole English-speaking world, "Down where the Würzburger Flows!":

Down, down, down where the Würzburger flows, flows, flows—
Everyone knows, knows, knows.
Rhine wine it is fine,
But a big stein for mine!
Down where the Würzburger flows!

It was the national beer-anthem of my youth, and the bit I have just quoted rings out in my mind like wild bells to the now sadly blue sky.

James Huneker immortalized Lüchow's in "Steeplejack." August Lüchow is indexed in the book along with Mozart, Byron, Chopin, Gautier, Swinburne, Schopenhauer and Shakespeare. "I took a walk and got as far as Lüchow's," says Huneker. He was always walking and never getting any farther than Lüchow's. All beer-drinkers' walks ended at Lüchow's. Huneker and Lüchow, indeed, were almost interchangeable terms. Although Lüchow himself is now safe in the bosom of Gambrinus, Huneker's name is always mentioned with reverence by his successor, Mr. Eckstein, along with those of the other celebrated patrons of the place, which sound like a Who's Who of genius. There were De Pachmann, Anton Seidl, Ignace Paderewski, Vance Thompson, the De Reszkes, Leopold Godowsky, George Luks, William Glackens, Rafael Joseffy, Heinrich Conried, Victor Herbert, Georg Brandes, Edgar Fawcett, Antonin Dvořák, O. Henry, Max Alvary, Emil Fischer, John Quinn, William Butler Yeats—the list irks and dazzles. It was in Lüchow's that Huneker threw a seidel of Pilsner into DePachmann's face because the "great Chopinzee" called Joseffy an unprintable name. Lüchow himself was one of the party and led the bizarre Vladimir to the lavatory to rid him of the Huneker-Pilsner douse. (Huneker later told me that he always regretted having named DePachmann "the Chopinzee.")

Lüchow opened his place in 1881. It was dedicated to beer. In all the years I frequented it, I do not now recall ever having seen a highball or a straight whiskey on the tables or at the bar. It would have been as incongruous a sight as Bishop Manning tending bar. There are one vast room and a number of smaller rooms on the first floor. Somehow the big room always conveys to me the mirage of vast thirsts. It is a room that has always been wall-lined in my beer-mind's eye with casks and shining spigots. For thirty-eight years a quartette thundered Beethoven, Liszt, Brahms and Strauss (the Strauss, Johann) to the gurgle and deep Rhineflow of millions of quarts of Würzburger and Pilsner. The orchestra still thunders from the Steinway and the Strads, but the gurgle and the guzzle and the flow of Würzburger and

Pilsner have become cautious lip and throat wettings of depressing imitations suggesting the Gowanus Canal.

It was in Lüchow's that the Bohemian Society and the Society of Authors and Composers were organized and met for years on the second floor, where vast problems of enchanting blab were settled in skuttles of imported suds and to the yelp of George Luks' hoarse Ride of the Pennsylvania Dutch Valkyries from the top of a table. Blessed freshet!—now dissolved in the runnels of near-beer. The Steinway room, also on this floor, was of, for, and by the Steinway beer-boys. Mention of it will recall to all enlightened beer-drinkers the name of "Baron" Ferdinand Sinzig, of the house of Steinway, and the Würzburger and Pilsner ace of aces. Sinzig was from Cologne, and wherever imported beers were drunk in New York he was known.

He passed away, God be praised! before the Blight descended on the land whose liberty was achieved (so 'tis said) by a gentleman who left his Mount Vernon stills and vats to do the job. Sinzig could drink beer for a solid week without sleep. Pounding out Liszt, Bach or Debussy on the piano, he would exhaust the bungs of Lüchow and then start uptown, seeking for more seidels to annihilate. With his long, flowing moustache, his slouch hat, his broad tie, his hair that flowed into his ears and hid his collar, his eyes always a-twinkle, an anecdote ever on his lips, he was the incarnation of beer heartiness. His favorite *mot* was "Schopenhauer is a local issue."

August Lüchow was the greatest benefactor that the American kidney has ever had. He was the American agent for Würzburger and Pilsner. His whole life was given to putting America on a German-beer basis. His place in Fourteenth street is now a cenotaph buried in a Sahara.

III

I have before me as I write a booklet that should be filed away in Washington with the original draft of the Bill of Rights and other such obsolete documents. It is a large booklet of sixteen pages, beautifully printed and illustrated, and from its back dangles a small black seal on a cord stamped "Hofbräu Haus, New York." It is a twenty-year old beer-and-eats menu presented to me lately, with some pardonable lachrymose gutterings in both our throats, by Herr Schmitt, who has charge, in Mr. Janssen's absence, of the famous port of the pre-Volsteadean beer-parched at Broadway and Thirtieth street, "opposite Daly's Theatre," as this most precious of my rare incunabula saith. Almost everything that has been written in America since 1900— except checks—has been written with tongue in cheek, including Dr. Wilson's declaration of war, the Volstead law and "Abie's Irish Rose." But not this illuminated ritual of the gullet! It is a labor of love, conceived and wrought by the priests of Pilsner. Merely to look at it whets and wets the appetites of the present population of the Ginmillennium. Perpend:

Bürger Bräu Pilsen—light, bitter, slightly veiled.
Münchner Hofbräu—dark, sweet, creamy.
Würzburger Bürger Bräu—a little lighter in color than the Münchner; not quite so sweet.
Nürnberger Tucher Bräu—called the Burgundy of all beers; very dark, creamy and full of character.
Following the old German custom, as it was in the days when Albrecht Dürer and Hans Sachs drank in Nürnberg's famous inn, the old bell in the *Schenke* is rung whenever a new cask is tapped.

Sitting with my cronies in the Hofbräu Haus annexing imported sausages with sauerkraut, and half-liter steins of deliciously kept Pilsner, I have heard the old joy-bell ring a thousand times. There is no more satisfying sound to your real beer fanatic. On Saturday nights the ringing was almost continuous. For the Hofbräu Haus, like Lüchow's, was not a preparatory school. They were post-graduate courses. August Janssen opened the place in 1898. He says he knew I was to arrive in New York in 1899, fresh from my conquest of thirty thousand quarts of Peter Schemm's dark, in Philadelphia—a beer, by the way, that came nearer to the great German beers than any that has ever been produced in America. Old Peter so loved his brew that until he committed suicide by leaping into Niagara Falls it was sold to only one out of every ten saloons in Philadelphia.

Mr. Janssen made his establishment—and it still is—one of the show-places of New York. It was dedicated to Fine Beers Kept Right. In this pious work he spared no expense. It is a replica, inside and out, of the famous inns of the medieval towns of Munchen, Nürnberg, Leipzig and Frankfurt. A trip through its rooms is like an excursion into the soul of the muzzy, lushy, Devil-be-damned past, when Beaker, Flagon and Bung were the Trinity of priest and peasant and all good swizzle-nicks. The wainscoting in one room is from a three-hundred-year-old Nürnberg church, some of the stained window-glass is dated 1538, and there is a clock to be seen that is 195 years old. There are burned-in pictures on the walls of singing lobsters, their faces mad with satyric glee, and of grotesque maidens of eld, soaked to their crowns of glory in wine. There are dancing steins, fat serving wenches who know not Parsifal, cocks that crow "Let there be drink!" and sly eyes that peep at you from tangled grape-vines.

The Hofbräu Haus, in a word, is a Cathedral of Bibulous Joy—that was. To sit in one of those half-darkened rooms, as I have lately done, produces in me the identical emotions of quiet ecstasy and peace, mixed with a soft and pensive melancholy, that I get when I sit alone in St. Patrick's Cathedral long after the service is over, as is my wont. And, indeed, the service *is* over in the Hofbräu Haus, as it is everywhere else in my country 'tis of thee.

IV

Terrace Garden! My psychometer registers a tremendous quake of joy in the breasts of thousands of New York beer-drinkers at seeing those two words. I can even hear the burbled sighs of old grand-dad—*he* knows!—for Terrace Garden, at Fifty-eighth street and Third avenue, was one of the oldest uptown open-air beer gardens in the town. My mother has told me that she used to visit the place on her trips to New York during the Civil War.

The garden was an immense affair that ran through to Fifty-ninth street. In a patronage of many years I have never seen anything but beer on the tables. It was a family drinking-place, sacred to the stolid bourgeoisie and their progeny, even unto the third generation. The diapered generation was given sips from the glasses and steins of the elders and allowed to nibble the mystic pretzel. The band played German and American airs, but no one ever paid much attention to it. Terrace Garden was, every Summer night, a beer gabfest, a box-plant grove of laughter that billowed its way up to the bead-winky stars. Domestic beers were drunk there in vast quantities—a nickel a glass, ten cents for a huge seidel or stein, and the honest Heinie always threw in a basket of small pretzels free. In dark and remote corners of the gardens one could hear four or five good beer-pates exgurgitating, *pianissimo,* some old German air or maybe "In the Gloaming, O My Darlink!" The building still stands, shot to hell by the illicit plum-brandy and whiskey distillers of the Western Farm Bloc and the Southern corn-mule rot-gutters.

Scheffel Hall, at Eighteenth street and Third avenue, was also a famous beer-hall in its day. It was patronized by the literati from Irving place and Gramercy Park. A seven-course dinner was to be had for forty-five cents—without water. If anyone—literatus or illiteratus—had ever ordered a glass of water in Scheffel Hall, Billy Allaire would have had him ejected. I was a regular attendant for many years at the services in the hall. An anecdote sticks out.

I spent an evening there with Murray Schloss, amateur Socialist and culture-hound *de luxe.* The conversation ran to poetry. After my tenth seidel I delivered my well-known dithyrambic glorification of Swinburne straight in the face of Schloss. He called Swinburne a lyrical loon and solemnly announced that Rudyard Kipling was a far greater poet. I quit the bird.

The following night, while I was seideling alone in the hall, Jim Huneker blew in. He squatted with me and ordered three seidels *pronto.* I told him that Schloss had pronounced Kipling a greater poet than Swinburne. Jim threw himself back, his chest expanded like an athlete's, his little gray eyes narrowed to a slit, his right fist doubled up for battle, and bawled at me:

"Didn't you smash the —————?"

At Ninety-eighth street and Broadway there stood Unter den Linden, an open-air beer garden like Bob Tagg's of blessed memory at Franklin street and Fairmount avenue, Philadelphia, where we used to fish for minnows in the fountain after midnight. Unter den Linden was only a neighborhood garden, but no doubt it will be remembered by all those who have travelled the great trunk lines of beer in what is now the Volsteadean Pompeii.

Pabst's Harlem Casino, up in 125th street, Feltman's at Coney Island (where the caterpillars dropped into your seidel; but who cared?), the Atlantic Gardens on the Bowery (where they threw in pretzels, *Leberwurst*, pickles and a whole vaudeville show with a five-cent beer), Schmitt's rathskeller in Fourteenth street, Madame Hoburg's at Third avenue and Fourteenth street (where Sadakichi Hartmann danced his epileptic boleros with a full seidel perched on his Gargantuan head till 6 A.M.), the Zumpraellatten in Thirteenth street, the Kaiserhof, Mock's, Buck's—

But I simply can't go on. It is to weep as only strong men with home-brew kidneys can weep over the emasculation of a god.

Red-Ink Days

THE excavation of ancient New York goes on with great emotion and energy. The Pompeii of beer, whiskey and red ink that went down under the sudden explosion of the Vesuvius of venom, poison gas and mephitic booze in 1920 is gradually coming to light. The more intelligent magazines and Sunday newspapers have begun to teem with stories of the Lost Atlantis. The corpses of Old John Barleycorn, Papa Gambrinus, King Burgundy, the Princess Coraline Claret, Uncle Mumm, the Pied Piper of Heidsieck, the Dowager Mother Sauterne, Little Eva Absinthe with the green eyes, and Little Rollo Cognac have been fished forth piously by a band of scribes and laid in the sun for all the flask-toting Boy Scouts and Follies flappers to behold, while the palaces, kitchens, bars and back-yards in which they were wont to revel and set the table and mirrors on a roar are being reconstructed in half-tone, black-and-white and dry-point for the Volstead Museum of Ancient American Customs.

The old-time bibulous, sin-adventuring New Yorker thought pretty much in reds. There were the red lights, red eye and red ink. Red ink was the name given to table claret because it looked like red ink. It now tastes like red ink and often looks like fermented carbon paper. A red-ink joint was New-Yorkese for a place run by an Italian, a Hungarian or a Frenchman—but in most cases by an Italian—where you got a seven-course meal for forty-five cents with a small bottle of claret thrown in. Red ink joints still flourish by the thousand in New York, but since the collapse of liberty and the rise of stomach ulcers (*circa* 1920) meals in them are of five courses only, the price has been tripled, the diluted and fermented carbon paper runs to two dollars a quart and up, and the only thing that is thrown in is the free use of the roller-towel in the wash-room.

I have been informed by ancient but still articulate human containers of red ink that the first veritable joint in New York of which we have any knowledge was Niblo's Garden, once on the outskirts of the town at the corner of Broadway and Prince street. This was a large open-air drinking place *(circa* 1823) with bird-cages and lanterns hanging from the trees; it served mainly ices and clarets. As a solid institution, the red-ink joint, with its chin-chatter, brain-expansion and festal grin, was born at Mulberry Bend and Paradise Park at about the time of the second discovery of America by Italians *(circa* the Pierce-Buchanan Dynasty?). It was here—. at least, so I have been informed by venerable *ban vivants*—that the table d'hôte that began with antipasto and minestra, that went to great gobs of spaghetti and chicken, and thence to spumoni and coffee, with oceans of red wine, was first known to the uitlanders from uptown.

When the literati and the painters—followed, as they always are, by the solid Macedonian phalanxes of illiterati, culture-hounds, fame-danglers, college Babbitts and brawling Sancho Panzas—invaded the claret-and-spaghetti cellars of the Bend, the Italians began to hie nor'-nor' west in the direction of Fourteenth street, hoping to retain the old flavor of their meeting places. But pretty soon, seeing that it was impossible to keep out the Americans, and getting a taste of the fleshpots of the West to boot, they declared open pool. Thenceforward spaghetti and red ink became the touchstones of arts and letters in New York, and the kitchens of the Italian snuggeries became the bullrings of Philistines, sales-agents for barbers' goods and that vast hoard of burns on the lower slopes of Parnassus who seek the Horebic gleam by night.

Whiskey, beer and ale had preceded wine as regular souse-aiders in New York by many generations. Whiskey, beer and wine had up until the Blight their separate worlds. They overlapped but seldom mixed. Whiskey was for Dutch courage, for stock-and-barrel Americans and black-eye Rembrandts. To your real, prenatal whiskey-lifter, Art was and is sodomic. The New York whiskey drinker had an ecliptic all his own. Beer, as I have pointed out in a former lamentation in this place, was for the soft-souse, the singing, human, weeping-sleeping fellow. But wine produced gayety, expansiveness, an ethereal simper, a laudable desire to give away wife and fortune, a superb indifference to time and check-book. It had the power to fertilize a thousand stale cell-eggs in the brain—a phenomenon which I have seldom observed in whiskey and beer partisans. The metabolistic influence of wine that I have observed as a student of myself builds tissue, rinses the brain of all Schopenhauerean clog, tunes up the larynx to mighty efforts, and transfigures the plainest Jane into a mirific Isolde. Red ink may have spread uric acid among us occasionally, but the cure was found in the cause. There was no headache in it. There was no fight in it. And I never heard of an alcoholic case at Bellevue caused by wine.

If you want to jolt an old member of the New York Ink Guards out of his stoical and gin-wrinkled hide pronounce in his ear any one of these magical words: Guffanti, Riccadonna, Maria, Roversi, Little Hungary, Cabaret Francis, Moretti, Mouquin, Martin, Carlos, Black Cat, Mori, Gonfarone, Petit-Pas, Poggi, Marabeni.

These were only a few of the names that blazed in bulbs and were magnets to thousands who came from the uttermost boundaries of the five boroughs and even from beyond the great waters that divide Hoboken and Jersey City from the Island of Souse's Desire.

II

Most of the old and well-patronized Italian and Hungarian red-ink table d'hotes were in private houses. The ground floor had a small bar and dining-room, with a kitchen in the back wherein the wife of the proprietor—fat, garlicky, matriarchal—cooked. The daughters (if any, and there were generally some) waited on the tables, and were treated by the intelligentsia, and even by those in trade, with the same degree of respect that the Englishman offers to his bar-maid. Wine idealizes even the wench. The proprietor—generally, in the early days, a heavy-set, good-natured Italian with a Kitchener moustache and a non-stop, belly-broad watch-chain—kept the till and the cigar-stand. There was sometimes a cat that slept at the end of the bar. Some of these restaurants flowed over on to the second floor, used generally by the Junkers of Bohemia and the owners of watch-case factories who looked askance and askew at the rather free-and-easy ways of the talented proletarians in the basement. Almost all of them—especially in Greenwich Village—had Summer gardens, which were the backyards of the houses rebricked and decorated with potted plants and Brooklyn rubber-plants, with night-blooming tom-cats walking the spiked fences. Many of these gentle sons of Napoli had skipped the detail of taking out a liquor license, but they were seldom bothered, for some one always got the license-money.

We drank our cocktails in the kitchen and kidded Mamma until our appetites became sharpened to the biting point. Then we went to the table, which looked like Joseph's coat when we arose at midnight.

After the coffee and cognac (the latter ten cents extra, I may as well remind the rising Boy Scout generation) some one sang a song, often a professional singer of either sex. A Neapolitan love-song, maybe—melodious, dream-evoking; or perhaps two or three of them got together with mandolins and we had "Funiculi-Funicula," while the whole place took it up, including the ribbon clerks from Yonkers. Our shirts were dyed in the blood of Bacchus and our voices walloped the welkin when the Famous Neapolitan Trio (always Famous, always Neapolitan, even after the invasion of the Greeks) was doing "Funiculi-Funicula." It was the Marseillaise of the Red Ink Army, which will neither die nor surrender as long as "real, old, genuine Chianti" is funnelled from tub to bottle in the cellars of Houston street.

The Hungarians, like the Italians, were strong on red table wines. The most renowned as well as one of the very oldest of their retreats was Little Hungary in East Houston street. Its early name was Liberty Hall—no doubt chosen by a countrymen to honor Louis Kossuth's revolution. It was the most curious place in New York. Peddlers of shirt-studs, neckties, socks and hairpins had their stands in the restaurant. They went from table to table with their wares, just as the cigarette girls do now in the pimp-infested night clubs of the White Lights. Rigo, after his great publicity stunt with the Princess Chimay had worn off its edge uptown, led the orchestra there for years, giving clown-like performances with his violin. He was a pre-Charlie Chaplin and a great drawing card for Launcelot Gobbos out of the West. Those who did not care for him went into the cellar. Here there was a treat for the red inksters. You sat at a long board and drew your wine out of a glass tube just over your head by pushing a button. You literally pumped it into yourself, and paid according to the number of tubes consumed.

Theodore Roosevelt, when he was police commissioner, was a patron of Little Hungary, and one evening, in a dee-lighted state of mind, he told the proprietor that he would still dine there, even if he became President of the United States. The finger of Fate having done the business, the proprietor reminded President Roosevelt of his red-ink remark. Teddy was as good as his word. The streets were roped off, a thousand cops were swung into East Houston street (there were dangerous Bryanites, single-taxers and referendum nuts on the soap-boxes in those days) and he was dined and wined in great state in Little Hungary. I have not been there for many years, but I believe the chair on which the God of Blare sat is still on exhibition, and that the plan of the Holy Supper is still on the wall.

Memories of Little Hungary draw me over to Second avenue, once the most picturesque and European-like street in New York. Hungarian red wines, steaming hot or ice-cooled, were consumed in the sidewalk cafés far into the Summer nights, and in Winter they were got down indoors, while a violinist strolled around, stopped at the tables and played some of the weirdest and most beautiful airs I have ever heard. What has become of these exquisite bits? Second avenue preserved its air and entity almost to the dreadful end. Few uitlanders ever visited it. It was seldom invaded by New Yorkers. There were the Café Monopole, Balogh's (happy, laughing Balogh, who one night went behind a cask of red and blew his brains out!), the Orpheum (steaming red Hungarian wine and a whole play in Hungarian, Yiddish, or something, for ten cents), the Café Royale, with its extensive sidewalk café, and the Café Boulevard, with its wine cellars lighted by candles, and its grotesque cymbolum player: Huneker made him the central character in one of his fantastic short stories. The Boulevard was not, strictly speaking, a red-ink joint. It catered to the Vere de Veres of the East Side. It was just a little too respectable and formal for me, although I once slept on one of the long tables in the cellar after a grand party. It was at a dinner of the Sunset Club at the Boulevard that Sadakichi Hartmann delivered his epoch-making lecture on temperance and monogamy.

Maria's! A tocsin, a trumpet of resurrection in the ears of all Bohemian, winebibbing, roystering New Yorkers. Maria's was in Twelfth street, and for many years it was a club of the arts and letters. It has become a legend. For thirty years it was a whole Boul' Mich in itself. Who has not dined, wined, sung and high-jinksed it at Maria's is not in the Golden Book of New York Bohemia. It was the central red-ink joint of every writer, painter, sculptor, architect, composer and newspaper man, including Ibsenists, Marxists, Stirnerites, Shavians and Swinburnians, that heeled it around New York. On Saturday night after ten o'clock you couldn't lower a boat in that heaving Red Sea. At four o'clock in the morning you could attach a fire-hose to any mouth in the place and put out a fire a block away.

It was in Maria's that a lady whose name shall be inviolate here laid her face on my collar, crinkled to a string, and wept and wept. I inquired. She pointed to a big fellow (a well-known painter) who stood at the piano, his arm around the waist of a young woman, bawling out a song.

"That's my husband," she sobbed to my neck-string. "Look at him! For two years after we were married he didn't drink a drop and we used to read Nietzsche and Schopenhauer to one another every night. Now he sings in bed, and our dear Nietzsche and Schopenhauer nights are no more!"

Maria's had a recognized toastmaster. For years he was Mickey Finn. Anybody called on had to do something—a song, a story, a dance, or a recitation. "Gunga Din" was done to death there. I once recited "The Ride of Paul Revere" in order to soothe the Dingle-Dangles who frequented the place.

If Maria's was local, Mouquin's, at Twenty-eighth and Sixth avenue, was cosmopolitan and universal. It was known to artists and litterateurs throughout the world. (I except Philadelphia, for I never knew a Philadelphian who had heard of Mouquin's. The Quaker City was never strong on wine or Bohemia. It sticks, immemorially, to the sacredness of the home, the back-alley speakeasy, and the Sunday poker-party). I defy any habitué of Mouquin's to write objectively of that celebrated emporium of wines, snails, onion soup, bouillabaisse and the mazagran. Little Hungary and Maria's were places. Mouquin's was home. You tossed your hat anywhere, you lolled, sprawled, cushioned yourself for a long session on carafes of *vin rouge* or *vin Mane*. The waiters were your cronies. Sometimes, when they got tired standing on the marble floor, they sat down with you, bought you a drink and discussed the election of Maurice Barth to the Académie Française. Joe Harri was the chum of every Mouquineer for thirty years. Joe was captain of the waiters an one of the managers. He was a well-educated Parisian. After a couple of carafes of red quietly impounded in the kitchen, or a few social cognacs with one of us, he would recite Victor Hugo, Alfred de Musset and Paul Verlaine by the yard, dramatically or sentimentally as the case might be. He would go to Jack's with us after Mouquin's closed and tear off Lamartine and De Vigny to the vast astonishment of Jack Dunstan, whose highest flight was "Mother Machree."

III

Mouquin's was fundamentally a wine house. Wines were cheaper there than at any other place in New York. The artists, poets, wastrels and radicals to whom Mouquin catered achieved mighty feats of metabolistic transubstantiation with the ruby hippocrene, from plain red ink to sparkling Burgundy. His three-story place was a Hall of Fame. I recall, offhand, Jack London, Ernest Lawson, Robert Henri, Arthur B. Davies, Vance Thompson, Charlie Chaplin, James Huneker, Richard Le Gallienne, Paul Bartlett, Emma Goldman, Jo Davidson, Homer Davenport, Arthur Brisbane, Michael Monahan, Enrico Caruso, Jean de Reszke, William Butler Yeats, Theodore Dreiser, Stanford White, Bob Chanler, William Glackens, John Barrymore, O. Henry, Lincoln Steffens, Augustus Saint-Gaudens, Tito Ruffo, Victor Herbert, Charles Macauley, Clive Weed, Don Marquis, Leon Trotzsky, Frederick James Gregg, Booth Tarkington, Francis Grierson, David Belasco—and, and, and. The place vibrated with talk. It is now a cloak and suit cafeteria. It is to weep!

When Francis Savoureau left Mouquin's in the early part of the century he opened, with the backing of James Moore, the Cabaret Francis in Thirty-fifth street near the Garrick Theatre. Moore was a real estate lawyer, but he cared only for the company of painters and writers. Finding that he could not meet them all at once at Mouquin's, he opened a four-story house with a café in the basement, a restaurant on the first floor and sleeping rooms on the upper floors so that he could surround himself with Parnassians day and night. Jim Moore was a royal waster, a royal houser of the down-and-outs, and a unique dispenser of red ink for thirsty brush and pen men, for he didn't care whether you had money or not. He wanted you there. The walls of the café were lined with originals by Sloane, Glackens, Lawson and others. It was a gay, wild place of stormy sessions. There was a piano in the café and the usual Famous Neapolitan Trio. Savoureau himself, at midnight, would grab a tinpan from the kitchen and start parading around the place with all of us behind him, with our carafes of red ink in our hands, singing to split the walls. The Famous Trio would sometimes join the procession with their mandolins if they were able to walk. After the place closed, nominally at one A.M., Moore would invite a bunch of his boys over to his house in Twenty-third street, where the gayety was continued until they flopped into his many beds. The Cabaret Francis burned out one night with all of our checks, and Jim Moore has gone to Heaven. There are many famous American artists who could tell just how good he was at periods when a meal and a pint of red ink stood between them and suicide.

When J. B. Martin was at Ninth street and University Place he had a famous red-ink stand. The night before he closed to move to his highbrow store at Twenty-sixth and Broadway he brought a mule into the place at three A.M. while the crowd was swilling its way into a vinous Nirvana, and had the animal kick hell out of everything, to the frenzied howls of the mob. The Village, of course, swarmed with red-ink bazaars, and does yet—even more so. The most famous were Guffanti's in Seventh avenue; Gonfarone's, in Eighth street (I have been told that this place was the residence of Aaron Burr, but I do not know); Mori's, in Bleecker street; the curious, macabre Black Cat in West Broadway (a place that always gave me the Schopenhauerean willies), and Ricca-donna's. Uptown, further, there were of blessed memory the Carlos, Moretti's, with its delightful Summer garden, and Roversi's, which still stands at Twenty-seventh street and Broadway, the name in bold electric lights—a sad, lone, solitary, Cambronnic survivor of a halcyon and hyperborean past.

Resurgam

MY RESPECT for all drys is zero. My respect for nearly all wets is zero minus. A dry and his friend, the bootlegger, know exactly what they want, and they belch it out. But nearly all the so-called wets I have met have a sneaking suspicion that Prohibition is a "little bit right." Their very souls blush guiltily at the word saloon. They stand aghast at the idea of the complete repeal of the Amendment and the Volstead Act. "There may be something sinful about rum, after all!" they murmur to themselves.

The vision of the saloon wide open again is so pleasurable to them that, like the sound Christians that they are, they feel it is a sin even to dwell on't. This is in line with American psychology: anything that is free-and-easy, that is unrestricted, that can make you unrestrainedly happy is somehow wrong. A hatred and a fear of freedom are inherent in all the descendants of the original squatters in this Land of the Free. The unblended American wet is inevitably tainted with such qualms. Visions of Joe Morgan spending his last cent in Simon Slade's bar-room fittingly pursue him and "Frank Slade, you have killed your father!" booms dramatically down the corridors of his timid soul whenever his mind dallies with the programme of the only real wets: A saloon for every block!

And by the saloon I do not mean just a beer-saloon. To put this country back on a civilized basis, to bring back happiness and adventure, romance and forgetfulness, *to restore* the *democracy of* wit, good humor and equality between Mike and Fritz, to reduce crime, to destroy the hip-pocket flask, to provide comfort-stations for man, woman and child, to strike a death-blow at the universal corruption caused by Prohibition, to provide again free-lunches to the unemployed and the financially embarrassed, to set up clubs for home-sickened men, to give the Boy Scouts ocular and gustatorial proof that all the heroes they reverence were nursed on bottled fire and that the greatness of Our Country rose to the song of ten-bottle men—to do this the saloon must, will and *is* coming back in full canonicals: beer, whiskey, gin, cocktails, brandy, wines and Mamie Taylors.

The saloon is coming back because it is an organic necessity. It is essentially and peculiarly American. It was born of our hurry, our hatred of leisure, our disdain of elegancies, manners, table-cloths. In Europe the people from time immemorial have sat down to drink; they have made of it a sacrament to go with leisurely eating. But "Sacrament be damned!" said the early men of the Republic, "I want five fingers quick—and then another!" Europe sips her drinks. We sip nothing. We throw in a whiskey, a beer, a cocktail, just as we gulp down Haiti, Cuba, the Philippines, Nicaragua, a World War, all the great musicians of Europe, Proust, Trader Horn, fifty million automobiles a year, and four or five new religions.

The saloon was thus a healthy growth, a normal growth, an organic extension of our healthy gullets and bellies. "This is hell!" said a four-generation American friend of mine when he *first* hit Paris. "I've got to sit down to get drunk! Where's that American Bar I heard about?" An American seeing the word Bar in any quarter of the globe immediately returns to his tribe. His eye dances, his mouth waters, his spine runs up the Stars and Stripes. In going toward that sign, he is going home. He'll see Chicago Jim or Bowery Pete behind the long mahogany. He'll stand before a bottle and a glass, and with his foot on a shining rail he'll salute with loving thought the spirits of Andy Jackson, Kit Carson and General Grant—all grand American bar-flies in their day. You can no more ultimately dissever a real American from the saloon than you can part Herbert Hoover from his decorations.

II

The saloon-root in the American soul was never better exemplified,

I think, than in the following incident. It is all the more significant in that I had never considered myself a patriot—until what I am to tell revealed to me that patriotism lies deeper than reason, and that wherever there's a bar there's at least one wandering, erring American who will come home to the bosom of Old Abe.

I went to the City of Mexico when Porfirio Diaz, the most pro-lific founder of cemeteries that the Western World has begotten, was in power. I arrived in the city without knowing anybody, without knowing the language, and without even being able to read the signs. I saw *cantinas* and *pulquerias* without number, and terraces where dull-eyed Latins and Indians sipped their drinks while staring at the gutter. I was lost, depressed, home-sick. I thought of ending it, like Empedocles, by plunging into the crater of Popocatepetl. Then, sud-denly, on the third day, turning a corner in my melancholy walk, I saw a tremendous sign, "Coney Island." *Te Deuce Laudamus!* It was an American saloon, run by Carl Spitzer, a German-American from our own Coney Island! Swinging-doors, sanded floor, white apron, brass-rail, spittoons, and everything, including a pyramid of bottles behind Carl labelled Old Crow, Belle of Nelson, Trimble, Wilson, Black Label and Holland Gin!

My loneliness was over. This God-sent saloon, where Carl pro-vided all the paraphernalia of a regular Sixth avenue free-lunch, per-suaded me to remain in Mexico. Everything about the man became of profound interest to me—his modest birth in the great city of Brooklyn, his matriculation at Val Schmidt's booze Mahal just over the bridge, his babies that he had left behind, and—when did your hair begin to fall out, Carl? Carl's only regret was that he could not let his patrons have Ehret's beer. (Mexican beer is very fine, and most-ly made by Germans.) But the point is this: "Coney Island" made me a red-hot American while I was in Mexico. I understood for the first time the profound affinity between the saloon and My Country.

It is because of this adventure that I believe the one way to destroy radicalism in America and calm the fluttering hearts of the D. A. R.'s is to reopen the saloons with their whole pharmacopoeia of infallible cure-alls. I can promise the Ohio, the Indiana and the Pennsylvania Gangs that they can get away with anything in Washington and no one will care a damn if they put a saloon on every corner in every city throughout the Republic. It should be done forcibly as a patriotic act, to silence those of us—millions—who have a grouch against "the way things is goin'." At bottom, none of us *cares* a bootlegger's oath who gets away with anything. Our howling assumptions of rectitude are merely defense mechanisms to hide—"light wines and beer" hypocrites, hear! hear our firm determination to bring back the saloon, which we are *going* to do—if the spirits of Jackson, Webster, Grant and the other great American patron saints of the brass-rail do not fail us—if it takes the rest of our lives!

In the olden days when My Country was really true to the thirst of the Fathers any one who desired could die a drunkard's death, the best, the most painless of all deaths, seeing that most of us have to die of something terrible. But to-day one cannot even die a decent drunkard's death. Instead, millions of us are being slowly poisoned and our entrails are slowly rotting because of the liquids administered to us by the Volstead Borgias. The restored saloon—cheap pure whiskeys, gins, beers, cocktails, brandies and absinthe drips—at least will allow us to go to Heaven or Hell in our own way, a fundamental constitutional guarantee.

The saloon is, again, necessary for a revival of the humanities of Our Country. For eight years there has gone on a steady commercialization and standardization of good fellowship in the form of Rotary clubs and other such mechanical pumpers-up of almost-dead instincts. The saloon in its palmiest days came nearer to realizing the Brotherhood of Man ideal in its most natural and masculine form than any other institution which the Christian era has littered. If among the millions who assembled before Mike and Heinie year in and year out there were some who would knock that ideal into a cocked hat, or even a cock-eye, by "offering to clean out the ranch," they were quickly brought to terms by the Presiding Bishop, who, quickly divesting himself of his canonical apron, took a miraculous leap over the bar and propelled the misguided brother through the door in less time than it took to change water into wine at Cana.

At the moment of entering a saloon one immediately became flooded with the Christmas spirit. Pockets, hearts and lips opened and poured out their treasures on a brother, on all the assembled brothers at times, while Bishop Mike or Bishop Fritz, his face melted to that of a beneficent Allah, pontificated with the waters of life. "Ruined homes!" the Salvation Army used to tom-tom in the streets, showing us decayed exhibits of "saved" pseudo-human beings who would have made better looking whiskey corpses. Ruined homes! All homes are now in ruins from the Salvation Army's point of view. Every kitchen is a gin-mill and the decencies of the old saloon are put to shame.

Before I describe some of these delightful American sanctuaries so that the rising generation, and especially the ecclesiastically captained Boy Scouts, will know what their manhood will miss unless they throw off the yoke of the Methodist-Baptist speak-easies—before I show the post-war generation something of the glory that has passed away, but which must return as surely as God made us primarily to sin and transgress, I will recall the loveliness of New York after sunset when the lights from fifteen thousand saloons on twelve thousand corners threw their fires like guiding beacons into the dark streets and lit the way to spirituous redemption from the day's cares, worries and grouches of a million tired business men, solitary hall-bedroom thinkers and the gnarled and twisted men with the hoe, shovel, pick and spade, not to mention the day-weary proofreaders, watchcase engravers and cloak-stitchers (there was the redemptive Family Entrance for drooping corset-models, sales-girls and actresses who supported John MacCullough). On cold, snowy evenings, when the streets were deserted, these brilliantly lighted saloons made a veritable fairy-spectacle set in the midst of a dark and deserted world. Merely to look at them glimmering *and* gleaming down Sixth avenue or Broadway after all unnecessary lights had been turned off evoked a warmth of soul and a promise of joy that must have lured, alas! I know not how many good men of the cloth on their belated errands of spiritual comfort to the joyous damnation of their souls.

III

Some men's first memories of the happy, unbuttoned life of the appetites may go back to grandma's puddings, others to the first little girls they kissed behind the sofa, while still others may remember their birth in sin as a surreptitious pull at father's pipe while the old man was frisking a drink of whiskey out of the medicine-closet. My own first memory of the Larger Life is on a more nearly epical scale. It is of Pop Ziegler's saloon at Eighth and Berks streets, in Philadelphia. At the age of five we moved to within three doors of this great neighborhood amusement cathedral (for there were no motion pictures, uptown theatres, radios or jazz parlors in those days, and any one who possessed even a telephone or a typewriter was what Pop called a *Grossmaul*). He kept a real, old-fashioned lager-beer saloon. In Summer (he was a tremendous, be-whiskered beer-barrel of a Fafner) he used to run his establishment openly and himself unashamedly, for he never had any glazed windows and he always appeared in nothing more than an old pair of trousers and an undershirt which never had any buttons.

In cataleptic awe, I used to stand at the door and watch Pop lining up hundreds of handles of beer. The foam from the glasses tan over everything, for he would have nothing to do with the new-fangled sud-shavers that were coming into use in the aristocratic downtown saloons. As a result, his bar was a Bridal Veil Falls. Pop himself was an eclectic. From seven in the morning until midnight he drank beer, whiskey and brandy. I used to watch him from the street doing his colossal stunts with the Twentieth Ward Falstaffs that lined his bar. That was my movie, and I dreamed of the day—and it came, for I lived on the block for fifteen years—when I could stand before this mighty, good-natured god and laugh and spit without let or hindrance just as he did.

Ziegler was one of those gorgeous ancients who lived without thought of the morrow, whose to-day was a seventeen-hour feast in honor of Gambrinus and Barleycorn, and whose yesterdays went into oblivion through his nether waste-pipes. On a stove at the back of his saloon he cooked meat-balls, fish-balls and corn on the cob. We boys used to run in the back way from the alley once in a while and filch a meat-ball from the stove. This amused Pop immensely—and it all came back to him in family orders for bottled beer and from alley growler runners. I do not remember ever to have seen or heard of a fight in Pop's place. It was one of hundreds of thousands of similar shrines throughout the country. Chester A. Arthur, with a full cellar, was in the White House, Grover Cleveland was putting away the stuff in Albany. All was well with Our Country.

Ah! the delicious odor of tripe and pigs' feet that greeted one on entering Gus and Frank's Old Halfway House, in West Thirty-fifth street, New York! This was one of the middle-of-the block saloons that held their own for decades against the cloak-and-suit invasion. Drinkers came from many blocks around to *Gus* and Frank's sawdust-and-sand arena. Gus was tall and looked something like the late Dan Daly, while Frank was a fat, happy pate. Schooners were a nickel, and good, healthy red-eye was a dime. Pigs' knuckles, sauerkraut and immense hot dogs were served all day at ten cents a plate. Between the whiskey bottles at the back there stood for some years a photograph of a soldier in the blue of the Union Army. It was Papa Frank (neither Gus nor Frank had a last name that I can now recall), "who fought mit Sigel." My whole being drips with mnemonic rapture over the pickles that Gus and Frank gave away. Gigantic, succulent Zeppelins lifted out of a tub of ice-water! A mouthful of beer and then a bite, another mouthful and then another bite, and so on, until my whole internal being became so highly and poignantly ecstasized, my esophagus became such a Ninth Symphony of fleshly hallelujahs, that I am sure I must have lost my place in line at the Second Advent.

A type of saloon which all Broadway will remember with purling gullets was the so-called business men's lunch. It began at the Battery and punctuated every block to Twenty-third street. Outside of these places there generally dangled a big slate. Chalked on it were sausages, krauts, stews, soups, rare cuts, and other lures to the bar, where one sat on a high stool and for ten to twenty cents got one's fill of business men's food (a little tougher than Olympian guttle) and all the drinks one could carry for a nickel or a dime apiece. There were about forty such places from the Battery to Twenty-third street, and I was sib and hep to about ten of them, the best being Solly's, somewhere near Reade street. To describe the mosaics of beer, whiskey and twelve different kinds of foods that I have inlaid at noon or as the shades of e'en-tide fell while a-squat on one of Solly's leather-capped stools would require a miraculous upswirl of my early dithyrambic style, which deserted me when Holy Man Bryan *successfully* walked the sea of grape-juice in 1920. Solly himself was of the old school. He did his own bar-tending and food-digging, and with meticulous conscientiousness. He was always shaved and groomed to a whisper, his big black mustache lolling all over his lower face. I have never seen such politeness and *savoir-faire,* even in movie European drawing-rooms.

In the financial district the aristocratic sideboard bar flourished. A single small sideboard often of rare wood—was all there was to it. A butler of stern phiz and in demi-evening clothes opened mysterious doors for your special label. He made your favorite cocktail with the concentration and seriousness of an idealist confecting a new republic. He never spoke unless he was spoken to, and then with a high-class accent and a Ward McAllister smile. I regret the passage of these sideboard bars, for I always patronized them on the days that I was a gentleman. They, too, will return with the Renaissance, I hope.

Lipton's saloon, at Park Row and Nassau street under the old *Times* Building, was a famous newspaper hang-out until the very year that the Blue-Nozzle Curse fell on us. This eminent saloon formed an arcade from Nassau street to Park Row and was presided over by Pat Croley, who could tell the city editors of the *World,* the *Sun,* the *Press,* the *Times* and the *Tribune* just what their reporters and copy-readers were doing—just how much and far they were doing it, too—at any hour of the day. It was a House of Call. When we got tired of *standing* at the bar we used to put our drinks on the floor and sit on the bar-rail. There were booths with victuals for the newspaper intelligentsia, but these were patronized only by Don Marquis, Frank O'Malley and other such three-figure check men.

A homey saloon on the Bowery was Pat Farley's place at Canal street. Pat's theory was that nobody could possibly make a whiskey that was worth fifteen cents. He was an Irishman of parts, would tolerate no obscenities or the use of the Saviour's name in his place, and always passed around five-cent Henry George cigars after the third round with a "Have one on the house, gentlemen." When the day approached the vespers hour Irish stews appeared mysteriously from under the bar and a dainty fishball was aimed at you on a fork. The place was secretly open all night for newspaper men, politicians and the quieter sort of Bowery actors. I never saw a disturbance there, and I was actually present when Pat quietly asked Big Jack Zelig to take his trade elsewhere.

IV

If I could transport some millions of the adolescent generation back to those gorgeous all-mirror, circular-bar palaces they would, in mere esthetic frenzy, decree the instant return of the saloon when they came to exercise the inalienable right of every American pussy-head. For those of us who couldn't do Europe such establishments were the Versailles Hall of Mirrors and the Crystal Palace. Their great virtue was that they drove men from home, From mud-colored wallpaper and Brussels carpets made up-State, with their holes and baby-spots, to Jerry Donohue's marble floor, glistening mirrors, shining rosewood and impeccable glasses in pyramids, cones and squares—that was many a man's retreat from the thought of murder or suicide. I do not speak of the bars in the big hotels, generally frequented by Westerners and Southerners who came to New York to get bawling, crawling drunk and then return to their Methodist lairs with tales of the wicked Sodom-on-Hudson. Such bars never belonged, not even the one at the Knickerbocker or that at the Imperial. They had an alien air.

Thousands will no doubt recall two of the most celebrated all-night saloons in New York. They both operated under the ten-dollar all-night license, which I hope to see come back also with the return of the saloon. One of these places was Furthmann's, at the corner of Forty-second street and Seventh avenue. The bar was circular. I have done a total revolution around it in two hours, dragging my satellitic drinks with me. When the place was packed the motion was slower; it then took three hours for a normally laden planet to demonstrate that Galileo was right after all. I have seen a gorgeous necklace of jewelled drinks around Furthmann's bar—rainbow-tinct pousse cafés, cardinal Manhattans, amber Ehrets, opalescent absinthe frappes, heart-bleeding clarets, saffron highballs, incarnadine Bourbons, with the lights beating down so fiercely that you could see all the freckles on the brain of Pat the bartender.

The other place was Tim Shine's, at the corner of Thirty-sixth street and Sixth avenue, opposite James Gordon Bennett's daily ship-news bulletin, the New York *Herald,* whose proprietor, be it said in reverence to his shade, never discouraged drink in himself or others. We inmates of the *Herald* worked exclusively and in twenty-four shifts for Bennett and Tim. The corner was famous for forty years. The saloon was originally the lair of Paddy the Pig (né O'Brien), whose Negro bartender, Bob, was a continuous commuter between the bar and Blackwell's Island. Tim took over the place after Paddy and Bob went a-frisking for the watches and gold cigarette-cases of the angels, tore it out, threw on the lights (Paddy, like all deep, brooding thinkers, liked drawn curtains day and night) and made it the most famous corner *salon de joie* in New York. It was in Tim's, one morning, that Corse Payton, who by his own confession is America's best bad actor, swapped a pup and his pants belt for a collection of South American postage stamps.

Nor will the old-timers ever forget Andy Horn's place at the New York entrance to Brooklyn Bridge. Andy's bar never closed except for a few hours on Sunday morning (a slight but well-meant tribute to God), when he put everybody upstairs. Straight drinks here, no lunch of any kind, and mind your own business! The Bridge crooks were always out in force around Andy's place. This gave it a tang. Nothing, to me at least, is more pleasurable than to have a small slant on and know that murder or a dirty deed is in the atmosphere. To be on the *qui vive,* to suspect the guy standing next to you at the bar, to know that one word may cause an explosion—those great days are gone. Now, our lives are so safe that life is hardly worth living. Murders and accidents to-day are drab. The saloon was Expectancy. It was Adventure. It was the Unknown. It was the romance of everyday. And until *Eggnog* Monday, the bock-beer signs, the May-wine cards and the swinging doors are seen again in the land, we shall drift lower and lower in the stews of peace.

But the saloon is coming back. It was prophesied of old in the Blessed Book, Psalm II, 1 :

"Why do the nunkey-donkeys rage and their leaders imagine a vain thing like Prohibition in New York?"

Lüchow's

I took a walk and got as far as Lüchow's. —JAMES HUNEKER.

THAT walk was taken in 1886, on the same day that the future Stee-plejack of the Seven Arts took up his permanent residence in New York at the Morton House, at the corner of Broadway and Four-teenth street. August Lüchow had then had the place for four years. Lüchow's beer-house, kept by an old German couple, was several doors to the westward. This latter was Huneker's first stopping place, so the walk was merely out of one saloon into another.

This was the classical way of walking in Fourteenth street in those golden days. One simply walked from beer-saloon to beer-saloon, and in the Summer from beer-garden to beer-garden. Fourteenth street was as completely beer and pretzels as Maiden lane was diamonds and Baxter street second-hand clothing. From river to river it was one vast beer gullet, one great river of malt, the alimentary canal of Gambrinus.

All these places were run by Germans, Austrians or Hungarians. Pretzels, cheese, sausage and pickles were given away with dripping schooners of cold beer that cost five cents. Almost every saloon had a piano in the back room. In fact, Fourteenth street at the time of Huneker's walk was not only the beer centre of the town but also its musical centre, for hard by Lüchow's and Lienau's there were Stein-way Hall and the office of the *Musical Courier,* not to speak of the old Academy of Music.

Another walk. Ten years after Huneker's entry into Lüchow's—a place he was to be entering regularly for thirty-five years afterward—I, having cast my first presidential vote for Bryan, free silver and the salvation of the *chandala,* felt, like any other young Philadelphian, that my manhood would not be complete without seeing New York. For a Philadelphian to visit New York for the first time is to experience a second puberty.

An old rummy who worked on Alec McClure's *Times* and who declared that in his New York days he had often got drunk with Henry Ward Beecher, drew up for me a Baedeker of New York in which the only public building that he wanted me to see was Tammany Hall. All the rest of the points of interest were beer saloons, gin-mills and what were known in those tongue-tied days as houses of ill fame. Tammany Hall was described as being "cata-cornered from Lüchow's and three doors west of Carl's place at the corner of Third avenue and Fourteenth street." I asked him what and who was Lüchow's.

"It's a place," said McClure's best drunken reporter, "where you get beer that'll make blond hair grow on your esophagus and your gizzard sing 'Die Wacht am Rhein'". That sounded fine to me, for even at that early age I was an adept and conscientious beer drinker.

I rounded into Fourteenth street at Third avenue and walked straight to Lüchow's, giving Tammany Hall and Tony Pastor's a negligible once-over. I had reserved my thirst from the time I landed at Liberty street. As it was a warm November day and I had walked up from downtown via the blatant Bowery, I had a regular horsehair edge on.

As I entered the place the cells of my pylorus and the psychons of my memory clicked, for my maternal grandmother was born in Munich, and so my hereditary will-to-guzzle chortled with the delight of recognition. In Philadelphia, I saw at a glance, there was no such place as Lüchow's. The dark wood, the high ceiling, the ultra-Teutonic waiters, the dripping bar, the mounded free lunch, the heavenly odor of pig's knuckles, sauerkraut and *Paprika Schnitzel*—all these things saturated me with an indescribable feeling of contentment.

I anchored at the bar and discovered at once that the quality and the upkeep of the beer in the place were all that my crapulous newspaper friend had told me. As it went down—*Seidel* after *Seidel*—every atom of my body bloomed with radiant philanthropy. Dill pickles and tiny raw onions burst in my throat and sprayed my brain with a fine tickle. I guzzled not like an epicurean—an epicurean is always an invalid, a flannel-belly —but like a healthy animal, like a man who salutes his gullet, his tongue, his appetite, his thirst, reverently and joyously. I was then and there a Lüchower forevermore. *Hoch!* I went straight back from Lüchow's to the Twenty-third street ferry in a four-wheeler, singing at the top of my voice. That was all I saw of New York on my first visit. I never got above Lüchow's. I believe I topped Huneker's walk.

II

Still another walk, thirty-five years later. I walked down Irving place, where, facing that famous street of famous people, Lüchow's still stands like a Memory surveying ruins.

Everything in the district has changed except Lüchow's. Its three-story, buff-colored, quiet exterior, with its lace-curtained windows and its refined air, is in striking contrast to the blatant, blarish, blowsy note of modernity that surrounds it. In place of the old saloons and beer-halls—such as the Alhambra Garden, which was only a few yards east—we now have tango gardens, chop-suey dumps, cheap music-stores where radios spew all over the sidewalks the Morton Downey and Rudy Vallee caterwaulings (on the very sites where on back-room pianos or in Steinway Hall Joseffy, Huneker, Sternberg and Neupert used to play Music!), fly-blown cafeterias, gutter vaudeville, putrid speakeasy bars, and all the other appurtenances of cheapjack Prohibition America and a New York gone Main Street.

The ancient gayety of Fourteenth street has departed, and in its place there is the hectic, convulsive, drooling, lickerish look of an old man trying to simulate a youthful gayety with a smelly glandular serum bought in some shady drugstore. Lüchow's is about the only dignified place in sight. To me—as I stood looking at it on this particular afternoon from in front of the Consolidated Gas Company building across the street—it seemed to be a symbol, an admonition, a kind of funeral oration on our lost liberties, our lost gayety.

And as my imagination is always a thousand horse-power stronger than my sense of reality, I flung down the walls and the gin-sodden nineteen-twenties with them, and saw again a beer-happy humanity seated at tables or standing at the bar in a Lüchow's that blew the bung out of the carcass of Care and drowned in millions of gallons of Pilsner and Würzburger the rotting hulks of Work and Worry. I heard again the shouts and laughter of the beer-laden and the mirthful hosannas of millions of dill pickles and squares of cheese as they committed euthanasia in beery tidal-waves in hundreds of thousands of laughter-quaking stomachs.

I heard again the guffaws that lasted for hours when one was a-sosh with this blessed stuff that made Lüchow and beer as completely synonymous as Strauss and waltz or ale and England—festal howls, yowls and grunts, tornadoes, hurricanes and simoons of unleashed and boundless gayety from fat German faces as round as the moon gone cockeyed, and as delightfully silly as God's universe.

And the dishes—the palate-thrilling, belly-ravishing dishes—that Lüchow's served in those days! Perhaps the most famous was *Hannoverische Kalbsschnitzel mit Steinpilzen*. Marry this to two *Seidel* of Pilsner or Würzburger and not only was God in his Heaven but you would even concede the divinity of Theodore Roosevelt. Then there were *Rinderbrust mit Meerettig*, or *Rinderbrust gedämpft, en casserole;* grilled *Bratwurst mit Sauerkraut, Sauerbraten mit Kartoffelklösse,* and *Gänseweissauer mit Bratkartoffeln.* These were only a few of the masterpieces that Lüchow was famous for. Oh, yes—let me not forget *Hamburger Kücken in der Pfanne gebraten mit Gemüsen,* one of my favorites, to be flooded only with Würzburger. Or *lunge Taube mit Spargel.*

Lüchow's drew the finest class of patronage, not only from all over New York but from every section of the country. The very name of the place had the power of making one hungry, thirsty and mouth-watery. It conjured up images that directly affected the most delicate cells of the body. I had but to say Lüchow's if I were in Harlem with some of the boys—and we were on a Third avenue elevated in two minutes, bound to Fourteenth street!

Contemplating the street as it is to-day, I recalled my own nights of laughter in this place, when Baron Sinzig, George Luks and myself have laughed to the screaming point—those insane waves of beery mirth where you cry, "Oh, my God!," "Stop, or I'll die!," "My belly's bursting!" the wild, care-free, Dionysian, fulgurating, cleansing hysteria that is in malt and hops, my eucharist, wherein I partook of the blood and body of Immanent Joy. I used to rock for hours with gayety in my mellow Pilsner stews, my soul the buffoon of Gambrinus, my face twisted to ridiculous grins or convulsed as if a bomb filled with the Devil's laughing-powder had exploded in my brain.

This is the laugh that's gone out of the American soul forever—the laugh that's in beer and Rhine wines. As I left the corner after putting back the walls of Lüchow's I uttered an anathema on Prohibition and those who brought it about which, could it have been recorded, would have certainly landed my carcass in the same coffin that Benedict Arnold occupies.

III

Guido August Lüchow, a Hanoverian, was called to this country in his early twenties. He started at Stewart's place, in Duane street, in 1879. Stewart's was at that time one of the best-known saloons downtown, celebrated for its excellent domestic beers, its imported wines, and the proprietor's penchant for expensive oils, which decorated the walls. It was in existence until the war, and may still be serving food for all I know. What happens below Fourteenth street has never interested me very much—it is too commercial, even the drinking and eating. August must have felt, as a waiter reared in the good old German dogma that beer and wine and good food were put on earth to make us forget business, that his destiny lay uptown further, where there were music, actors and Laughter.

At this time a certain Baron von Mehlbach had been doing an almost one hundred percent beer business on the same site that is now Lüchow's. His establishment was only about an eighth the size of the present place, which runs all the way back to Thirteenth street (in those days and even up to the beginning of the Twentieth Century a thoroughfare notorious for its vast number of ladies of uneasy virtue, both housed and free lance). Young August took a job in the baron's place as bartender and waiter in 1880. The baron—probably only a beer baron—was getting old, had cleaned up a tidy fortune in Fourteenth street, and wanted to end his days in a native beer vat in Munich. He saw in Lüchow just the sort of fellow to succeed him as papa to the beer-buddies who patronized his place, and in 1882 he sold out the saloon to the thrifty August.

So down came MEHLBACH and up went LÜCHOW on the front window in the one-hundredth-and-sixth year of American Independence, the thirty-eighth year before the Bootleg Amendment, the thirty-seven hundredth year of King Gambrinus' reign on earth, the year one of Chester A. Arthur and his sideboards in the White House, and the twenty-sixth year of August Lüchow's life. *Hoch!, Prosit and Gesundheit!*

There are several self-evident truths that escaped Thomas Jefferson. One of them is that an honest seller of food and drink is the noblest work of God. When to this honesty is joined a scrupulous regard for clean beer pipes, then we have Civilization Triumphant. We had it, generally, in the old German saloonkeeper before the Stinkball Amendment. We had it preeminently in August Lüchow, the most famous—and certainly, in the annals of New York thirst, the only immortal—of these beer dispensers; the meticulous honesty of a man proud of his business, proud of his association with the word beer, and proud of the fact that nothing was ever misrepresented either in liquids or food in his place. His pride was the pride of the artist, the *maestro*.

He lived in a time when it was inconceivable that people could ever cultivate a palate for poisonous drinks, as they have to-day. If Prohibition is ever knocked out, it will take a whole generation of Americans to rediscover the taste for fine beers, wines and liquors. (A young friend of mine who is a post-Amendment drinker, belonging to the generation that knows only speakeasy beers, wines and liquors, got deathly ill several times on his first European trip from drinking pure beers, ales and whiskies.)

Lüchow knew, of course, the inferiority of the American beer to the German article. They used to tell me that the difference was in the water. What it really was I never knew, for I have never concerned myself with analyzing why I like or dislike things. But American beer always left a brassy taste in my mouth, while Pilsner and Würzburger (of which I have drunk enough to drown both Dayton, Tennessee, and Westerville, Ohio) never carried that taste with them. Pilsner, especially, was, to me, always like drinking moonlight.

It was as early in his career as 1885 that Lüchow, greatly concerned over the threat to the American kidney (for we Americans are naturally adulterators and cutters of everything), became the American agent for Würzburger and later one of the American agents for Pilsner. He wasn't the first man to import German beers, but he was the first to popularize them, to found a genuine Pilsner and Würzburger cult—so much so that a song was written about thirty years ago in honor of him and his place called "Down Where the Würzburger Flows" (which I have sung exactly 2,841 times at 1,718 bars):

Rhine wine it is fine,
But a big stein for mine,
Down where the Würzburger flows!

The whole country danced it and sang it. It promised to nose out "The Star-Spangled Banner" as the national anthem. Lüchow himself remarked at the time, "I feel like a kind of Beer Columbus!"

Along came also, about this time, or a little later, a musical comedy, "The Prince of Pilsen," the music of which is still played over the radio. It helped to make Lüchow immortal. Würzburger and Pilsner were Europe's greatest gifts to America, and, personally, if I had the power I'd junk the Statue of Liberty and put in its place a colossal effigy of Guido August Liichow, with an o'erflowing *Seidel* of Würzburger held high in one hand and a *Seidel* of Pilsner in the other, and crown his head with a wreath of pretzels, for greater love hath no man than to preserve the kidneys of his brother. Pilsner preserved mine, and therefore will *I shout* hallelujah to his *name until I am* forever beyond the reach of that *eau de skunk* which we call beer to-day.

The domestic beer (up until the war) that Liichow sold was negligible. He had one tap for transients who rustled in and shouted "Gimme a beer!" and slung it in in the usual American fashion. Why try to save the livers of pigs? The old German beers should be allowed to sing on the palate, fiddle arpeggios on the tonsils and gurgle ecstatic God-bless-yous as they glide slowly down the esophagus. No good beer is ever drunk; it is consumed. It isn't swallowed; it is ingurgitated. It is a softly lapping, shoreless sea on which float millions of happy dill-pickles.

For that portion of the rising generation that is naturally beer-minded; for those Boy Scouts, still uncorrupted by the teachings of their scoutmasters, who have latently in them the beer-and-ale thirst of the Fathers of the Republic; for all those who have grown up this side of the Feculent Eighteenth and to whom these things of which I speak are Eleusinian mysteries, I must write it down that Pilsner was a light beer and Würzburger a dark. But it probably means nothing to you who were born under the dynasty of the Bootleg Borgias. For while Lüchow was a real man and Lüchow's was (and is) a real place, they are also symbols and slogans of a Lost Cause. The future historian will date the transformation of the Republic into an Imperial Plutocracy from the Spanish-American War, and the transformation of what was the finest democracy the world has ever known into an Oligarchical Plunderbund from the day the selling of beer was declared a crime. For me, a beer drinker for many years, it was the Second Fall of Man.

Going back to the matter of domestic and imported beers, or the distinction between such places as Lüchow's and the Hofbräuhaus and the common corner saloon, there was a great difference the next morning. A night's bout with the purely domestic product, of miscellaneous breeds and species, left you filthy, with a tackhammer going in your head and your heart pounding and yelping for a dose of *Schnapps*. But after a night of Pilsner (and I seldom drank anything else) I used to be as fresh as a Dutch cherub the morning after, my metabolic contraptions all dressed up for—more Pilsner!

Lüchow was also a connoisseur of and importer of wines. These he bought in person in his trips back to Europe—Förster Jesuitengarten, Deidesheimer, Eltviller Sonnenberg, Rüdesheimer Berg, Niersteiner, Rauenthaler and how many others, from the humble Laubenheimer at $1.50 a quart to Steinberger Tröckenbeer at $25! In all the years that I patronized Lüchow's I do not recall ever seeing hard liquor on a table. It was sometimes asked for and served at the bar—especially the pre-brandial cocktail. But whiskey at Lüchow's seemed as out of place as a stein of Würzburger on Tom Sharkey's bar, further down the block. However, a pony of brandy after dinner was often seen, August himself sometimes topping off his dinner with one.

Personally, he was one of the finest types of Germans—or Europeans, for that matter—that ever came to this country. For my part, you can have your Baron Steuben, your Franz Sigel, your Carl Schurz, and even your Lafayette—give me the European who raises the level and sharpness of our pleasures, who brings with him Continental manners and the unbuttoned, un-puritanical conception of life. Freedom and liberty end with Prohibition. The two most civilized men who ever came to New York were August Lüchow and Henri Mouquin.

Lüchow was a joyous, overflowing, live-and-let-live fellow. He fairly glistened with good nature. The main characteristics of his face—at least in his middle years—were honesty and merriment. In later years, as you may note by the hand-painted oil painting (with a pouring electric light on it) that now hangs on the wall of the restaurant, a somewhat severer and more settled look came over him. Good fellowship costs like everything else in this world; but it is a payment always given without regret. For myself, I might say with Nathan Hale, that my only regret is that I have not four kidneys to give to the service of Gambrinus. And to that sentiment I think I hear August Lüchow from the *Rathskeller* of the Mansion in the Skies shout *"la wohl!"*

He was not a man for stunts; but he pulled off one that attracted great attention at the time. It was typically Augustan. When Prince Henry and his party left America on March 11, 1902, Lüchow chartered a river steamer almost the size of the old *Grand Republic*, rolled on board enough imported beer and wines to irrigate forever the God-forsaken State of Kansas and invited everybody to get on board who had a mind to trail Henry out to sea. Was there a party? A German band, mountains of frankfurters, pyramids of sauerkraut, *und—und—und—Well, Gott im Himmel!*, there has never been a real floating beer party since. Nobody remembers coming back. *To-ho-yo!*

As all his employees will testify to-day, Lüchow was an extremely charitable man. Next to the upkeep of his place, his passion was enjoying the society of his friends. He never married, which probably added to his popularity. His only romance was Beer and Friendship. He lived with his sister, who looked after him like a mother. He died in 1923, leaving behind him an institution the character and flavor of which I here attempt to convey, although it would take the pen of a Huysmans and the brush of a Hals to do it rightly.

IV

There was nothing Broadwayish about Lüchow's. On entering I always got a sense of vastness. The center room was very large and open, a sort of closed beer-garden. In the old days the smell of Würzburger seeped all through you as you passed the door. As you got deeper and deeper into the place, with its many rooms, your cells were beered up before you even got your face into a *Seidel*. There was a pastry-counter opposite the bar. I recall at least five pantrymen in the busy hours cutting off great hunks of cheesecake. There was a constant non-stop flight between the bar and the lunch counter.

It had a family air, enhanced by the wholesome, kermess-looking faces of Lüchow and his raft of German waiters. Everybody drank leisurely, as though he or she had nothing else on earth to do. (Indeed, what is a worthier occupation in a world invented by some insane Tyl Eulenspiegel than the drinking of fine beers?) The air was always one of freedom and good-will. Papa Lüchow, if he knew you, would take a seat with you and inject a remark—and a round of beers.

In the evening the Vienna Art Quartette played some of the best music I have ever heard. Indeed, Lüchow's to this day carries on the high musical traditions of old Fourteenth street and its famous patrons of the past, who included De Pachmann, Caruso, Paderewski, Ysaye, Dvořák, Richard Strauss, Victor Herbert, Rafael Joseffy, the De Reszkes, and almost everybody else you can think of. Jazz has never been heard in the place.

About twenty-five years ago Louis Zucker, the pianist of the quartette, was killed by a Third avenue cable car. Another pianist took his place in ten minutes. The present conductor is Edward Fink, who has been at the piano for nineteen years. Everybody who goes to Lüchow's knows him as Ed. I have heard him smash out Liszt and Wagner in a way that actually caused me to stop drinking my Pilsner. The quartette always gets a big hand and is profuse with encores.

Irving place, which has housed in the past more famous persons in the arts than probably any other street of only five blocks in the world, poured its beer-thirsty crowds into Lüchow's night and day. The place was the headquarters, of course, of Heinrich Conried and his German actors in the old Irving Place Theatre, now given over to legs and painted barkers. The Steinway Room on the second floor Lüchow made over to the employees and patrons of old Steinway Hall. I never had the privilege of attending any of the feasts there, but my old friend Baron Ferdinand Sinzig, of the House of Steinway, used to regale me for hours with tales of the gay jinks in the room. It was this same beloved Baron Sinzig—whose beer-feats I am never tired of recording—who had a record of thirty-six *Seidel* of Würzburger in Lüchow's—*without rising!* A native of Cologne, he was absolutely kidneyless. And it was this same Sinzig who gave a piano recital in Rumford Hall, and who, after playing three pieces with three encores, told the audience the recital was over, as he had an engagement with Anton Seidl at Lüchow's. But he went on, as his manager, refusing to see the pun, threatened him with a black eye after apologizing to the audience.

In another room on the second floor the famous Bohemians were organized by Rafael Joseffy and James Huneker. The Society of Authors and Composers, still in existence, was also organized at Lüchow's.

Of the dreams that were dreamed and the stories that were told there over oceans of Würzburger and Pilsner there is no record.

One hears of only one unpleasant incident in the whole history of the place. Let its hero tell it himself. The story appears in Huneker's fascinating autobiography, "Steeplejack":

One night at Lüchow's, sitting with Ed Ziegler, August—Himself—Joseffy and De Pachmann, an argument was started. De

Pachmann, who had been especially irritable, turned vicious, and spitting out his rage—he was a feline person—he called Joseffy an unprintable name. Before Joseffy could answer the villainous attack, I, with a recklessness unusual for me, let the Chopinzee have the contents of my glass full in the face. If I had been sitting closer I would have slapped his mouth; as it was, the wetting might cleanse it. Sputtering, he was led away by a waiter and presently returned, smiling as if nothing had happened. Joseffy was disgusted with me, as well he might be. It was unpardonable, my conduct, and I promptly apologized. Then De Pachmann explained it was jealousy, as I had mentioned Joseffy's name seven times more —he gave the exact figure—than his in my Chopin book. It sounded childish, but it dissolved the disagreeable business into laughter. After all had gone away except Ziegler, Joseffy turned to me and severely reproached me, but ended his sermon thus: "And you, of all men, wasting such a lot of good beer!" I can recall the diabolic twinkle in his eye yet.

Mr. Victor Eckstein, the present proprietor of Lüchow's, still points out the exact spot where this took place. He was present, although not sitting in. Mr. Eckstein has been in Lüchow's for thirty years, and so great is his reverence for his old boss that he named his son Guido August Lüchow Eckstein.

To-day Lüchow's is run precisely as it was in the days of its founder. It still serves excellent food, the old waiters are there to wait on you, the quartette still gives you Liszt and Wagner—all is there except the one important thing—German beer. In the middle of the restaurant stands a ten-gallon stein, which I hope to drain at one draught the day Lüchow's puts in German beer again.

The place has the air of waiting for a miracle. Standing before the picture of August Lüchow recently I was conscious of almost saying out loud—"waiting for a miracle!" The lips of the picture opened and I distinctly heard come forth, *"Apfelmus!"*

Mouquin's

THE Legend of the Free City of New York quickens in the arteries of the national imagination. Wherever three New Yorkers meet beyond the boundaries of the greater town tales are exchanged and round boasts are uttered and Rabelaisian laughter is heard and deeds of alcoholic derring-do are thundered of pre-1920 New York. For it was in that year, *mes enfants* of the present gin-sodden, stomach-boil generation, that the happy Atlantis of our memories disappeared in a tidal-wave of Methodist waterbrash, and the New York of brutal senility, poisoned beers and whiskeys, female bar-flies, cesspools called speakeasies, and Blossomy Youth with a Kansas sour-breath rose in its place.

Great booze legends of the Big Town are in the building. They may some day rival the Thousand and One Nights, the Niebelungenlied, or the Song of Roland. I hear, in my prophetic ear, children who still repose in the womb of the Noble Experiment, children who will be born when America is a Gunman's Sparta, children who will be alive in the reign of Vachel Lindsay's Cocaine Buddha and Slick-Slack Kopenskys—I hear them whimpering at the knee of some ham-sagging centenarian uncle, "Tell me a tale, uncle, of the days of Mouquin's, Lüchow's, Jack's, Joel's; of Terrace Garden; of the good Prince Burgundy, of the Fairy Princess Absinthe, of the big fat Gambrinus, of the funny clown Gin Rickey, of the playmate of all the world, Little Sauterne; of the mighty deeds done nightly in the great Castles of Laughter in Broadway and Sixth avenue." And I hear the old gaffer, one of the few survivors of the Booze Bull Run of 1920, begin once again his bedtime story of the magical wine-sacks and human beer-bungs of pre-pussyfoot New York. And I see the dear little ones in that hideous era of communistic Cromwells going into Blanket Bay murmuring, with seraphic looks on their faces, Mouquin! Lüchow! Burgundy! Sauterne! Pilsner!

As for me, the word Mouquin evokes, as it must do in thousands of others, a magic, a charm, a warmth that neither Lüchow, Jack, Joel, Martin, Breevort nor Hofbräu can evoke. I am flooded with the sorcery of bibulous exaltation when I conjure up that building at Twenty-eighth street and Sixth avenue whereinto I entered a three-dimensional buttoned-up being and departed a five-dimensional wide-open bacchant for nearly twenty years. The other places bring me pleasant enough recollections, but the image of Mouquin's causes the detonation in me of thousands of tiny wine-cells; and the men I knew, the songs I sang, the talk I talked and the grins I grinned become transfigured in an ocean of gushing red and white wines to something akin to a hasheesh dream, wherein I can hear myself shouting in mingled rage and ecstasy: *Ave,* Mouquineers!—To arms, Burgundians, Sauternians, Pommardians, Chambertins and Saint Juliens! *Evohé,* Mouquineers—arise from your *châteaux* and *caves* for one more revel of iced buckets and carafons while we hang in the middle of the big room upstairs the last Baptist parson with a rope made of the ticker-tape of the last Methodist bishop!

And we'll crown Papa Henri Mouquin in his ninety-fifth year—a veritable Bacchic Methuselah!—Prince of Hosts, and then drench him in Chateau la Tour Blanche and Chablis Moutonne!

II

The elements of this unique quality of magic which bathed Mouquin's uptown place and set it apart from any other French, German or American restaurant in New York were frivolity, a total absence of all formality, *cameraderie,* the subtle suggestions that came to the nostrils and the eye of wines, wines shimmering and winking at you in every conceivable kind of glass; the wall-mirrors and shiny marble-topped tables in the famous café downstairs, and, above all, the feeling that soaked into you on entering that here was a place where business was never discussed. One entered Mouquin's to shed all forms of seriousness. Here was the real Abbey Thélème of New York: *Do as thou wilt!*

Mouquin's was essentially and profoundly French—hence a wine house, although excellent German beers could be had there. It was the Left Bank in New York. No matter at what time you entered the door blasts of gayety came to you from the tables. The quality of intoxication varies. There are exquisite degrees and kinds of it. I believe in the Spirit of Place; therefore I believe that one place will produce a form entirely different from another place. The faces of the beer fanatics in Lüchow's were blithe but yet somehow serious; in the Hofbräuhaus you heard the bituminous Kulmbacher guffaw; in Joel's the plastered looked sinister and perverse; in Jack's their faces were either split with a furious, insane laughter or drawn up like a pill—ready to give up the ghost. But in Mouquin's the quality of intoxication was always vinous—which is to say, radiant. Every face sang. There one always found that lightness, that mobility, that *gaieté de coêur,* that dancing, Dionysian will-to-folly that can only be discovered among the Latins, and which those two super-Latin non-Latins—Erasmus and Nietzsche—declared to be the profoundest of wisdoms.

Even during the war, with many of the waiters' sons at the front, with many of the waiters themselves at the front—Mouquin's had seventy-six volunteers from the uptown, downtown and wholesale places in four years, many of whom never returned—the gayety went on unabated, the wines flowed as they had never flowed before, and "Sambre et Meuse" and "Lorraine" rang out every night over thousands of bottles that also had contained the blood of France Wine!

No two things are farther apart in the world ethnologically (except it be an Esquimo and a Hottentot) than Americanism and Latinity. The Yankee is nearer the Jew than he is to the Mediterranean man. He has affinities with every race in Europe except the Latin. To him France, Italy and Spain, with their old cultures, their noble art, their spacious concepts of life, their heroic drinking habits, are Original Sin. Our "friendship" with France is the most ridiculous piece of hypocrisy I know of. I have never met a blown-in-the-bone American who was in France during the war (or since) who doesn't secretly, or overtly, hate France and all Frenchmen. The cause? The American hates everything that is not bootleg—everything that is open, loose, amoral. He hates genius, the imagination, beauty, mirth. Why again?

Because it is the opposite of Work, the Moloch-god of the Nordic countries.

This was one of the reasons why Mouquin's spelled magic to me. It was a retreat from America. It was going back home. It was getting away from my accidental self to my real self. It was release. I frequented Mouquin's for the same reason that New York is the only city in this country I would live in—because it is non-American. And this is what drew thousands of Americans to this great French house: the desire to taste, even artificially, the Latin spirit. But the hundred percenters who went there, even many of the soil artists and writers, never seemed to fit into the place. They plainly didn't belong. They managed to feel at home in any other restaurant in New York, even the Brevoort, the Lafayette or Lüchow's; but in Mouquin's they plainly had the air of slumming, just as the Kansas Crô-Magnon has when he tours France.

What added to this perpetual magic of place in the eye of all real Mouquineers (and must have been an added stench in the nostrils of all wind-machine patriots) was that the place was the greatest rendezvous for artists, writers, newspaper men and—whew!—poets that America has ever had. Henri Mouquin, his son and his part-ners catered to the men who painted, wrote or mauled granite *a la* Jo Davidson (whose coal-black beard, hair and eyes used to stick out from the marble and the mirrors like a *tête de nègre* in a monstrous charlotte russe, the while his voice boomed the canons of his art and his gullet lowered the drawbridge ever and anon for the passage of another bottle of Clos Vougeot or Volnay Santenot).

I acquired there, from my first visits in 1906, a kind of second innocence of brain and body. When I went to Jack's I went to get soused; when I went to Joel's I went to purloin a girl from the *corps de ballet;* when I went to the Brevoort I went to meet the nuts; when I went to Lüchow's I went to mush in beer and the nimble pig's foot; when I went to the Café Francis I went to sober up—but when I went

to Mouquin's I went for mental and physical levitation; to play bat-
tledore and shuttlecock with Art, Literature, Philosophy, the Cos-
mos and all points south and west; to shut out utilitarian America as
one slams a door in the face of the President, and to watch my face
in the mirror expand from a sucker of a proofreader to a monstrous
wine-bubble.

For Mouquin's had the atmosphere of vinous exaltation and intoxication even if you drank only Vichy Célestins or Saint-Galmier.
It was a secret of the very rafters and beams of the place, which is not
the exaggeration of a divinizer of Bacchus but a literal fact, which I
shall show as we go on with this Tale of Tokay.

III

Henri Mouquin—now living on his farm (on a tract once held by the
Washington family) at Williamsburg, VA., in his ninety-fifth year—
was born at Aubonne, Switzerland, in 1837. Six generations of hotel
proprietors were in back of him, so Henri was born of the grape, for
the grape and by the grape. This salty and witty old man once said to
me: "The celebrated *caves de Mouquin* are really the blood-cells of my
ancestors. I am an old bottle out of those cellars!" He still brags that
as a boy he used to pour the wine for one of the guests at his father's
hotel—Prince Louis Napoleon, afterward Napoleon III. When Henri went to Paris with his parents shortly after the *coup d'etat* he took
up Louis's challenge to come to see him, and he was received by both
the Emperor and Eugenie.

Asked what he was going to do, Henri said he thought of going
to America.

"That's a fine idea, young man," said the Emperor. "I've been there,
and those people are rapidly becoming whiskey sots. Teach them to
drink wine—it will civilize them."

It was, indeed, Henri Mouquin who was first to popularize wine
in America and put it within the reach of everybody's pocket. Before his time it was something for rich men only—something to be
drunk at weddings, balls and inaugural orgies. He performed the
same service for America in the matter of wines that August Lüchow

performed in the matter of sound German beers. But he did it much earlier, for he came to New York in 1854 and established himself in a cellar in Fulton street in the very year that Lüchow was born, 1857.

1859 is generally held to be the most important year in that decade, for in it Darwin published *The Origin of Species*. I will always insist, however, that 1857 was the greater year, for it was then that the Gallic Bacchus and the Teutonic Gambrinus conspired to take us off the old American whiskey diet. If H.M.S. *Beagle* had sunk with Darwin on board it wouldn't have made a particle of difference; but if the boats which carried Henri Mouquin and August Lüchow had sunk, the quantity and quality of joy in New York would have been appreciably changed for the worse in millions of gullets, stomachs and brains.

The importance of our theoretical origins is as nothing compared to the unbelievable *fact* that for years in Mouquin's I drank Beaune, '89, at $1 a quart, Chambertin, '89, at $1.75, Deidesheirner at fifty cents, Chateau Yquem, '94, at $1, Margaux, '90, at seventy-five cents, Chateau la Tour Blanche, '90, at $1.15, and Chablis Mous seux (which was my favorite) at $1.80. As I write this I have before me an old wine and food list. Here are names of drinks and dishes at prices that compel you to believe that once upon a time in New York City God *was* in his Heaven and all was right with My Country 'Tis of Volstead. O ye post-war grown-ups, ye suckers and fungi on the rotting bottom of the old hulk of our liberties, listen to these yarns from that little-while-ago:

Chicken fricasse with rice *a la* Henry IV, forty cents (with a pint of Listrac Medoc, '93, twenty cents extra); broiled English quail with peas *au beurre,* fifty cents (wash it down with a pint of Médoc Supérieur, '93, sixty cents extra). Top off things like these with a cognac, '54, for fifteen cents!

My memory weeps. My parched pylorus weeps. From gizzard to *caput* I'm all Niobe. This Mouquin menu is more precious to me than the signature of Greta Garbo or a newly deciphered Babylonian brick. There are 175 wines on that list, and on each one the eye of my memory rebuilds a Pleasure House that makes the seraglio of Kubla Khan in Xanadu look like a cowhouse in Indiana. The printed letters rise out of their inorganic life and shape themselves into full bottles before me. The corks pop in rhythmic thundertones and I am again at my table in Mouquin's amid the lightning of Chambertin-loosed brains and the tintinnabulation of tongues that Chambolle-Musigny has whipped to *mots* and epigrams minted in the belly of the grape. And nowhere on this wine-list do I see Gordon Gin, the *eau bénite* of our godly Republic.

Mouquin's hadn't been long in Fulton street when his place became a newspaper and political centre. He not only popularized wine but was the first New Yorker to bring down certain famous French delicacies from heaven to earth. Downtown New York during the Civil War began to talk of *bouillabaise,* truffles, *escargots,* French mushrooms, *ceves,* artichokes and mushrooms *sous cloche* and to swallow cheeses that were before the advent of Mouquin only names: Camembert, Gorgonzola, Port du Salut and Pont l'Évêque. And along with these marched the tall Mazagran, hot black coffee in a long glass that one sipped with a spoon. Throw a pony of cognac, '54, into this tumbler and you began to float like a spirit over all your numbed metabolistic machinery. Take three and you were in hypostatic conjunction with what old man Plotinus called the Transcendental Luminosity.

It was here, in the Fulton street place, that Madame Mouquin seventy years ago, then being two years married to Henri, made from her own recipe that onion soup which did so much to make Mouquin's famous. It was the greatest pick-me-up after a night-of-it that my stomach has ever known. It saved hundreds of newspaper men, artists, and even judges of the Supreme Court from an early enforced sobriety. This thick redemptive mixture of onions, bread—and what else, Mother Mouquin?—not only put you back instantly on your feet but also caused a delightful yelp of the belly-juices for a carafon of *yin Blanc*. And that famous sauce Madère! If you do not know what it was, made by Mother Mouquin, then your palate has missed an almighty kick.

There was a little bar on the Ann street side (the place went through the block). At this bar—and at the tables—there were present at various times Charles A. Dana, James Gordon Bennett, William Cullen

Bryant, Henry Ward Beecher, Cardinal McCloskey, Whitelaw Reid, Amos J. Cummings, Horace Greeley, John Hay, Chester A. Arthur, General Grant, Larry Godkin, Walt Whitman—almost everybody who was anybody in that era save Neal Dow and Frances Willard. Mouquin himself often sat with Dana at lunch and split a bottle with him. The noisiest person in the place was young Jimmy Bennett of the *Herald,* who, always deckle-edged from the night before, insisted on running in and out of the kitchen to see how Mother Mouquin was getting along with his order.

The waiters were all taken from France and Switzerland when they were boys and grew up with the place. A waiter seldom left Mouquin's. They were all known as Emile, Max or Pierre. Sometimes an Edenne showed up, but he soon became Emile, Max or Pierre. On the street window and on every bit of china and glassware in the house was printed *In Vino Veritas.* So closely did Mouquin adhere to this motto that the famous establishment shut its doors forever twenty-four hours after the Eighteenth Amendment became a law—the fine gesture of an eighty-three-yearold public benefactor in front of the Borgias of Morality.

"Eating in public without drinking wine or beer is piggery," said Mouquin as he slammed his door in the face of your Uncle Sam.

IV

Fulton street thus surrendered without a shot, but the Sixth avenue place fought on to Waterloo. It was padlocked in April, 1925. It was this uptown place that I knew best. It was, under Louis Mouquin, Henri's son; Ulysse T. Delisle, Peter Chaffard and Joseph Herry, *tout* New York—that is, the only part of New York that counts, the New York of art, letters and music.

The building at Twenty-eighth street and Sixth avenue was literally saturated with wine and ale. In the memory of the oldest inhabitant in that section of the city it had never been anything else but a tavern. It had been built by Isaac Varian on the old Varian farm a hundred and fifty years ago between two cowpaths, one of which is now Broadway and the other Sixth avenue. Its tavern history goes back authentically to 1810, when it was the first stop for drinks for the stage that left Bowling Green. Some of the original timbers of the old Varian mansion are still supporting the back of the building. It became known afterward as the Knickerbocker Cottage, and was run by a Captain Fuller, founder of the Thirteen Club, the traditional feasts of which survived down to Mouquin's tenancy, when annually Louis gave a party for thirteen on the top floor. It was the first home of the New York Athletic Club. After that it was Jacquin's restaurant, a French place modelled on Mouquin's downtown restaurant.

Henri Mouquin himself took it over in 1898. There was the regulation mirror-and-marble Parisian cafe downstairs and large dining-rooms upstairs. There was music once a week, on Friday evening from 6 to 8:15, in honor of *bouillubaise,* which was always to be had on Friday in the Mouquin restaurants. This gorgeous fish chowder, first concocted in the south of France and made famous in Anglo-Saxon countries by Thackeray's "Ballad of Bouillabaise," brought them a-runnin' to Mouquin's from Staten Island to Yonkers. It was (can it be had anywhere since Mouquin's closed?) a dish that fired every cell in me to vinous derring-do. A fine Burgundy or Rhone would do the job honorably and well.

The place was essentially and absolutely New York. The same persons went there year in and year out. It was off the line of transient travel and millions of New Yorkers never heard of it (thank heaven!) and it was unknown in the sticks. People were taken there; no one ever found it. I lived in New York for four years before I ever heard of it (although I worked and lived less than a mile from it) and it was seven years before I ever entered, which was in 1906. Once having found it—I was towed there by Lou Glackens—I had literally to be pried loose at closing time. And always those eternal Emiles, Maxes and Pierres!

It was there I met Jack London. (It was there I met almost everybody I've known since.) Jack was dining with Richard Le Gallienne and Michael Monahan. Mike ambled over to my table, where I was sitting with Henry Charles Lee (Harry Lee), a painter of immaculate Barbizon buckeyes. Mike had a habit of sitting on your table when he came to talk with you, sometimes sitting in your pie and carrying it away with him on his rear. He said that Jack and I should get together. We did. It was too much for Le Gallienne, but Mike, Jack, Harry and I died facing the enemy that morning.

This Harry Lee, who looked so much like Maeterlinck that in Paris he was often taken for him, was the greatest and most continuous laugher that I ever met. He spent his nights and days chortling, gurgling, guffawing, yowling. At one in the morning he was shaking like a huge tapioca pudding. Tell him he painted buckeyes and he'd yelp with glee. A man of means, he never cared where he slept. He never had a plan or an appointment that I knew of. He was the most totally unleashed, unfettered, unmoored bohemian I ever met. Life was a colossal joke to him. He was in Paris during the war and he spent huge sums on what he called canteen comforts for the girls who followed the allied armies. He is dead. Peace, Harry!—you were a great Mouquineer!

It was in Mouquin's that the famous revolution was plotted—in 1908, I believe—against the National Academy of Design by Lawson, Sloane, Glackens, Arthur B. Davies, Henri, Shinn and two others whose names escape me. These were the Eight. They all became famous. The night they issued their defiance to the academic nunkey-donkeys Sloane rode on the back of Shinn on the marble floor while the century-old rum-soaked rafters quivered and quavered with our war-shouts (I was not a painter, but I'm for all rebellions). In the cellar of Louis II, there are marble slabs on which Glackens, Lawson, Sloane, Henri, Homer Davenport, Tom Powers, Arthur B. Davies, Leon Dabo and Winslow Homer have drawn faces, bottles, dogs, cats and Rabelais-knows-what! Blow the man down! Sink the ship with all on board!—such were the slogans of those days, with the wine-bottles lying all around, all around, with the wine-bottles lying on the ground, on the ground!

Stories of the glorious place crowd upon me so thick I can't remember them. Here's one:

Mook's was almost empty. It was Monday. Must have been a hard week-end for the boys of the pencil and brush. I squat, order a sandwich and a carafe of *yin Blanc*. I must talk. I had several epigrams to unburden on some one, beside some brilliant ideas about anything else that might tickle my well-oiled tongue. I looked around for a human cuspidor for my bursting brain and I noticed a man sitting at the table to my left who was lapping up some red-eye. I aimed at him and unloaded. He was receptive, but not very loquacious—in fact, politely morose, I thought. I emptied all that was in me, swinging the battle-ax at many a famous head in literature, art and politics. I got around to the short story—Poe, De Maupassant, Chekhov, God knows who. Finally, I got to O. Henry. Lightly entertaining, splendid New Yorkese, but without depth, background or universality, I stormed. Then there were those tricked endings. That Columbia professor who called him the American De Maupassant was a ninny. It was the difference between tragedy and clever vaudeville.

I had exhausted myself. My acquaintance had poured down several more whiskeys and I had secreted four more carafes. It was one o'clock.

"Well, I think I'll hit the hay—you've had a bully talk," said my acquaintance, shaking my hands. He left. Delisle, the manager, came to my table and said:

"That's the first time I've seen O. Henry here in several months."

One night, in a highly creative—so to speak—mood, he sketched out on a tablecloth the plot of his celebrated short story, "Four Millions." He then, after another bottle, presented the tablecloth to young Louis II. Louis was later offered $1000 for it, but he refused. He recently went to look for it to show it to Bob Davis, but it had taken wings.

"And not moth-wings, either," said he, telling me the story.

V

The great beauty of Mouquin's, and of all such places, was the apotheosis of the nonsensical, the trivial, the inconsequential. Your real Mouquineer was acolyte to Baron Munchausen, Tartarian, Jerome Coignard and Colas Breugnon. At the south side of the cafe was a table which for years was consecrated to a group of writers and artists, of men of the long-bow and topsy-turvy anecdotes, of heady, scabrous wit mixed with the blood of the Musa. The founders of this table were Fighting John Flanagan, sculptor; Paul Bartlett, sculptor; Ernest Lawson, painter; Frederick James Gregg, editor of the old *Evening Sun,* a man who fought all over the editorial pages for the red-coats in the arts; Jo Davidson, sculptor; Homer Davenport, cartoonist, and Robert Henri, painter. The table was occupied by these men and other members of this informal club at lunchtime and every evening from six o'clock on. If sometimes cloak-and-suiters or a crowd of leather goods salesmen preempted the seats they were ordered cleaned by Paul Bartlett. Those were the mirific days of *a bas the boojewah!* What a telescoping of sublimities and humbug! What an intellectual *pétarade!*

One night we were all sitting at this table discussing which one of us would outlast the other in the mouth of the old strumpet, Fame.

"There's one at the table next to us that'll outlast all of us," said Jim Huneker.

We all turned to an empty table and saw, crossing its surface, a giant cockroach.

Another evening I dropped in rather late and saw Huneker glued against the mirror with the immense hairy artist (whose name I'm forbidden to mention) from Jersey City whom we called Abracadabra. Junior because of his brilliant but incomprehensible juxtaposition of words and ideas. Abra Junior was pouring his sesquipedalian sauce into Jim's ear in an attempt to demonstrate that "The Merry Widow" had better music in it than "Tristan and Isolde." I sat with them and ordered a whiskey. "But this is Yom Kippur, Ben, and whiskey isn't kosher anyhow!" boomed Jim, the while Abra Junior kept threading his unmarried words through the needle of Jim's ear-drums. Jim was a great stickler for Jewish holidays. He was right. Yom Kippur had begun at sundown. "Well, be kosher for your sake, Jim," I said. So I ordered a port wine while Abra Junior continued—"and the potential blast that that music conceals would, if let loose, blow the whole of Erin to all the shores of Mercator's Projection, and still there would remain a soft holocaust to breathe a quiet curse to the god behind the eye of Leonardo da Vinci."

There was a singing quartette in Mouquin's in the old days before Prohibition whose great stunt was the sextette from "Lucia di Lammermoor." We all used to join in—even the strange lone drinker who was known as Tête-de-Veaux and the mysterious absinthe drinker, always in black, who was known as Croque-Mort. Again the old shack would quiver under the fusillade of a hundred alcohol-dilated lungs and throats dripping with Sauterne and Chablis.

And every Mouquineer will remember the rat that used to come out from his hole under the seats on the north wall precisely at 1:40 A.M. and skip down the room into another hole. It was noticed that two o'clock closing time was approaching. We time this rat dozens of times. It never missed by a minute. According to Arthur Leonard Ross, a celebrated Mouquineer, it proved that time was absolute and put Einstein and his theory on the shelf. Discussion is invited.

In the early days of Prohibition Mouquin's uptown place went on as if nothing had happened. Henri retired to his Virginia farm to meditate on human stupidity and to look after his chickens. Louis, Mouquin, Delisle, Chaffard and the Only Joe Herry—captain and manager and twelve-bottle man who, when things got dull in the cafe, would recite yards of Victor Hugo and Alfred de Musset in French—tended to our wants.

During the Democratic National Convention of 1924 in Madison Square Garden the house was so wide open that it looked like a French Wine-Growers' Convention. Buckets! Buckets! Buckets! Dry snoots from the South, dry McAdoodles from California and Texas slushed and sloshed and died in the place, soaked, drunk, plastered. We worked on them night after night for Al Smith. We sang "The Sidewalks of New York" into their sodden, hypocritical brains. We even drew recruits from German Hoboken through the Hudson tubes to swing the dry swine for Smith.

But all carnivals must end, my children. So the house of revels, this abode of fantasy and joy, was snapped shut in 1925 by agents of your Father who art in Washington. But history was not done with Mouquin's. In padlocking the restaurant Mr. Emory Buckner left seven cats in the place. The Society for the Prevention of Cruelty to Animals protested to the government. Finally, Mr. Buckner sent up some agents to break in and rescue the cats. When they were about to smash, the cats were discovered in a coffee-house next door. Such,

ladies and gentlemen of posterity, are the important matters that oc-
cupy the time of what has been called in some editorials the greatest
country on the face of the globe.

The Mouquins, father, son and grandson, have faces that are
abloom with the joy of living. They are of the earth and have the wisdom and laughter of it. Henri, at ninety-four, is a retired Cincinna-
tus of the Vine; Louis travels in Europe, dining and wining on the
best, and Louis II conducts the wholesale French delicatessen house
in West Broadway. All Mouquineers are welcome wherever you see a
Mouquin.

England had its Grand Old Man, Gladstone; France had its
Grand Old Man, Clemenceau; Germany has her Grand Old Man,
Hindenburg. So I nominate for the Grand Old Man of America, not
Thomas A. Edison or John D. Rockefeller or John. R. Voorhis, but
Henri Mouquin, of Williamsburg, VA., the man who first put wine
within the pocket-reach of even the children of America (who should
be brought up by law on a half-pint of *vin rouge* or *tin blanc* a day). It
was Henri Mouquin who for sixty-eight years put that in our mouths
which destroys seriousness, the disease and curse of all Americans.

Joel's

EVERY once in a while before 1920 New York was swept by an anti-rum and obey-the-law spasm. All-night licenses were suddenly rescinded. Saloons were ordered closed at one o'clock and restaurants were commanded to sell nothing but food after that hour. Strong men wept and fat madames bawled before heavily chained back doors. These concessions to rectitude would last for several weeks, when, sufficient moral publicity having been achieved for the officiating police captains, everything would open up wide again. During such spells of cataleptic virtue it was sometimes far harder to get a drink between the prohibited hours of 1 and 6 A.M. than it has ever been under Prohibition, which so beautifully abolished the Raines law, Sunday closing, and the Lord's Day compulsory sandwich.

But during these sporadic outbreaks of the pox of holiness two places in the Broadway district never quit selling the Blessing: Jack's, at Sixth avenue and Forty-third street, and Joel's Bohemia, in Forty-first street just west of Seventh avenue. They were the white-headed boys of the Police Department. At times, it is true, they went through some comic motions of closing at one o'clock, but they never were really closed for a moment. Jack's went so far as to take out an all-night license, but Joel's never had such a document.

"Why bother with something they can take away from you?" said Joel to Jack one morning. "Besides, there is no all-night license for Saturday and Sunday nights, and that's when I do my biggest business."

As a matter of fact, they did take away Jack's all-night license for six months because of a row in the place in which a young fellow had his eye knocked out. But nothing ever happened to Joel's, although from 1902, when he opened his six-story Bohemia, until 1926, when, still selling the stuff, he disposed of the place, there was never a time during the twenty-four hours that you couldn't get a drink.

He was the mystery, the superman of the Tenderloin. "How do you do it, Joel?" I once asked him from the depth of my open-mouthed naivete. For answer I got a duplicate of that enigmatic smile which it took Leonardo da Vinci twelve years to paint on the lips of the wife of Francesco de Gioconda. The thousands who recall the subtle but impassive mask of Joel Rinaldo—a pale, intellectual, Latin face—will know exactly what I mean.

As Joel's Bohemia was absolutely unique in Twentieth Century New York, so was Joel himself. It was easy to conceive of August Lüchow, the Mouquins, Louis Martin, the Shanleys and Jack Dunston behind a bar or serving food. That was their born business. But no one ever saw Joel Rinaldo serve a drink from behind his bar or act as waiter. Among the restaurateurs and purveyors of the Blessing he was the intellectual, the aristocrat.

This Portuguese Jew, born in New York, was always in formal dress. There was always a flower in his lapel. His whole make-up was stunningly immaculate.

Tall, dignified, with gold nose-glasses, low-spoken, seldom taking a drink in his own place, he always looked like the guest of honor at a party. When he put you out for unbecoming conduct he bowed you down the stairs as though the honor were all his. If you fell on the way, he hurried to assist you, and with a solicitous smile and some low-murmured words of apology conducted you to a taxi. But go you must! Jack Dunston used a flying wedge of six waiters to remove his cantankerous Yale boys, and they were often landed on the sidewalk bottom down. But it was an honor to be put out of Joel's by Joel himself.

Once I wrote him a testimonial for this favor which he had bestowed on me. He had it framed. Why was I put out? Simply because I had started a theological war in the dining-room by arguing that the good Nazarene had been betrayed by the waiters at the Last Supper because He had neglected to tip them. It would have been all right, said Joel afterward, but it was Good Friday.

The things that gave to Joel's its unique odor were its celebrated *chili con carne,* its immense scuttles of beer ("five scuts!" they used to sing out downstairs at the bar), and its literary and revolutionary flavor. Joel not only played for the literary, newspaper and artistic cream of New York and the nation (of course, a lot of intellectual skim milk got mixed with the cream), but his Bohemia was also the meeting-place of heretics and radicals of all breeds: fleeing, out-at-heels generals from Mexico; hunted, unshaven admirals from Honduras; common, every-day White House dynamiters from Guatemala; bawling Egyptian Anarchists; loudmouthed sappers and miners of the social edifice in general who would shut up for a beer and a load of beans; barroom Napoleons and millennial crackpots of all nationalities. Add to this a raft of actors and actresses, mainly from the country of Ham, and you will have but a faint notion of the most colorful, the most romantic and the most vibrating place in all New York.

II

Joel's was the town's Jacobin Club, its House of Farces, Fantasies and Fumisteries, where revolutions, fake newspaper and magazine stories, and even presidential booms were hatched and launched. Nothing was too absurd, too amusing, too nearly inconceivable to be spawned there. Joel himself was known as the Chili Con Carrie King, and when I asked for *chili con carne* in the Café Gambrinus in the City of Mexico in 1906, Belatto, the proprietor, said, "You'll have to go to Joel's, in New York, for that!"

I have seen everybody of note that I have seen anywhere else in New York at Joel's. It was the melting-pot of all nations and all races. It was ultra-democratic, ultra-New York, ultra-cosmopolitan. Joel never had imported draft beer in the place, but his waiters were Jews, Gentiles, Germans, Hungarians, Italians, Greeks—anything. No one, however, ever spoke anything but English. "We are Mongrelians here," Joel said to me when I first met him in 1904, having been taken to his place by the caricaturist, Carlo de Fornaro, and Roy McCardell, the Dostoievsky of the Jarr family. Fornaro not only hatched the overthrow of Porfirio Diaz in Joel's after he came out of Blackwell's Island, where he had served ten months for "libelling" that famous bandit, but also founded the famous Literary and Revolutionary Table in the northeast corner of the dining-room. A sign was fixed on this table every night at 11 o'clock. It read "Reserved for Literature and Revolution."

Joel worshipped intellectuals and revolutionists of all kinds, and one of his fantasies was to stake any man to a meal, a room, a five-spot, or all three, if he had anything at all to do with the arts or had exploded a mine somewhere. Thus he nosed out Jim Moore, of the Café Francis, in West Thirty-fifth street, who would stake you to anything if you could paint. So far, indeed, did he distance Moore in these good deeds that the Lord rewarded him in the end by bestowing on him for a small sum all the pictures on the walls of the Francis. Among them were a Glackens, a Luks and a Sloane. Ernest Lawson recovered his after a terrific battle in which the waiters at Joel's were divided into Lawson and anti-Lawson camps.

There is a picture made by Fornaro of a Sunday morning at the Literary and Revolutionary Table. At it are seated Booth Tarkington, Edwin Markham, Leon Trotsky, E. Haldeman-Julius, Robert W. Chanler, Leonard Charles Van Noppen, Jacob Coxey, Charles Willis Thompson, Michael Monahan, Leon Dabo, Arthur Leonard Ross and Emma Goldman. The Grand Old Man of American Poetry, Edwin Markham, when he came to Manhattan used to put up for the night at Joel's, whose three upper floors were the Hotel de Rinaldo. Naturally, he who gave us that rollicking ballad, "The Man with the Hoe," was always an honored guest at the revolutionists' table. Markham, however, never drank anything stronger than coffee. He didn't need alcohol, for his spirits and his body were always leaping like the hart from the depths of some cosmic joy not perceivable to the rest of us. But we always had a diabolical curiosity to see any professional sobersides in his cups. So one night I passed Big Fritz, the word to dump a slug of brandy in every cup of coffee our Poet Laureate ordered. Around 2 A.M. Markham was pounding the table, signalling joyously to the singers, and rising to execute a Highland fling when Papa Joel, who had got hep, towed him up to the Poet's Suite on the floor above. Markham told Joel to order ten pounds of that coffee for Mrs. Markham. Led by Charles Willis Thompson, we serenaded the poet outside of his door with the national anthem of Forty-first street, "One grasshopper jumped right over the other grasshopper's back."

III

About Big Fritz, the favorite waiter of the Happy Few who were permitted at *the* Table. Every one who ever went to Joel's will recall that big, heavy Prussian ex-cavalry officer. When we went into the war in 1917 the Table became the Newspaper and Literary Table. The word revolutionary was quietly dropped, and everybody in the place turned patriot overnight except Big Fritz. He kept on drinking to the Kaiser right out loud whenever we asked him to have a beer with us. His audacity awed us. So we protected him from the onslaughts of the uniformed boys who were going over to make the world safe for Lenin, Mussolini and Harry Daugherty. "Why, it's only good old Fritz —he's—" and we'd tap our foreheads significantly. Fritz came out of the war without a scratch. Maybe he was a kind of vicarious atonement for our frenzied patriotism.

The first floor front of Joel's was given over to the bar and the hotel desk, behind which was a towering safe in which reposed the checks and I. O. U.'s of what Shaemas O'Sheel used to call "Joel's authors." It was known as the Iron Cemetery. In back was a drinking and eating room and the kitchen. The second floor had a balcony overlooking Forty-first street, from which point we used to spy into the dressing-rooms of the Ziegfeld Follies girls across the street, or salute them and drink to them with scuttles of beer when, on Summer evenings, they came out on the fire-escapes to air themselves. With a purely æsthetic eye, of course, we men of the Foaming Grail thus took our peep into the Venusberg. Sometimes, at about four in the morning, Sadakichi Hartmann, George Luks and I would toss our *chili con carne* bowls from the balcony into the street to find out just how many cops were sleeping in Forty-first street and where they slept.

The rest of the floor, a very long one, was made up of tables, a musicians' stand, and a dancing floor. It was on this dancing floor that Sadakichi, after he was pumped up on many brandies, would execute those exotic dances which would stop the works. He looked like the Grand Lama of Thibet gone nuts. One night he passed around a seven-gallon hat for what he called "substantial recognition of my genius." The hat was rapidly assuming its original shape from the load of silver that the all-night cloak and suit revellers were throwing into it when it reached Bill Reedy, coshed to the crow's nest and right off the St. Louis pickle-boat.

Bill had the largest foot ever owned by a Single Taxer. He aimed it straight at the hat and sent ten pounds of coin high into the air. The waiters and the musicians scrambled for the windfall while Sadikichi aimed a table filled with scuttles of beer at Bill's head. It missed and smashed Glackens' picture, "The Prix de Rome." Sadakichi was ordered to the floor below, beyond the bar. This place was for first offenders. The broken glass in the Glackens picture was never touched. It became known as the Sadakichi Glackens, beer-stains, cracked glass and all. Where is it now?

If downstairs in Joel's looked like a Teniers kitchen—especially on Saturday night—the second floor at its riotous apogee, which was between 1 and 4 A.M., was smelly glamour, stuffy sensuality, blasts of beer and *chili* sauce, a Babel of talk, song, girls (ah! Vic with the marvellous teeth!) and the blare of detonating laughter. I always threw myself right into it as I hope to do some day into a Munich beer vat. Joel would have no lone sitters in his place, no mopes, no Johnny-stare-in-his-dregs. He was a *Schadchen* of joy.

But he would never introduce a banker to a writer, or even to a proofreader. He was against frisking. He was strong for vibrant harmony. It was thus in 1912 that a lanky, red-headed fellow from Sauk Center, Minn., was put at my table by Joel. It was there and then that Sinclair Lewis presently issued a challenge to out-swill me in *chili con carne*. Bugs Baer's arrival settled the argument, for Bugs ordered a large bowl of *chili con carne,* emptied two highballs into it, stirred the mess with a fork, and swallowed the whole thing. He challenged Lewis and me to follow. We refused. The conversation then turned to higher things. The three of us were sentenced to the first floor back at

4 A.M. for aiming oyster crackers at the electric fans.

Joel had the most penetrating eye that I ever knew any human being to have. He advanced in all his open boiled-shirt grandeur to greet every writer, newspaper man and artist as the visitor came up the steps. He had to. For many of us, on occasion, hadn't a cent, and we were out to bum a jag and eats off of the house. Joel's eye knew, in one rapid survey of your face, just about how much money you had in your pants and what your intentions were and instantaneously on surveying you, he prepared his defences. His eyes said *go* or *stop*. A grand game of cat-and-mouse then began.

But Papa Joel was the best fellow that ever was. He was the Otto Kahn of the cafes. Of course if, in his crying need of intellectual cronies, he deliberately set about, in 1902, as he did, to cater to the Literary Barrel-House Gang, he had to stand for a frisk now and then. Anyhow, I said to him, as he looked one morning with pained eyes at my check, "It is prestige, magic, brains that we bring you, Joel. Like Maggie Murphy's organ, *we* give the house a tone!" It was then that he issued his celebrated *mot:* "If you do me once, damn you! If you do me twice, damn me!" But Papa was really our Corn Exchange. Every one will recall the framed sign that greeted you at the head of the steps: "Let Joel Be Your Banker." No one needed a receipt from him. He was sounder than any bank.

In the middle of the floor upstairs, opposite the music-stand, there was a large cigar-case. if you looked in the case you were astonished to see the poems of Shaemas O'Sheel, Fornaro's *Diaz, Czar of Mexico*, Hippolyte Havel's *La Guerre Sociale* and my own *The Shadow-Eater* between the Coronas and the Cremos. Sam, the Hungarian waiter, presided over this mixture of smoke and letters. He tried to sell a book to every customer who displayed a five-dollar bill and seemed the slightest bit lit up with Joel's famous Blue Moon cocktails. There were other books of the gang's, the titles of which escape me, in the case. At every sale to some maudlin guy from the sticks we used to collect our 15% royalty from Sam.

Joel took over fifty copies of my book of poems, and he sold every one at $5 apiece. (The book retailed at $1.) If we were in the place (and some cigar-case author always was) we were requested by the purchaser to autograph the book. Then he would generally set up wine in honor of meeting Fame in person, and the night ended by the author frisking his book from the sleeping jewel salesman and putting it back in the case. One toothpick manufacturer from Pennsylvania thus bought one of my books three times over in a year. Thanks to Our Joel, those were the Golden Days of cash royalties and quick turnovers. His *mot* concerning this matter was: "An honest author is the sorriest work of God."

It was in 1910 that this most fantastic and colorful of New York's Prosperos (in these gray years such men of the Drink Elysium shimmer in my memory with the splendor and the magic of a tale out of the glamorous skull of Scheherazade) put forth the most astonishing book over his own name that ever emanated from a seller of food and drink. It was called *Rinaldo's Polygeneric Theory: a Treatise on the Beginning and End of Life*, and was a serious attempt in eleven chapters, with diagrams, to upset the Darwinian notion of evolution. There was an exhaustive bibliography at the back.

What drew me to Joel at my first meeting with him was his disbelief in all modern science. The book was a powerful (and to me conclusive) argument against the theory of the mutability of species It was received by the reviewers at the time just as the books of Charles Fort are received to-day—with open-mouthed incredulity. I challenged Joel on his authorship. In reply, he showed me some of the original manuscript in his own handwriting. In 1921 he issued another book, *Psychoanalysis of the Reformer*, one of the most drastic and penetrative pummellings the Prohibitionist and bluesnoot have ever got. In it all puritanical inhibitions are traced directly to sexual perversions. There is an introduction by Andre Tridon.

Were these books really written by Joel? There are some who doubt the authenticity of Shakespeare's plays and the sacred inspiration of the Bible. Oh, ye men of little faith! The man who invented the Blue Moon cocktail and drank it every evening has a brain, I claim, that could eject anything. In this famous controversy I was, and still remain, pro-Joel. Joel, it must be remembered, had his enemies, too; for could he not smell the rubber burning in a check before the holder of it had even set forth Joel-ward?

IV

After Sadakichi Hartmann, the most picturesque fellow who frequented the place was Hippolyte Havel, who, variously, ran *La Guerre Sociale* in Chicago, was Emma Goldman's editor of *Mother Earth,* lectured in jail and out on Anarchy, was the first banner-carrier in every strike, and was, at bottom, the gentlest humanitarian who ever tried to break my skull because I was a Tammany realist in politics. Long black hair, a coal-black mustache, a flowing black tie, gold-rimmed glasses, behind which were gentle satanic eyes; and barely over five feet. Havel was almost always broke, was a great spender when he got it, and a whale of a guzzler. There was, however, something so sinisterly charming about the fellow that he was welcome everywhere.

I once saw a sight in Joel's that cannot be repeated even in Nietzsche's *Eternal Return.* I entered at about 11 o'clock and saw at one table Hippolyte Havel, Konrad Bercovici, Jo Davidson and Carlo de Fornaro. Havel's black hair, mustache and tie; Bercovici's jet-black mustache *a la* Nietzsche, his fierce, black eyes and swarthy complexion; Jo Davidson's bituminous beard and hair and eyes that spit pitch; Fornaro, who looks like the last of the Borgias on a milk diet—well, it seemed like the Ethiopian Day of Wrath split four ways.

Havel soon discovered that he had a great nuisance value. He knew Joel's gentle and long-suffering nature and his love of decorum (hilarity to the limit, but decorum, boys!). Havel needed (always) a dollar or two. He would mass his swearwords in battle formation down at Hell's Hole, in Sixth avenue, and move on Joel's. He would advance down the dining-room emitting oaths until Joel gave him two dollars to get out. It never failed. For all that, Joel loved Hippolyte. "Although he believed my grandmother barked, still do I revere him," said Lord Rinaldo.

During the periodical closing spasms that New York had before the Speak-Easy Amendment Joel's used to go through an elaborate manoeuvre at 2 o'clock. At quarter to one the waiters would take all the customers, upstairs and downstairs, both the bar-flies and the sitters, together with the five musicians and the singing women, and herd them all into a small room on the third floor. Here, standing or sitting, we would hold our breaths behind locked doors while the cops went through the two floors to see that everybody was out. Joel was innocently at his desk pretending to add up the day's receipts, and one by one the lights were extinguished by the cops. As soon as they left to report the place closed for the night Sam would let us down to the second floor, the music would begin, the booze would flow, the panels would be thrown around the bar, now wide open again, the *chili con carne* would send up its pungent vapors again from vast boilers—and the rouse would go on till 8 A.M., or 10 or all day if you wanted to stay. As then, so now: the Thirst is mightier than the Law!

It was this *chili con carne* that lured Caruso into the place. He came over in tow of Fornaro. Naturally, the works stopped. Everybody pressed him to sing. Joel rubbed the dust off a bottle of his old Chianti. The chef made a ton of spaghetti. But sing he would not, not even for Vic of the glorious teeth. His contract, it appeared, wouldn't permit it. But when he got good and mellowed he stood a bowl of *chili con carne* on his head and drew caricatures of Joel, Sam Hoffenstein and Bob Davis. And as he left the orchestra struck up and we all sang "My Cousin Caruse!" For answer Enrico grabbed up Vic and carried her down to the street. Further deponent saith not.

Of those who went to Joel's who does not recall Uncle Morales? He turned up about twenty-five years ago, and must have been about seventy-five. He was a distinguished and ultra-English old swell from somewhere in the West Indies. He was more British than *rostbif.* Well, one of Joel's specialties when it was in season was hot corn on the cob, which he almost gave away to the *chili* and beer boys, especially if you were of the Table. One night we made Uncle Morales a Table guest. In the centre was a heaping plate of corn on the cob. Joel, in his blitheness and generosity, pushed the plate over toward Uncle Morales. What a treat for Uncle!, shone in Joel's eye. Uncle Morales put on his monocle, looked at the steaming cobs and said with an air of infinite disdain, "In the West Indies we feed *that* to the swine." Joel was wounded to the gizzard. But quick as a flash there came out of his mouth, "That's the reason, Uncle, I pushed it in front of *you.*"

This same Uncle Morales was a perpetual and mortal offense to

Corse Payton, of Council Bluffs, Iowa, America's best bad actor, who when he was asked by a soldier in uniform during the war why he wasn't Over There replied that he was too tall for the trenches. Corse used to show up in Joel's with a huge lily in his lapel, a perfecto as long as a blackjack in his mouth, and a grand air of *Ecce Homo!* The minute he would spot Uncle Morales he would stand in front of him and say, "Salute the three greatest Americans: Abraham Lincoln, Jesse James and Gorse Payton!" Papa Joel always smashed this Anglo-American conflict in the egg by planting Corse facing the mirrors at the end of the dance room, with America's best bad singer, Wilson Mizner.

V

But in the mental kaleidoscope of Joel's Bohemia there rises—there towers—above all my memories Robert W. Chanler—Sheriff Bob. I first saw him there more than twenty years ago. He was at his peak. He looked like some one who had just come from an orgy on Olympus. A giant with a fat, round face fired by the rays from the Sun of Alcohol, a sun that knew no dawn or setting. A corona of thick grey curly hair. A voice that stoned your ears, eyes, brain. An impediment in his speech heightened the effect of his bombilating larynx. He was pandemonium; a magnificent hang-over from the Renaissance; a Dutch satyr such as Frans Hals never conceived; an Astor who smashed with his cobblestone fist the frowning mug of the whole landed "aristocracy" from which he descended.

At the head of the table he was Gargantua-Silenus. He guffawed at the universe. He loved the world drunk, soused, stewed, frenzied. To be sober at his table was an insult to him. His murals and panels are gorgeous nightmares, alcoholic and Venusan color-blasts. Baudelaire, Rops, Redon and Poe were in his work. But he was only tainted with them; he was not of them. He offered to paint Joel's ceiling with pink butterflies, red monkeys, green serpents and plastered Jezebels. But Papa said no. He could brook no rival to his Blue Moon cocktails.

Here's the way I met Bob Chanter. The waiters weren't fast enough for me in Joel's on this night. So I myself was carrying the beers for our table from the bar. Bob howled at me to bring him some brandy. He thought I was a waiter. I laughed at him. He complained to Joel about his impudent waiter. Joel introduced me. Chanler ordered me to sit down and drink with him, uttering a string of oaths at me that made me gargle blood the Olympian blackguard! It was soon afterward that he threw Walter de Shoto's (the Great de Shoto!) trombone out on Forty-first street. Elohim!—what fantastic nights!

There was the picture that Carlo de Fornaro painted when the Cubistic craze came out of the skulls of the artistic Acephali. It was hung on the wall over the literary-nicotine showcase. Joel offered a prize of one hundred free bowls of *chili con carne* to the person who would divine what it was about and give it a title. This set to work all the lace-curtain brains and even the papoose skulls of the culture-hounds from the Suit and Cloaka Maxima. Some of the guesses were "Gettysburg Before the Battle," "Trixie Friganza in the Subway," "Strindberg Milking a Cow," "Benjamin DeCasseres in Conference with God," "Daniel Frohman Speaking," "Snowstorm in Mott Street." It was General Jake Coxey who guessed right and won the hundred bowls with "Prophetic Vision of the Fall of Yonkers."

General Jake, by the way, always made Joel's his headquarters when he was in from Massillon, Ohio, or back from Washington, where he had been trying for years to make a purse of plenty out of the Congressional sow's ear. Jake was a perfect example of the hick political miracle man, the philistine on a radical souse. His bugs were many and proliferous. In 1920 he launched his candidacy for the Presidency at Joel's bar to the jingle of a set-up of New Orleans sazaracs. We were all for him so long as he paid. When he quit shelling out (which was soon) we literati remained like Shelley's Mont Blanc—remote, serene, inaccessible. But nothing ever dazed Jake.

On Christmas Eve, before the war, Papa would assemble by invitation the Biggies among the lace-curtain Intellectuals and the thick cream of the Way-Outers, Fiat Luxers and Barricade Bombers. A grand spread in the second-floor back room. A high trellised screen was thrown across the front of the room. Through this screen the Acephali from Queens and the business marts were permitted to peep. Joel would serve steaks, *chili con carne,* beer and the Blue Moon thing. What a memorable logorrhea those suppers were! Everything from the sex-life of the amoeba to esoteric Anarchism was belched out. It was at one such party that Hip Havel tried to choke the life out of Don Marquis because Marquis said he didn't think he loved *all* of the human race, and Arthur Leonard Ross was attacked by Jo Davidson because Arthur had mildly averred that all the arts aspired to etching. Joel sat at the head of the table at these feasts commemorating the birth of the good Nazarene. His only remark that I can now recall is "How embryonic!"

His generosity sometimes winced. There suddenly appeared on the wall downstairs one night 'round about 1917 this sign: "According to the style-card of the New York *Herald*, 'A *Patron* of a hotel is one who pays for his bed, eating and drinking. A *Guest* is one whose bed, eating and drinking are paid for by the host.' We love our Patrons; but damn our Guests! Joel Rinaldo." But for all that Joel knew as many guests as he did patrons. He has helped hundreds of cultured gentlemen (and newspaper writers) over the cobbles. And as for the actors of New York, he was their post-office, their banker and their angel.

The ethical ladybirds and tumblebugs put over Prohibition in 1920. But that made no more difference to Joel's than it did to Jack's or Mouquin's. As a matter of fact, Joel's, like thousands of other places in New York, was already a speak-easy during five hours of the night. Prohibition merely extended the five hours to twenty-four. We drank out of cups for a while as the snoop-snouts looked on pleasantly for a few minutes and then left us. Gradually the cups were abandoned and the glasses reappeared. Scuttles of beer were always to be had. It was in 1922 that Tom Geraghty, the playboy of Broadway; Charlie Chaplin and myself landed in Joel's one night, dismissed the orchestra (for a consideration) and gave a concert of our own—Tom playing the trap-drum, Charlie the violin and I the piano (I can play Liszt and Chopin by using only the little finger of the left hand and the thumb of the right hand). Joel was attending a dinner at Barney Gallant's Village Inn. The Great Walter de Shoto again lost his trombone on that night.

Joel sold out in 1926. He now lives the retired life of South Brooklyn. Surrounded by books—from Aristophanes to Ben Hecht—by rare pre-war cordials and exotic brandies, himself never touching a drop, as hospitable as ever, he dreams of the Pleasure House that he, the Kubla Khan of the Tenderloin, decreed and the revels and charivaris of twenty-four years, a few of which I have tried to indicate to the gin-sodden growing generation of our Comic Republic.

Jack's

JACK'S, at Forty-third street and Sixth avenue in New York, was for thirty-five years the most celebrated all-night booze playground in America. It opened in 1891 and closed in 1926.

I was myself a practitioner there for twenty-six years. I was in the place oftener and for longer hours than I was either in my furnished room or at the *Herald* office. Well, why not? Like hundreds of others who called Jack's home, I ate, drank and often slept there: When John Dunston opened the house he threw the keys away. Once, when he was closed temporarily for three months between the hours of 1 and 6 A.M. for a nasty row, he had to have new keys made to lock up. One of his chairs was bed and board to a lot of us. The ordinary sessions lasted from ten at night to noon the next day, with intermittent naps.

Jack's had no duplicate anywhere in New York, for there was no music, no cabaret, no clock, no dancing: just good, low-priced food and drinks morning, noon and night, and a moving and continuous parade of novelists, artists, prizefighters, judges, newspaper men, scientists, business men, politicians, soldiers, Governors, Senators, actors, Presidents-to-be (Roosevelt, Taft and Wilson used to dine and wine there), mayors, revolutionists, gamblers, the most opulent madames (and the most eminent of their parasites), labor leaders, song writers, racetrack touts, and wine agents.

Jack himself told me in 1918 that he had $90,000 worth of unpaid checks in his safe. Paradoxically, that's what made him and the place. He knew you had to come back to his store, for after 4 A.M. there was no other place to go—that is, no place that was not a mere bar and where you didn't have to knock on the door. Jack's was a walk-in. All ages were on exhibition, from the bawling young generation with its first jag—the nurslings and yearlings of Good Mother Booze—to the most venerable, viscid, vacuous, bowed, bent, spent, rheumy, rubbishy old gaffers that you can imagine.

At four o'clock in the morning Barnum's three calliopes would have sounded like a flea's sneeze in this tempest of tosspots. Many were carried from the field by Jack's privy councillors, and many more were propelled none too lightly into Sixth avenue by the famous Flying Wedge, a rightangle-triangle with six of Jack's waiters constituting the side-lines and the offending client the hypothenuse. Six A.M. was *siesta* time for the newspaper men, artists, song writers and actors. The monied aristocracy had practically gone by then, and only the gamblers and a few stray Jezebels remained to watch over the sleep of copy-readers, reporters, proofreaders, ham Hamlets, Broadway Mozarts, and others of Jack's *illuminati*.

Presiding over this happy restaurant was the aforesaid John Dunston. He was physically and psychically a part of his kitchen, his bar, his oyster counter. He had his apartment on the second floor of the Forty-third street wing. (The house formed a perfect L.) It was his personal, and sometimes loud, supervision of everything that made the place. He walked from table to table every evening inquiring about your food: "Is it just right?" "How is the beer?" "Is your wine as you wish it?" Sometimes he sat at the cashier's wicket, which surveyed three rooms and part of the fourth. He always seemed blossomy. Tall, distinguished looking, with cheeks ruddier than his friend Tom Lipton's in the latter's prime, wearing a heavy military mustache which, like his hair, turned to a silver gray in his latter years, always in evening clothes after 6 P.M., a white flower in his coat, Jack Dunston would have been observed anywhere.

I made my hit with him way back in 1902 when I told him he ought to be Ambassador to the Court of St. James. I slyly entrenched myself still deeper on the credit side of his books when I hailed him as Sir John. He was the only Irish Catholic I ever met who was proud to be taken for an Englishman. During the war he actually denounced the Irish rebellion. He was well grounded in history and religious matters and I have spent hours with him in verbal wrestling matches. Like his colleague, Joel Rinaldo, he liked to sit with the stewed literati. He had the Irishman's nimble wit. It was dangerous to fence with him, for he had a memory like a tax-gatherer's. Deep in his cups, just before he went to sleep he was sometimes handy with his fists. It was generally nothing more than a love-tap, but I was told by the venerable Frank Ward O'Malley that one night back in the 90's Jack reached John L. Sullivan at the pivot of the jaw while both were in liquor and that John L. rolled on the floor, bellowed like a baby and then hulked out. Jack was always in high fettle. He swore by something he called Cockles' English Pills. He gave me one once. It was a compressed Vesuvius.

II

He was born in Cork in 1853. He came to America via the Canadian route, bringing with him the municipal air of Cork, "McCarthy's Daughter," a corrosive chant which he always sang for the boys when he got corned. It was the only music ever permitted in his place. He would weep while singing, for McCarthy's daughter, according to the saga, got the raspberry from some white-collar Kerry man and destroyed herself in the River Lee. We *savants* and pundits always rose respectfully while Jack intoned this frightful tale —mainly because we were all in the deep red in the big book under the desk.

The first job that he got in New York, according to the record at the Hall of Fame, was that of waterboy at the Old Fifth Avenue Hotel. This was during the Grant administration and Grant himself used to put up at the hotel when he came to New York. "Twice," Jack once told me, "I was waterboy at his table—do you get it? *Water-boy* at General Grant's table! Why, I was of no more use than a toothpick to a hen!"

The next we hear of one of New York's greatest benefactors he was a partner in Dunston & Kennelly's Manhattan Oyster Bay, at Seventy-fourth street and Columbus avenue. This was as far north as any cruising rummy ever got in the 80's. On a clear day you could see the aurora borealis by standing on the bar-rail. Tom Healy—afterward the owner of Healy's restaurant at Sixty-sixth and Broadway—was one of the waiters. All three men—Dunston, Healy and Kennelly—died millionaires.

In 1891, with Kennelly and Tim Hurley, Jack opened the Manhattan Oyster House at Sixth avenue and Forty-third street. The opening made some noise throughout the then free and happy Republic. Its salient event was the wedding breakfast of Frank Jay Gould and Helen Kelly. This was the beginning of the House that Jack Built. However, somewhere between Seventy-fourth and Columbus avenue and Sixth avenue and Forty-third he had been head-waiter transiently at a place almost as famous as his own. This was Sam Burns's restaurant and boozery three blocks further up Sixth avenue. There is a tale that Sam fired Jack after a row and that Jack said, "Some day I'll buy this place over your head." Twenty-four years later he bought it for $225,000. This Irishman, in fact, never had any bad luck in his life. Curious how God loves the vendors of booze! They are blessed beyond all men.

The most curious and esoteric property of Jack was his apostolic blessing. When he came toward you two fingers on his right hand were raised just over your head if you were sitting. But watch his face closely! The blessing might precede the statement that your credit account was closed until you put a five-spot on your last add-up. Or it might mean, "I extend to thee the limit." With a waiter standing alongside your chair it might mean "We desire to be relieved of this man's presence. Wedge!" If the arm was raised at an angle of forty-five degrees it meant "I am going to sit with you." To the inmates of Jack's his fingers were veritable fingers of Fate.

There were six keys to Baldpate and four doors to Jack's. Three were on Sixth avenue and one was on Forty-third street. The three Sixth avenue doors entered different rooms. Every old Jacobin will recall the importance of this seemingly trivial arrangement. Put out of one door, the offender would walk around the block, get a shave and a shine, brush his hair, sometimes buy a little malacca cane, and an hour afterward he would come in, all snapped up, through another door, take a seat, order an ale and smoke up. The waiters in the room wherefrom he had been catapulted seldom discovered that he was now in another room, passing idle quip and jaunty quiddity and oiling up for another bounce. Ah! how often I have played that delightful game!

However, members of the newspaper guild were never, or seldom, flying-wedged. When they had to be expelled there was great pomp and ceremony and no laying on of hands: the uniformed coat-boy, still hoping against hope for a tip; full canonicals for the forced exodus of "lettered men," as Jack called us in his o'er-ripe satire. Full canonicals and fanfare—but into the street!

The quality of Jack's food and drink was famous. And at what prices! He was one of the few Irish hosts in New York who knew how to keep and serve German beers. His scrambled eggs and Irish bacon (the 5 A.M. dish of the gay all-nighters) were perfect. His Manhattan sirloin steak, with all the fixings (and what a whopper of a steak!), for sixty cents—you remember? Put a bottle of Bass' ale (thirty cents) on top of it and you had set sail for all cosmic and comic ports.

His twenty-cent brandy was the best at that price I ever tasted. I used to pick rainy nights for brandy. (Beer for women, wine for men and brandy for the gods, said old Sam Johnson.) With John O'Brien of the *Herald* (who could twist his long legs so corkscrewy around the legs of the table that to remove him the waiters had to take the table with them), I have passed sessions on Jack's brandy until our combined luminosity burned up our bar-checks.

O'Brien, who was variously known as Jack O'Brien, Oby, Spanish O'Brien, Mexican O'Brien and Tom, was one of my cronies in Jack's for years. I first met him in the City of Mexico. He was a man of many talents and languages. A Parisian by birth, educated at the University of Edinburgh, he loathed all forms of sham and hypocrisy. Pointing one of his long, bony fingers one night at some fat-faced business smugmug, he said: "I loathe those men who will never admit they have been drunk! I have been boisterously, stupidly, weepingly, dancingly, singingly, brilliantly, asininely, triumphantly, morosely, pugnaciously drunk a thousand times. My kidneys have wrecked whole breweries. My gullet has swallowed whole distilleries." I hallooed my approval. Arthur Leonard Ross voted his oke. Frank O'Malley and John Barrymore conducted the fragment of the Respectable Element to the door. It was upon this very night and date, children, that Corse Payton slept on his planked steak.

My stomach and my gullet have palpitant memories of some of Jack's dishes—creamed chicken-hash with sliced green peppers and small onions, in a chafing-dish, enough for two, seventy-five cents! The tremendous murphys with a fat wad of butter stuck in their entrails that you got free with your steak! Those kidney stews, piping hot, with a foaming seidel of Pilsner, fifty cents!

But, above all, Jack's was noted for its sea-food. It began as an oyster and lobster house and always remained so, primarily. No matter what you ordered, a dish of oyster crackers and a sauce of piccalilli was set before you. Jack took great pride in his fish. There was a special oyster-bar, presided over by an Italian who was known to everybody as Caruso. Those monstrous Lynn Havens!

III

There were football nights in Jack's when the Princeton, Yale and Harvard rowdies invaded the place. What souse cantatas there were! The brandied hiccough met the hooligan howl of the highball, and the beer belch mingled with the hoarse roar of the rickey. There was a fight a minute, and the Flying Wedge was kept busy flinging these students of Homer by the hundreds clear across Sixth avenue and up against the doors of the Hippodrome. The uproar sometimes was so great that it roused the denizens of Frank Case's sedate Algonquin, around in Forty-fourth street. They would pour out in nightgowns, nightcaps and berettas, believing that some great catastrophe had overtaken our quiet city.

The college intellectuals were picked up on the sidewalk by the fleet of hansom cabs, with their high-hatted Irish drivers, which lined the whole block in front of Jack's after 12 P.M. I'm happy to report to the boys and girls of to-day that these Harvardians, Princetonians and Yalensians were frisked to a whisper by the cabbies before they got back home. A finer set of thugs, blackguards and drink bilkers than those college boys I've never met. Jack never wanted them, but he could not get rid of them. On one of the football nights Boies Penrose (Harvard) was present. Ach! Ach!—but that's another story.

In those days the wine agent was the Biggie of Broadway. He was always thought of as a Croesus. He was followed everywhere by a gang of picaroons, yes-smirkers, rakehells, Doll Tearsheets, and other *pediculidæ*. Necks craned and knees crooked when the king of them all, George Kessler, entered Jack's in high hat and full regalia, with something red slashed across his shirt front which signified that he was O.K. with the Shah of Persia. Jack always welcomed him at the door with a military salute, for the awesome words were always telephoned ahead, "George Kessler's on the way!"

Black-bearded and tall, Kessler enjoyed the His Majesty stuff immensely. He was conducted to a seat by Jack, who himself took his order. We underlings of the pen and brush held our breath bated, for we were soon to hear from our waiter, "Mr. Kessler would like to know, gentlemen, whether you will wine with him." Ah!, those magnificos! Those Kesslers, Wally Murphys and Garners—the *pier sang* of the Booze Dynasty, the Castilians, the Samurai of Thirst! *Aye! et de profundus!*

Comedy! No end of comedy. Like Mouquin's and Joel's, Jack's was a Temple of the Absurd. This one has stuck in my head after twenty years: two young fellows, both Vere de Veres, and both lushy, got jammed in the narrow door which led to Uncle Daniel Murphy's washroom. After a few mutually mumbled apologetic words one said, "Well, anyhow, I can see you are a gentleman." "No," said the other one, "I don't think I am a gentleman." "But you are—I know a gentleman when I see one." "I don't think you do—for I'm not a gentleman." "You insinuate I am a liar? —I say you *are* a gentleman."

Immediately the one who accused the other of being a gentleman had the throat of the one who insisted he was not a gentleman. Jack stepped up hurriedly to the scene, and in his kindest and most drippingly Gaelic tones said, ripping them apart, "I believe you are *both* gentlemen." Then suddenly changing from a treacle soprano to a foghorn bass he thundered "Wedge!"

So the Flying Squadron landed the two epicenes on their roundhouses out in melancholy Sixth avenue.

This Uncle Daniel Murphy, who tended to the sick and wounded in the gents' washroom, was the best known person in Jack's next to

Jack himself. Jack had imported him from Halifax when the house was opened. He was as much a part of it as the keyless door. He was one of those little old shrunken men who by no stretch of the imagination could you ever imagine having been born a baby. He was like that old fellow in Balzac's "The Magic Skin," the fellow who sold the ass' skin to the hero. He lived in his little atelier; he died there. He had towelled and chinned with more famous men than probably any other person in the country.

He remembered them all. He was a chatterer *de luxe* who for thirty years withered away in a toilet-room. He had tidied up Roosevelt, Wilson (when he was a Princeton professor Woodrow used to go to Jack's), Taft and Prince Henry of Prussia, beside a list of dukes, marquises, Prime Ministers, authors, Senators, Governors and whatnot that would make a who's who of the traveling world from 1891 to 1922, when he keeled over. Uncle Dan'l was well beloved by all. He was known as the Privy Councillor. And he pouched a small fortune. He was only once angry past the forgiving point. Then his anger was directed at Frank O'Malley, who sent the page-boy into his domain to page Cardinal ———.

On a certain morning four of us gave an exhibition in the middle room (which was variously known as the Café, the Psychopathic Ward, Matteawan and the Straitjacket) which drew all the *booze-wahzie* from the White, Green and Gold rooms. Tom Geraghty, then a reporter on the *Herald,* rolled up his sleeve and balanced two full ponies of brandy, one on top of the other, on his elbow. Andrew Mack held a gin rickey on his protruding tongue.

Hype Igoe planted a glass of ale on his nose. And I did my stunt of standing two seidels of beer on my head, one on top of the other. We had held them there for ten minutes when Mack's glass crashed. Jack was fortunately absent.

Hype Igoe, one of the noblest playboys of those gorgeous days, put music into Jack's. Hype had been brought up on the ukulele. He always had one hidden on him somewhere. Well, we—Hype, Tad, John O'Brien, Tom Geraghty, George Luks, Fornaro, Jack Francis, Stuffy Davis, Wilson Mizner, and who else? would wait for Jack to go upstairs to bed, generally about 5 A.M. Then we would assemble under the steps in the Gold Room, and Joe Nincompoopulous, from the cellar, would bring up Hype's uke. He stored it in the fishbin at a dollar a week. Hype would always start with "Ten Thousand Sheep" and then go into "How deee-lightful to be m-m-m-m-married!" Drinks! Drinks! Drinks! By 6:30 we were in full cacophonic blast. Jack, trying to sleep, never dreamed that this "music" came from his place. He put in a complaint against some neighbor in Forty-fourth street.

Alas!—one day Jack found the uke in the fishbin and smashed it. But he died without knowing whose property it was. Besides, Hype always had another uke.

One of the reasons for Jack's success was his strict order about the sexes mixing. He had an inflexible rule that no woman with a man could leave her table and sit at another man's table without her man accompanying her. This, no doubt, prevented many murders. Another rule was that no unescorted women were permitted in the place after 9 P.M. Of course, some of the girls used to get there at 8:50 and squat. "Oh, we're waiting for Freddy Gebhart," was their wheeze even after the frisky Freddy had passed away. What could be done?

But after 3 A.M. the newspaper men had to be entertained, so three women were permitted to come in unescorted—the Old Gray Mare, Salammbo and Cock-Eyed Dolores. (Jack knew we had no class.)

At that time in the morning the high gamblers—Lou Betts, Arnold Rothstein, Verney Barton, etc.—also used to come in with their beautiful molls all bedizened and bedecked like a Maharajah's harem. The men of the brush and pen were sometimes permitted to stew around with these morning débutantes. The gamblers had great respect for the Power of the Press, even when the Power was only half a horse. Arnold Rothstein, who came into Jack's every morning, was one of the most delightful beer companions with whom I have ever sat out a session. He impressed me as being a great executive who simply took the easiest way in a country where craft and graft are all ye need to know.

IV

Jack's waiters Irish and German—followed him from his first stake and steak. They grew old and gray in his service. They were of the white-aproned, hello Mike! type. Broke? They'd pay your check if you were in too deep at the desk. Want a fiver? Sure! If you were good to them, they'd protect you to the death against the onslaught of some muscleinsky.

There was Torn Dunne (Dunney), who was old beyond guess in 1900 and still old (he couldn't get older) in 1918. He was Jim Huneker's favorite waiter. Tom read all of Huneker's articles in the *Sun* and the *Times,* and was mighty proud of the Cardinal, as he called Huneker. One morning I heard him say confidentially, "That was a great dish of words, Cardinal, you cooked in last Sunday's *Times!*" Then there was Joe, the literary waiter, who nearly lost his job through inattention to orders the night his Elohim, Jack London, sat at his table. Joe's favorite line to any customer who looked at all like a book-lover was, "Have you ever read 'Peveril of the Peak'?" He was an advocate of hot milk stews three times a day for brain-workers.

There's a parade in my mind; but it would take a book to describe what I see going past: A Lieutenant Governor of South Carolina—a dry—sleeping off a jag on top of Jack's fishbin in the cellar; the historic battle between Freddy Gebhart and Louis Tiffany in which Freddy lost a diamond pin, and how it was found eighteen years later; introducing Jack Francis to a plaster contractor from Westchester as Wanamaker's son, Jack promising this plastered plasterer a contract, by appointment, to re-plaster both of Wanamaker's stores from top to bottom, while the plasterer made the corks pop for the newspaper bunch; telling Jack in about 1908 that I would some day lead an orchestra in his place—Jack's unprintable answer—and how in 1928, remembering my promise made twenty years before, I mounted the orchestra loft in the Golden Room, the only part of Jack's left, which was now a restaurant run by his son, gave five dollars to the orchestra leader to give me his baton, and led the orchestra while I shouted "Me voila, Jack!" (Jack had then been dead two years); the government of the United States in 1922 putting back into Jack's cellars $90,000 worth of liquors seized in an illegal raid on his apartment while the trolley cars stopped and New York stood by on roof and in window in open-mouthed amaze; Brooklyn Jimmy Carroll and his letter from

John L. Sullivan that had dropped into every cesspool, beer glass and soup-mess for twenty years; the smearing with thick mustard of the sword-pommel of a Belgian general during the war and our retiring to carefully prepared tables behind the lines to watch him rise and caress it; George Kaucher, of the *Times,* going home with Berry Wall's high hat; Ed Simmons, the painter, paying off two years' accumulation of checks by painting twelve wall-panels in the White Room depicting the adventures of Little Red Riding Hood; the evening the Salvation Army set up its heavenly minstrel show before Jack's and a hopelessly saved lassie stepped out of the band and sprinkled a demonifuge on the threshold to the barroom; my nightly feasts of the eye on O. O. McIntyre, the sartorial Mardi Gras, with his green-and-gold vest and his cheetah, iris, nacre, cerulean, fulvescent, erubescent, glaucous ties, the while he spilled his Faustian principles of life into the Eustachian tubes of Herbert Bayard Swope; the ride up to Jack's from Brooklyn Bridge in a hansom cab with John O'Brien—John offering the cabby a dozen eggs which he was taking home and I a poem I had just written in payment—and what happened; Johnny Hughes, the famous Hoffman House cabby—bringing an expensive poodle into jack's that some fellow had paid him to take care of for several hours—Johnny falls asleep—we slip the dog from the leash and tie frankfurters to the chain—Johnny going out woozy, dragging the frankfurters.

Tyl Eulenspiegel was alive in New York in those days!—and he reigned in the Kingdom of Folderol!

When Jack died the New York *Times* ran an editorial on the man and his place. The title was "Jack of Jack's." It said "Jack's will become a legend unintelligible to a country forgetting the days and nights of civilized food and drink."

Drinks

*"New York Is Hell" themed
cocktail recipes from Peggy Nadramia
of "The Cocktail Vultures."*

Benjamin DeCasseres about to imbibe the first legal drink marking the end of prohibition, at the Waldorf-Astoria Hotel.

Blue Moon

To a cocktail shaker filled with ice, add:

2 ounces London dry gin
1/2 ounce Creme Yvette or Creme de Violette
1/2 ounce freshly-squeezed lemon juice

Shake vigorously, then strain into a chilled cocktail glass. Garnish with a small curl of orange peel, or nothing at all. The grayish haze of the drink is beautiful all on its own.

Ward Eight

To a cocktail shaker filled with ice, add:

> 2-3 ounces rye
> 1 ounce freshly-squeezed lemon juice
> 1 ounce freshly-squeezed orange juice
> 1/2 ounce grenadine

Shake vigorously, and strain into a highball glass filled with ice. Top up with sparkling water of some kind, stir, and garnish with some fruit wedges and a sprig of fresh mint which you've "spanked" a bit to release the aroma. A straw would be nice.

Tom and Jerry

In "Hot Tom and Jerry and the Ghost Cop," DeCasseres relates a late-night ramble under the influence of this concoction; I don't know if you'll meet ghosts or see marble lions get up and take a drink, but you can consider it a mini-goal...

To a large heat-safe teacup or mug, add:

1 ounce brandy
1 ounce rum
1 ounce simple syrup

In a separate bowl, beat one fresh egg, then add it to the teacup. Stir, stir, stir.

Fill teacup with hot milk or boiling water, and garnish with freshly-grated nutmeg or other baking spices.

You can make this with all brandy or all rum, if you prefer, and I like to add a few drops of allspice dram.

The Tom and Jerry is often made as a punch, as your eBay search will attest; there are a lot of "sets" available. It appears that once upon a time, this was a holiday thing. If you do make a communal drink of this, I'd whip the egg whites separately and let them float around the bowl as a last touch to the presentation, then garnish with spices.

Wherefore hath the Lord smitten us to-day before the Philistines?

www.ingramcontent.com/pod-product-compliance
Lightning Source LLC
Chambersburg PA
CBHW031102030726
47496CB00002BA/337